The Lifegiving Home

THE *Life* GIVING HOME

CREATING A PLACE OF *belonging & becoming*

SALLY & SARAH CLARKSON

TYNDALE MOMENTUM

An Imprint of
Tyndale House Publishers, Inc.

Visit Tyndale online at www.tyndale.com.

Visit Tyndale Momentum online at www.tyndalemomentum.com.

Visit Sally Clarkson at www.sallyclarkson.com, www.momheart.com, and www.wholeheart.org.

Visit Sarah Clarkson at storyformed.com and www.thoroughlyalive.com.

Tyndale Momentum and the Tyndale Momentum logo are registered trademarks of Tyndale House Publishers, Inc. Tyndale Momentum is an imprint of Tyndale House Publishers, Inc., Carol Stream, Illinois.

The Lifegiving Home: Creating a Place of Belonging and Becoming

Copyright © 2016 by Sally Clarkson and Sarah Clarkson. All rights reserved.

Cover photograph of bread copyright © Barbara Dudzińska/Adobe Stock. All rights reserved.

Cover photograph of teacup copyright © Sandra Vuckovic Pagaimo. All rights reserved.

Author photograph copyright © 2015 by Joy Clarkson. All rights reserved.

Cover design by Joy A. Miller | FiveJsDesign.com

Edited by Anne Christian Buchanan

Unless otherwise indicated, all Scripture quotations are taken from the New American Standard Bible,® copyright © 1960, 1962, 1963, 1968, 1971, 1972, 1973, 1975, 1977, 1995 by The Lockman Foundation. Used by permission.

Scripture quotations marked NIV are taken from the Holy Bible, *New International Version*,® *NIV*.® Copyright © 1973, 1978, 1984, 2011 by Biblica, Inc.® Used by permission. All rights reserved worldwide.

Scripture quotations marked NLT are taken from the *Holy Bible*, New Living Translation, copyright © 1996, 2004, 2015 by Tyndale House Foundation. Used by permission of Tyndale House Publishers, Inc., Carol Stream, Illinois 60188. All rights reserved.

Scripture quotations marked NKJV are taken from the New King James Version,® copyright © 1982 by Thomas Nelson, Inc. Used by permission. All rights reserved.

Library of Congress Cataloging-in-Publication Data

Clarkson, Sally.
 The lifegiving home : creating a place of belonging and beoming / Sally Clarkson and Sarah Clarkson.
   pages cm
 Includes bibliographical references.
 ISBN 978-1-4964-0337-7 (sc)
 1. Home—Religious aspects—Christianity. I. Title.
 BR115.H56C53 2016
 248.4—dc22   2015036220

Printed in the United States of America

22   21   20   19   18   17   16
 7   6   5   4   3   2

In honor of the Girls' Club

Unless the LORD builds the house,
They labor in vain who build it.

PSALM 127:1

Contents

ACKNOWLEDGMENTS ix
THE ADVENTURE BEGINS xi

PART ONE: **Thinking about Home**

1. A LIFEGIVING LEGACY (SALLY) 3
2. MADE FOR HOME (SARAH) 13
3. A SYMPHONY OF GRACE (SALLY) 23
4. THE RHYTHMS OF INCARNATION (SARAH) 33

PART TWO: **Seasons of Home**

JANUARY 43
Creating a Framework for Home: Rhythms, Routines, and Rituals (Sally)

FEBRUARY 59
A Culture of Love: Growing Lifelong Relationships (Sally)

MARCH 79
The Art of the Ordinary: Finding Beauty in Your Own Backyard (Sarah)

APRIL 101
A Heritage of Faith: Engaging with God's Story (Sarah)

MAY 119
Days to Commemorate: Marking Growth with Celebration (Sally)

JUNE 133
Times of Delight: Creating a Value for Play (Sally)

JULY 149
A Heroic Heritage: Engaging with Story and History (Sarah)

AUGUST 165
The Story of Us: Shaping and Celebrating Family Culture (Sally)

SEPTEMBER... 179
When Seasons Change: Gathering In for Home and Soul (Sarah)

OCTOBER 193
Home Is Best: Serving Life within Your Walls (Sally)

NOVEMBER 213
Blessed and Blessing: Grace, Gratitude, and Generosity (Sarah)

DECEMBER.. 229
The Rhythm of Celebration: Seasons of Rejoicing in Family Life (Sarah)

NOTES 247
ABOUT THE AUTHORS 249

Acknowledgments

Many thanks to our wonderful Tyndale team; our editor, Anne Christian Buchanan; Joel Clarkson; and all our precious friends and comrades who gave love, encouragement, and prayers and helped us through the writing and ideas of this book. We are so very happy to be able to give you a book of our dreams and couldn't have done it without these wonderful people as a part of our team.

Most of all, we are so very grateful to Clay Clarkson, Sarah's dad and Sally's adventure companion for thirty-four years of marriage. You have dreamed, collaborated, cultivated, and worked so diligently to give our home a story worth telling. We are deeply thankful God gave you to us.

The Adventure Begins

THE ADVENTURE STARTED ON A WHIM. With a suitcase in my left hand, a laptop case and tote on my shoulder, and the luggage cart dragging behind me, I stumbled against the door of suite 209 and pushed it open with my shoulder. The cart lurched over the doorstep, propelling me farther into the room as I grabbed for the door, laughing at my decidedly ungraceful movements. With one toe balancing the cart and my finger just on the doorknob, I held the door open for Sarah, my nineteen-year-old daughter, who was lugging the laundry basket of extras we had thrown in for our week of retreat—electric teakettle, printer, candles, chocolate—all the necessities!

When she was safely inside, I gratefully dropped a few bags on the couch and breathed a sigh of deep relief. We were finally, blessedly here. After several months of planning, several more months of crazy living, and a four-hour drive through a mountain pass, we had finally arrived.

We had come here to Asheville, North Carolina, to write a book together. With my husband, Clay, busy with his own project, Joy, my youngest, off to a favorite auntie's house, and my two teenage sons away at camp, Sarah and I had decided to escape for a rare writing getaway. We were excited about this week of "girl time" and writing time in our favorite town.

Asheville, as I describe in the next chapter, is nestled in the arms of the Blue Ridge Mountains and has an air of mountain coolness that we absolutely love. Though it is famous for the incredibly beautiful Biltmore Estate nearby, it is also graced with dozens of lovely little shops, delightful cafés, and an excellent tearoom—just the places we would want to go in our moments of relaxation in between long hours of writing. Instead of holing up in the usual small motel room, we had even splurged and booked a suite complete with kitchen and a living room at a well-known hotel chain. We wanted everything to be beautiful and cozy as we sequestered ourselves away to do our work.

But now, as we stood in our suite with all our excited expectations chattering in our minds, we peered around, searching for the expected coziness. We had yet to see any sign of it.

First of all, as we approached the registration desk, we'd had to walk alongside construction tape that kept us out of a work area. Just as we initialed the final form, a jackhammer had begun to pound away so that we had to shout to each other to be heard. And as to our accommodations—well, the kitchen and living room were definitely there, but that was about all that could be said of them. The floor was covered in stained, thin, nondescript gray-brown carpet, with a large wet spot in the middle that smelled of Lysol. A cheap, stiff couch with nary a pillow was pushed up against one wall. Old, torn wallpaper covered the kitchen walls, and the unmistakable smell of strong cleaning solution from the sink assaulted our noses.

A sudden silence fell. It didn't last long, though, for we quickly realized our room was right next to the elevator. A metallic *ding, ding* sounded every two minutes or so, and through the paper-thin walls we heard the voices of the maids chattering in the laundry room next door.

I plopped down on the couch, a huge sigh rising in my throat, and looked at Sarah. Weariness seemed to hover as a cloud around both of us, and I let the sigh out with a sort of groan attached.

Well, I thought, trying desperately to be optimistic, *maybe if we light a candle the smell will go away, and if we borrow some pillows from the bed . . .* Then I just gave up. There wasn't much chance of making this room cozy. The excitement of the last hours suddenly drained from me, and my body and mind both went limp. Just sitting in that room made me feel lonely and depressed, neither of which is a good condition for writing a book on lifegiving. From the look on Sarah's face, I knew she felt the same way.

Now, you must know we are not picky people. In fact, traveling has made us quite flexible and resourceful. This room threatened to overwhelm our usual resourceful optimism. But what else could we do? I knew nothing of the other hotels around town, and I really wasn't sure this one would release us from our reservation. I reached up to my temples, trying to rub away an emerging headache.

Then it popped into Sarah's mind that we had passed a bed and breakfast on our way into town. Though our family had traveled extensively, we had never stayed at a bed and breakfast because they're rarely set up to handle six people at a time. But there were just two of us now, so maybe we could find a more personal and comforting atmosphere at a convenient B&B.

On this impulse, she grabbed the nearby phone book and flipped to the bed and breakfast section of the yellow pages. She picked three with large ads that were located in the part of town we knew best. Then we took turns dialing.

The first two were dead ends. As Sarah dialed the third, I kept trying to imagine five days in that barren, smelly room. *Please . . .*

The phone rang several times before the man on the other end picked up.

"Hello, I just arrived in Asheville this afternoon . . ."

"Well, congratulations!" said the friendly voice on the other end. With his deep voice, the man sounded like a radio host.

This is more like it.

"We need a place to stay and work on a project. Do you have any rooms available?"

We discovered, to our excitement, that he had a suite—a large bedroom with a small workroom attached. I explained that we needed a place to work on a book.

"So, you're writers," he said.

"Yes," I replied. "Actually, we're in Asheville expressly to get started on our book."

"In that case, you have to stay here!" he said. "This is the Wright Inn, and the room I have available is the Wright Suite—the perfect place for writers, don't you think? We're located in an old, quiet neighborhood, and once everyone is gone in the morning, you'll have practically the whole house to yourselves. Oh, there's a nice, big front porch as well."

(No, I didn't use writer's license to make any of this up! Every part of it actually happened.)

I think we were sold right then and there, but the proprietor said we could come and see the space first to make sure it was adequate for us. The dismal vision of five miserable days was fading fast away. Before we left, we checked at the front desk of our current hotel and found they would graciously release us from our reservation. (Others had also canceled their reservations because of the noise and dust from the building project.) So with a sense of new freedom dancing around us, we hopped in the car and zoomed to the downtown neighborhood where the Wright House was located.

The streets were narrow, shadowed by the branches of tall, old fir and oak trees that had watched a hundred years or more pass in those quiet lanes. The houses were a century old as well, with heavy wooden front doors and tall windows with antique panes gazing out from beneath deep covered porches that held rocking chairs and baskets of flowers. We rounded a corner and the Wright House came into view, a dignified, three-storied mansion surrounded by a small lawn, tall trees, lots of maroon and yellow mums, and some red roses having their last fling on that October day. We walked up stone steps onto a deep, rambling porch with white wicker chairs set in cozy corners.

The innkeeper, Mark, welcomed us at the door, carrying a silver tray with two crystal glasses of sparkling apple juice, as well as a plate of whole grain crackers, sliced cheeses, and Concord grapes. "Sparkling juice or a small bite for your refreshment?" he asked, ushering us through the front door.

I felt as if I had somehow jumped back one hundred years. Candles flickered on the mantle of a fireplace. Rich rugs and intricately carved furniture adorned the common rooms. And just beyond them, a tall, dark wooden door stood invitingly open.

"This is the Wright Suite," Mark said as we stepped through that door into a spacious room that glowed with soft light from the big windows and lamps on the bedside tables. A big Victorian bed was piled high with pillows and a comfy-looking duvet, the high windows peered out into a garden spot where squirrels played in the pine branches, and a beautiful fireplace occupied the left wall. A patterned rug covered part of the gleaming wood floor, and gilt-framed pictures hung against pale gold wallpaper patterned with yellow rose bouquets.

Beyond the bedroom, another tall door opened onto a little nook of a room with a small table and two deep chairs perfectly suited for a pair of laptop computers. I couldn't help but notice the many candles around the room and the CD player with a stack of instrumental music beside it. Beyond our nook was one last door that led out onto our own little stretch of porch with a view of the lovely autumn garden.

I honestly don't know if anything could have been more perfectly arranged for us. There was no question of whether or not we would take the Wright Suite—in my mind the *right* suite for *writing*—for the conviction was growing in our hearts that all this had somehow been arranged, that care had been taken to prepare a place for us, a rare and generous treat.

Now I am propped up on that high Victorian bed, writing this introduction, utterly surrounded by beautiful things that give life to my soul. We have been here for two days, and I can guarantee that you will be reading a much more inspired book because of it.

The air is chilled today, so our fireplace is filled with cheery, crackling flames. The candles are lit, a piano is playing in the living room, and there is a sense of warmth and beauty all around. The very richness of this room brings life to my soul, and that is what this book is all about—how to create a home that nourishes, nurtures, and sustains life and beauty. It is all about how to order your living space and what happens there to embody the joy and beauty of God's own Spirit.

In the end, God used our little adventure as a living illustration of what my daughter and I want to share in this book. We want to show women (and men, if they're interested) how to create a space that supports vibrant, joyful, productive living and supports growth of body, soul, and spirit. Sure, people can survive in the barren sterility of a chain hotel room, but the impact of such a place is soul deadening. Home was intended to be so much more than just a place of bare essentials.

If we look at the lovely world that God designed for us, we can see a pattern for what He has always intended for us—a home environment filled with color and creativity and order, a welcoming provider of laughter and refuge, a space where memories are made and shared. Instead of creating us to live in a house of weariness and colorlessness, God has made us to live in a home full of soul-beautiful elements.

I have a sneaking suspicion that these new discoveries of loveliness as I research and prepare this book will change me, you, and even the world because of lives that will ultimately be changed within a real, God-honoring, vibrant home.

That Was Then . . .

I wrote all of the above twelve years ago! That's how long this book has been on my heart—and how long it has taken for it to become reality.

Despite the loveliness of that week in Asheville, other projects and commitments soon took over, and *The Lifegiving Home* languished on the back burner. But those twelve years were not wasted. They gave my Sarah a chance to grow up and me a chance to grow as a wife and mother, a teacher and a writer, a woman of business and a woman of home. They gave us many Sunday afternoons to thumb through *Victoria* magazines over steaming cups of tea, to attempt new recipes and spring them on the family, to visit a variety of countries and stay in all sorts of homes all over the world.

Over those years, we invested countless hours talking, dreaming, and planning how to "make home" in a way that would minister beauty and rest, inspire study, stimulate conversation, and celebrate relationship. We also collected stories from our life together—stories that began on that profound moment more than thirty years ago when I held my newborn daughter in my arms.

The Story of Home

Dark blueberry eyes gazed intensely up at me, and I couldn't tear my own eyes away. I was starstruck with my first beautiful baby. And in a moment of startling clarity, I had a vision of the home I wanted to provide for her.

Truly, for me, it was a defining moment. My mind was suddenly filled with images of what home could be. I found myself dreaming of the kind of environment I wanted Clay and me to provide for this little seven-pound gift. I wanted us to do whatever we could to shape the potential locked in the heart, soul, and mind of this little one. Together we would create an environment that nurtured her and helped her grow.

No, we didn't know what we were doing. But with God's help, we were determined to try. So that's where our shared story began. With a baby . . . and a dream.

Before Sarah turned five, she had acquired two brothers—first Joel, then Nathan. Quite a few years later, little sister Joy came along. Our work took us to Vienna, Austria; California; and sixteen other places in between. Our home became noisy, messy, and full of life as our family began to celebrate what it meant to be Clarksons together. The vision of home that began in me the day Sarah arrived grew clearer and more compelling, and Clay and I worked to make our home into a place where our little ones felt a sense of belonging. We did our best to give them roots through creating and honoring family traditions, encouraging celebration, teaching them to cherish the ways and beauty of our God, and learning what we valued as a family.

Others began to step into our home. Single adults from divorced families who found themselves lonely and isolated in professional jobs and wanted a place to be in community. Married couples with houses full of children but no support systems. International diplomats who had never known the love of God. Teachers and musicians seeking kindred spirits. Folk who were broken emotionally or just longing for a place to be welcomed. We learned how to welcome them—how to help them *feel* the welcome.

Because I knew what it was like to live in a foreign country as a young, lonely missionary without a familiar place to go to when weary or overwhelmed, I wanted to provide a space of rest and refreshment for those who felt that way too. So we began to expand our understanding of what a life-giving home could be. With each new friendship, I had a deeper sense of the need for a place that "knows" us and welcomes us, with a family—genetic or otherwise—who will love us and be our companions through the ups and downs of life.

People from all over the world passed through our doorways and stayed in our beds and feasted at our table over the years. Hosting literally hundreds of people as guests each year, we cultivated our rooms into refuges for weary ones and places to celebrate births and weddings, to give solace to the sorrowing, to nurture and sustain those who were ill or overcome with grief, and to offer love, friendship, and even counseling for those who needed it. Our home was the venue for feasts, Bible studies, concerts, holidays, birthdays, and intimate times with friends. In the process, our home began to have a story of its own.

Years passed, and our children grew through each season of life. At times, we pulled in together behind closed doors to deal with heartaches, disappointments, abandonment of friends, or church splits—though we also celebrated joys and had lots of fun. At these times, home grew into a place of refuge, comfort, familiarity, safety, pleasure—a port to keep us safe through the storms.

During these years, God seemed to whisper to me in my quiet times, *Give foundations of strength and inspiration to these precious ones, but give them wings as well. Prepare them to take risks, to live by faith, so that they can take the messages and cherished values they learned at home and share them with a hurting world.* And so our home became a launching pad, a place of blessing, as we sent our beloved children on their way—hopefully strong, whole, and secure in the ideals, faith, and values that truly matter.

They were taking His light out into the darkness. But our home remained the lighthouse they could return to for rest and restoration in between the adventures that took them into the world.

This Is Now . . .

As Sarah grew from child to teenager to best friend, she began to catch my vision for sharing the adventures our home had lived to tell. She graduated from high school, became an author in her own right, and traveled the world. Now she's studying theology at Oxford University in England, far from our family home. But she probably won't be alone for long; Joy, our youngest, is considering doing her master's in the United Kingdom. Our two boys have landed in Philadelphia and New York for now.

And yes, there are days when Clay and I feel like we're rattling around in an empty house—but not often, because that house is still home base for our family. It's the hub to which we all return to refuel before venturing out once more. And it's the headquarters for ongoing works of collaboration—such as this book, which is finally coming to fruition after all these years.

You see, we never lost the vision that sent us to Asheville twelve years ago. If anything, the years have sharpened and deepened our convictions and our desire to share them. Finally, despite crazy schedules, hundreds of life interruptions, and chronic lack of time, we decided to make *The Lifegiving Home* a reality. We felt the world needed this book, and our publisher agreed it was a good idea.

So I decided to travel to Europe during one of Sarah's school breaks so we could do the bulk of our writing together. Joel was interviewing for a job in England and said he would love to tag along. Because international travel and living have been such a part of our lives, I found a lovely little apartment for rent just east of Paris, with a full kitchen and living room, for less than two hundred dollars a week.

The three of us landed there and immediately started making it home for our week together. Tramping through light rain to the closest village grocery store, we loaded up on crusty bread, local cheese, berries, yogurt, a sparkling bottle of juice, and three small quiches. Back home, we lit candles in our small living room, wrapped a scarf around a small jar of roses I had bought, and arranged our recent purchases on the table. We relished celebrating "home" together in this different place—the sense of familiar belonging, with a small feast laid out in the peaceful twilight. What a joy to be with those we know and love so well!

The next day, Sarah and I got to work—sharing ideas, outlining possibilities. And because we are a highly collaborative family, Joel joined in with many of our discussions. In a sense he is a third author of this book because he contributed so many ideas and stories. (Eventually he became coauthor of the companion planner, *The Lifegiving Home Experience*.) When it came to actually putting the words together, Sarah and I divided up the chapters. I wrote half, and she wrote half; then we responded to each other's offerings.

I hope you'll keep this collaborative process in mind as you read this book. Sarah and I have very different writing styles, and our perspective, of course, is different. I write as a mama who developed my home ideals through the years and applied them with trial and error and lots and lots of grace. Sarah writes as a young adult who grew up in our home and is learning to create home for herself. But the two of us (and Joel!) shared the same family culture and share much of the same vision.

You'll find that some themes will be repeated more than once because they reflect the same unique home environment and because each of us wanted to give our own impressions of what we valued. So you'll read a lot about teatimes (can there be too much mention, ever, of teatimes?), books and stories (again, never too much mention!), traditions, spiritual rhythms and practices, feasting, celebrating life, and understanding the importance of beauty to satisfy our souls. We hope you'll bear with us through this repetition and enjoy the dual perspective.

We also hope you will take the time to visit our dedicated website, www.lifegivinghome.com. We had so many ideas to share that we could not possibly fit them all into this book, so we have put them on the website. There you will find lists and links for books to read, movies to watch, resources to gather, and things to do with your family—plus a place where others can contribute their own ideas. Look for our website prompts throughout this book.

For the record, we did do everything this book recommends—at least once! Many of the practices were ongoing—we did them every year, no matter what. Others were enjoyed for a year or two and then abandoned as our family evolved. Some practices were suspended during times of stress—moves, illnesses, traumatic circumstances, or just the need to simplify. But others were what kept us sane during those same times of stress.

I suspect you will find the same is true of you. Don't hesitate to make adjustments and keep on learning as you and your family journey together. But always keep in mind that wherever you are, you can create a lifegiving home that will become a significant part of your family's story. How we need more "homemakers" so that all who live in this transient, contemporary world might have a place to belong, to feel loved and valued, to serve and be served, to give and receive and celebrate all that is good.

So make a cup of tea, light some candles, and sit down in your comfiest chair as you begin to journey with Sarah and me through the ideas and possibilities that take you right into the center of your own heart and home.

May God's richest blessings be with you as you dream, create ideas for your own family, and flourish in the creativity of mind and soul that comes with being God's child, made in His likeness, and destined for an eternal home with Him.

PART ONE
Thinking about Home

— I —

A LIFEGIVING LEGACY
(SALLY)

*The wise woman builds her house,
But the foolish tears it down with her own hands.*

PROVERBS 14:1

Leaves of crimson, gold, and brown drifted down upon the roof of our car as we slowly meandered on the winding road, gazing out at the mysterious woods on either side of us and the flowing stream that seemed to follow our course. The sweet, melancholy notes of a Celtic CD streamed through the car as each of us lost ourselves for the moment in our own dream worlds.

In that season of my life, as the mother of three teenagers and a bubbly little seven-year-old girl, I rarely had a quiet moment. This drive provided a soothing moment, a badly needed opportunity just to breathe. The soft music lured me to a secret escape inside, while the pathways leading through shadowy woods captured my imagination, providing a momentary break from mundane reality. And how I needed that! My heart was desperate for some new inspiration and rest from my draining and demanding days. Would I find it on this trip?

All six of us Clarksons had piled into our van to get away to Asheville, North Carolina, for a weekend of family adventure and escape. Now we were approaching the Biltmore, the famous home that George Washington Vanderbilt II planned and constructed more than one hundred years earlier.

We rounded a bend, and a stand of tall, shimmering ash trees opened up to a breathtaking view. The grand tree-lined entrance in front of us led to a four-story French château–styled structure. Designed as the dream project of Mr. Vanderbilt's life, Biltmore stood with castle-like grandeur against a dramatic backdrop of the Blue Ridge Mountains.

Completed in 1895, Biltmore was (and remains) the largest residential dwelling in the United States—with four *acres* of floor space and more than 250 rooms. In its heyday the estate covered most of four counties. Although some of the land has been sold since then, the house itself looks almost new, without the slightest evidence that the years have weakened or diminished the structure in any way.

Driving up toward Biltmore on that first visit, we found ourselves awestruck by the sheer size and beauty of the place in its breathtaking mountain setting. But as we toured the house and learned a little more about it and its creator, we came to appreciate the family dwelling and its builder even more. For Biltmore is more than just a big, elegant house in the mountains. It is the embodiment of one man's vision of home and his determination to make that dream a reality.

As the youngest of eight children, George Vanderbilt gleaned ideas for home design from his older siblings, from the family home in New York where he had grown up, and from prominent historical places he had visited in America and abroad. His vision for crafting a home grew over time, and by the time he got around to actually building his dream home, he knew exactly what he wanted—a solid structure built to last, a family home whose halls and rooms were filled with lively, rousing conversations; jubilant dances; and sumptuous feasts—a meeting place where friends he had met from all over the world could join him.

George Vanderbilt's monument of a lifework will last for generations, as it was built on solid foundations with good materials. As I walked its halls, I learned more and found my soul awakening, my imagination rekindling as I pondered my own dream of creating a lifegiving home, a legacy that would speak into generations to come.

Vanderbilt dreamed of designing a place that would be a haven for all who entered and a resource for the greater community. His family dwelling place would be a sanctuary for all who came upon it, crafted to meet the needs of people who longed for the solace of a peaceful life away from the demands of everyday living.

He especially wanted his home to provide a retreat for budding artists and musicians so they could create their works of art in peace. Vanderbilt dreamed of providing these folk with a place where they could find rest and renewal, then continue working on their art.

His remarkable success in achieving that dream was obvious with every step of our tour. Uniquely decorated guestrooms on the second and third floors were earmarked for friends and aspiring artists, authors, and musicians. A library of thousands of books stood at ready to support disciplined and curious minds—and prompted my own reflections as well.

How can I do that in my own home? I found myself pondering. *In what ways can I make room for those needing a place to be creative?*

Multiple living rooms were designed to provide his family and guests with privacy, companionship, and entertainment. Each featured a variety of cards and games, books piled high for escape and study, groupings of chairs where many friendships were forged in front of roaring fires, lit nightly for warmth and atmosphere. Guests delighted to congregate in these rooms to engage with new ideas, share stories, and enjoy one another.

How can I group chairs, couches, and tables in our home in a way that encourages people to spend time together?

A massive kitchen in the basement ensured that the dining and serving needs of all who stayed in the home would be easily met. Here elaborate feasts, elegant tea parties, enchanting birthday celebrations, and magnificent holiday celebrations originated. (Even the servants and their families were treated yearly to a grand Christmas party, and each child was presented with presents chosen just for him or her.)

How can I use my own kitchen and the rest of my house to meet both the physical and emotional needs of my family and those who might not have as much? What events can I dream up that help us celebrate life and make memories through meals and learning how to cook for groups with simplicity?

Culture and travel were important to George Vanderbilt, and he planned his house to reflect those interests. Art treasures and artifacts from all over the world, mostly collected by Vanderbilt himself, transformed each room into a visual feast. Beautiful, interesting objects adorned each corner and wall—robust statues, hundreds of pen-and-ink sketches, classic oil paintings, European tapestries, a grand organ, musical instruments, rare books, and fascinating relics. Each was carefully chosen to add beauty and interest, to capture the imagination and stimulate the flow of creative juices.

How can I arrange my own little treasure trove of items collected from the many countries where we've lived to refresh our decor and provide something interesting to see, read, or enjoy in every corner of my house?

Designed to Design

As I toured Biltmore, my imagination and vision were once again piqued by the idea of intentionally making my home a holding place for all that is beautiful, good, holy, and foundational to life—a place where those I love always feel like they belong, a place of freedom and grace that launches them into the persons they were made to be, a place of becoming. In the midst of demanding, constantly pressured lives, we all need refresher courses from time to time about what we are building and why we must be intentional about doing it.

My mom used to put it this way: "All people need a place where their roots can grow deep and they always feel like they belong and have a loving refuge. And all people need a place that gives wings to their dreams, nurturing possibilities of who they might become."

Creating such a place does not require building a mansion as Vanderbilt did. We are all capable of creating a lasting legacy in the form of a home that gives life to others who come under its roof.

A home that serves all who enter.

A home that reflects our own tastes and the values we treasure.

A home that meets the needs of family and visitors alike, that fosters beauty and creativity.

A home where the atmosphere, traditions, and celebrations give life to the hearts, minds, and souls of those inside its walls.

A home that provides a lifegiving legacy that will last for generations to come.

I believe God has designed us to do just that.

It was through the structure of home and family that God first gave men and women a chart for all of life, when it was perfect and untouched by sin. Adam and Eve received God's blessings and a mandate: "Be fruitful and multiply, and fill the earth, and subdue it; and rule over the fish of the sea and over the birds of the sky and over every living thing that moves on the earth" (Genesis 1:28). Family was God's original organization scheme for society, and home was the laboratory where human beings could learn to glorify God through the work, relationships, and purposes of their lives. Home would be the place where love for God and commitment to His purposes would be passed down from one generation to another.

A Homeless Generation?

Thousands of years later, in a world that rebelled against God's original intention, too many are left with no understanding of the Genesis mandate or the importance of home building. Broken families, divorce, abandonment, passivity, and abuse have plagued family history and have left scars on the hearts of children grown into adults. The vision of home as a place to flourish and grow fully into healthy persons has too often been lost in the busyness, distraction, and brokenness of both our secular and our Christian cultures.

Add to that the impact of technology in recent years, as social media tends to elevate *virtual* relationships over real-life, face-to-face encounters. Tweets, profiles, and statuses have replaced personal conversations. Gathering around the table for food and family discussions, lingering on front porches for long conversations over coffee, whiling away evenings with family and friends—all these have been replaced with quick trips through the fast-food drive-in or fifteen-minute meet-ups at a local coffee shop. There is little time or space for instruction about life or discussions about truth. Our souls seem to be filled with the sawdust of a lost generation.

Corporate moves have displaced people from their relatives; megachurches have replaced local congregations; and so many of us have become accustomed to growing up without a physical, local community of friends with whom we share life every day and who hold us accountable. Neighborhoods have become merely places to hold the dwellings where we sleep, grab food on the go, and meet our bare needs for existence. Sometimes we are lonely, and we do not recognize what has been lost.

As a result, in so many ways, we have become a homeless generation.

I am not even speaking of the poor who actually lack a place to live—though that in itself is a tragedy. I'm referring to a different kind of homelessness, one that is spiritual and emotional. It's the homelessness of those who have their basic needs for housing, food, and clothing met but do not have a sanctuary designed to preserve all that is precious in life.

People may have dwellings—apartments, flats, houses, dorm rooms. They may have roommates or husbands or wives or children or parents. They may even have architects and decorators. But so many do not have a place of refuge, a harbor for their wandering souls, a place where all that is precious about life is preserved, protected, and cultivated and the daily needs of their hearts and souls are satisfied.

More important, they have no idea how to create that kind of home for themselves and those they love.

What Makes a Home?

Each of us longs for a place to belong, a connection that gives roots to our wandering lives. Our hearts hunger for a community where we are intimate members, a sense of belonging to people who love us. Our souls crave a purpose bigger than our jobs, a connection to a sense of meaning. We yearn to know that our own stories have significance in the grander scheme of God's megastory. All of these may be found in home—a place to belong, a people to be a part of, and a purpose where God's righteousness and design are celebrated and cherished in community every day.

That's not to say the home or the people in it have to fit a certain mold or look a particular way. Whether single or married, parent or childless, student, missionary, working away from home, traveling as a way of life, or in between places while being transferred—anyone can "make home" amidst the ever-changing circumstances of life. But it won't just happen by accident. Homemaking—not in the sense of housekeeping, but in the broader sense of cultivating the life of a home—has to be done on purpose.

The essence of home, you see, is not necessarily a structure. What makes a home is the life shared there, wherever that may be. And cultivating the life of home requires intentionality, planning, and design. There must be someone (or several someones) to craft the life, the beauty, the love, and the inspiration that overflows from that place.

An architect who desires to build a distinguished edifice must start with a vision and then translate that vision into a blueprint that documents the design and placement of the structure's foundations, boundaries, facades, and enclosures. One cannot build what has not been imagined. And one cannot bring a vision to life without a plan.

Early in the life of our family, I realized I needed that as well. In order to build a vibrant, rich, lifegiving home, I needed to clarify my vision and construct a detailed plan for our own unique community called "Clarkson." As I pondered what I wanted my home to become, I jotted down thoughts in my journal. These became the essence of the Clarkson blueprint, my vision for what home is and should be:

- *Home is the haven of inspiration where the art of life is expressed and taught.* Color is strewn into every corner; delectable food is tasted; art, books, and other sources of beauty are strategically placed throughout its rooms and walls. Nature is observed from each window—flowers, plants, rocks, shells. The works of the Master Artist speak of the work of His hands.

- *Home is the place where the whispers of God's love are heard regularly.* The touch of His hands is given intentionally throughout the day, and His words of encouragement and affirmation lay the foundation of loving relationships.

- *Home is the place where stories of heroism, sacrifice, love, and redemption are heard, embraced, and celebrated.* These shape the dreams of the souls who live there.

- *Home is a place of ministry.* Redeeming words, thoughts, and actions are shared and taught, the wisdom and instruction of God is passed along, and God's love is offered to all who come under its influence.

My immediate motivation for building such a home, of course, was my family, especially my children. From the moment that newborn Sarah was placed in my arms, I felt the profound urge to create a safe and nurturing environment where she and, later, her brothers and sister could grow and thrive, where their spirits could be fed and their souls enriched.

But I needed that home for my own soul as well. I craved a place to belong amidst our nomadic lifestyle, a refuge from the draining practicalities and spiritual warfare I encountered out in the world. In order to thrive, I needed a place to be loved and restored, to find inspiration and purpose. The constructing of such a place was a way of seeing that my own heart, mind, and soul were filled up on a regular basis so that when I emerged from my home, I had resources to cope with the demands of my life.

Because of our missionary, job-oriented lives, Clay and I knew from the beginning that we would probably not have a static homestead where we could congregate over our life as a family. So we focused on creating home out of less tangible materials—traditions, habits, rhythms, experiences, and values. It was in the love and acceptance we shared, the comfort and warmth we enjoyed together, the spiritual and intellectual connections we fostered, and the traditions we celebrated together that we found both refuge from the world outside and the strength to engage it creatively.

We ended up moving seventeen times—six times internationally. We lived in a variety of houses and apartments—small and large, rural, suburban, and downtown. When we finally did move into a more permanent home in Colorado, our choices still reflected the values that already said "home" to us. And those invisible threads still tie our hearts together so that wherever in the world we are—and our bunch is likely to be found almost anywhere around the globe—we are united by the choices and experiences that knit us together as a family and define our very beings.

Today, as I observe the lives of our children, now adults, I see the construct of a palpable life we celebrated together. In their dorm rooms, hotel rooms, apartments, and cottages far away, they carry with them the life we shared, the traditions celebrated, the spirit of hospitality. No matter how small the place, how different the dwelling, the spirit of home is still alive in them. They, too, are intentionally creating lives that reflect God's beauty, the vast dimensions of the joys of life to be celebrated there, and the possibility of unconditional love made flesh. And they are learning, as I learned raising them, that to craft a truly welcoming, truly lifegiving home is a deeply satisfying work, one of the great glories of any life.

What greater joy can there be than to create a holding place for all that is sacred in life: faith, love, God, purpose, beauty, relationships, creativity, fun, the art of life, safety, shelter, feasting? To foster education in many realms of interests, a classroom of life where foundations of morality are taught and modeled and wisdom is learned. To build an environment that contains everything necessary for people of all generations—from babies to the elderly—to live healthy and well in community.

Building well is a long process. None of us will ever be perfectly wise or mature or loving. Creating a lifegiving home, then, is a long process taken one step, one season at a time. In the process, I've found, the home itself becomes wiser and more valuable.

This idea of being a home builder has drawn me forward, encouraging me to invest in worthy thoughts and practices. The intentionality of seeking to build my home piece by piece, day by day, has moved me and my family toward the goal of creating a great legacy of healthy people who live and grow within its walls.

Home should be the very best place ever to be. And the gathering of all of us together, including friends and those who would share our belonging together, should be the place we feel most at home. And whether or not you ever meet another person who has this kind of home to welcome you, *you* can create that sort of refuge for others. Not many in my life even invite people into their homes anymore, but I have found that almost everyone loves to be in a place that says, "Welcome! You will be cared for here!"

It is our privilege—and our God-given mandate—to make it so.

2

MADE FOR HOME
(SARAH)

*The ache for home lives in all of us,
the safe place where we can go as we are
and not be questioned.*

MAYA ANGELOU

I USUALLY FEEL IT upon the first moment of waking in a new place: the sense of disconnect. Sight, touch, imagination—my wakening senses grope out into the morning light for something familiar by which to pull myself out of sleep and into the new day. When a foreign surface, an unexpected corner, a ceiling or window, an unfamiliar slant of light meets my groggy eyes, I jolt awake, startled by the strangeness. And for a few moments I am afraid.

I've known that jet-lagged moment in my tiny student room in Oxford, where I am studying. Every atom, every surface and smell, declares itself foreign. I move within my new environs with a pained clumsiness, as if something vital in me were sick. I do not belong here. The gray walls and yellowed light are foreign to me. No known voice will break the silence.

I open my eyes and sit on the edge of the bed with an ache that is my longing for the people I love, for refuge from loneliness. I move among the shapes and surfaces of this room, this city, this new life as a stranger. A stranger in all the potent meaning of that word—someone who neither knows nor is known, regarded and regarding with a slight suspicion born of the fact that love is a kind of knowledge, and here I have none.

In the first breath of every morning, I ache for home.

I wonder how many of us wake up every day with just such a longing—perhaps not the sharp, obvious desire of homesickness but a wistful, lingering sense of need. How many of us bear a haunting sense that we are strangers in the spaces of our own lives, moving from place to place, from work to house to social gathering (real or virtual) without any true sense of belonging. Perhaps the ache is not so much a desire for something we miss as an awareness that something is missing. We have food, roofs over our heads, entertainment, friends, but still we yearn for something we can barely name.

That yearning is, at its core, a longing for home.

A Holy Desire

What is it about home that we long for?

We hunger to be deeply known and, in the knowing, held. We pine to belong to a place in which our story began, where the stories of others intertwine with ours in a history that sustains us through dark nights and winter seasons, where our loneliness can be comforted and we can encounter the affection of God and human alike. We yearn for familiar beauty, for the knowledge that the physical trappings of our lives, the spaces in which we breathe and suffer and love, have meaning. We want a refuge that is more than a house, with rooms that speak to us with a living presence and enwrap us with welcome when we return. We hunger for the rich community of love, the family that ought to fill those rooms.

But we are, most of us, so very far from home.

We live in a swift age, an impersonal age, an age of screens (phones, computers, TVs, and others), noise, and constant distraction. Ours is a hurry-up, check-your-goals-off-a-list, get-to-the-next-place existence. Many in our time have never known home at all, in the sense of something more than a collection of rooms. Some know only, as they say, a broken home, and few of us have any real sense of a local community or history. As a culture, we have disregarded the connections of physical place and personal relationship that named and defined our ancestors. We are busy and driven, and even if we have families we prize, we struggle to maintain connection.

We live in a profoundly lonely age, a homeless age. The noisy, happening, driven world draws us into itself through the never-ending presence of media, the sleepless activity of the Internet, the forward push of our cars and schedules and goals, the omnipresence of distraction and entertainment. And because the activity dulls the edge of our loneliness, masks the anguished desire for belonging that we cannot stare down, we allow ourselves to be swept away in all the noise and activity.

Until that one moment when the sight of a little child caught up in her mother's arms startles us into a grieved aching to be held ourselves.

Until that instant on an autumn evening when we step out of the car and the air is sharp with cold and wood smoke, when the windows of the houses nearby glow with invitation and we yearn to belong behind one of those golden panes, to be drawn into a refuge where we are known, where a table is set and candles are lit, awaiting our arrival.

Until the first morning in a new flat, a new life, when we wake and know ourselves strange to all we survey.

Suddenly we are homesick. And it feels as if we may never recover.

I don't think we were meant to recover—not entirely. I think homesickness is a holy desire because we were meant to be at home, to be profoundly loved and deeply known, to belong to a people and a place where our story can unfold nourished by beauty, formed by goodness, rooted in love.

Desire is no bad thing. The deep desires in our hearts are the ones that echo with the eternal, that tell us something of who God meant us to be back before the world was broken, of what He intends us to have once more in the life of the risen Christ.

When we recognize our homesickness as such, when we listen to what our hearts cry and sing about belonging, our desire can be transformed into hope, a holy conviction that becomes a creative force pressing within us, a muscled hope that challenges us to take the void spaces of our lives, the empty forms of a broken world, and fill them with love, beauty, and belonging. Hope then becomes our glorious challenge to make, in the wilderness of the broken world, a rich and lasting home.

Incarnation and Restoration

That is the heart and message of this book—a vision rooted profoundly in an understanding of physical place and personal relationship as extensions of the Incarnation.

One of the first obstacles I find in presenting a vision for the importance of home is the almost unconscious assumptions on the part of many modern people that home is inherently a sentimental notion and that beauty is peripheral to spiritual formation. We discount our own homesickness as a form of weakness. We marginalize the beautiful. We dismiss the aesthetic as second class. We think of beautiful spaces and comforting traditions as spiritually unnecessary and underestimate the profound importance of a safe place for growing minds and souls.

Action, mission, productivity, study—these are considered essentials. But beauty? Good meals? Gardens? Art? Gracious atmosphere? A safe haven for the spirit?

We tend to think of beauty as a niche interest in the Martha Stewart model, of home in the impossibly Victorian sense of an idealized past space that belongs to childhood and is not central to the happening realm of the modern adult. We look at home and the accompanying concepts of refuge from the world, of innocence, of quiet, as frivolous or extraneous because we misunderstand the fundamental reality of the Incarnation.

What I mean by the Incarnation is simply the fact that the gospel begins with God being born as a human baby. The Incarnation means that our salvation is accomplished within flesh and blood, time and space, and includes the physical spaces and particulars of our lives as well as the spiritual.

God didn't come merely to save us to a life beyond this world. He came to redeem the one we already inhabit. The message of the gospel didn't begin with death. It began with a world-startling life, the birth of God as a flesh-and-blood baby who lived out thirty-three years of robustly human life. The man Jesus showed us what it meant to live as creative, loving, constructive children of God, our Father.

The story of the gospel can only be fully grasped within the larger narrative of the Incarnation. Salvation itself must be understood as redemption—not merely *from* the effects of sin—but *to* life and love as they were meant to be: the world in its original goodness; the life that encompasses human relationship, work, and yes, home. The Incarnation was, in its deepest sense, a restoration of what God originally intended for humankind. And that includes a physical place of belonging.

What We Were Made For

Genesis makes it clear that we were made for intimate community, both of people and place. We were made to know deeply, in the light of many different days and seasons, both the people and the materials of our existence.

Those ringing words spoken by God to the new people of His image—*rule* and *subdue, fill the earth*—were a command to *act* in His image by bringing order and belonging to the world that He had made. We were made to delight and ground ourselves in the goodness of creation; to tend, cultivate, and keep a specific place on earth.

Do you see it? We were made for home. We were made for relationship and place. We were made for belonging in the physical world. The Incarnation affirms that this is part of the gospel—that belonging is restored because the life of God enters into the life of human flesh and physicality. The life of Jesus began in a particular little town, amidst people just like us, who ate and worked and laughed and hoped. The Kingdom came first to a stable in Bethlehem, not an abstract point of the cosmos, and the Incarnation continues to bring God's Kingdom about through us, in our individual lives, in our little houses scattered across the globe.

We must understand homemaking not as a retreat from the fallen world, not as a retrenchment from culture, but as a profound engagement with it. We must understand the creation of home as a work of incarnational power and creativity. "Kingdom come" doesn't happen on some cosmic scale; the whole point is that it invades the physical at the humblest level. As Christ was born a tiny human child of Mary, so Christ comes again, invading the human realm in and through our ordinary love of children and friends, spouses and siblings. His Kingdom comes in the way we celebrate, the shelter we make of our homes, the joy we put into what we cook and eat and create, our willingness to welcome strangers into our midst. As the Holy Spirit fills us, our families and friendships and the particular physical spaces of our lives become the spaces where Christ is born again and again—growing, ordering, renewing, healing.

Redeeming the Stuff of Creation

"The Incarnation turns stuff into love."

Those words were spoken by Mark Stafford, the chaplain of my Anglican church in Oxford, to me and a group of my fellow students. We had left the craziness of the city behind to spend two days, one in silence, in an old retreat house in the country. We were drawn into the quiet of the English countryside just as the earth began to stretch itself in the spring warmth. We ate together in quiet companionship. We worshiped morning and evening. We curled up in the old library to read some of the many books cramming the old wooden shelves. From our hurry-up existence as students, we were drawn into a space of fellowship and beauty in which God was made real to us again. The very atmosphere of the place communicated the truth of our chaplain's words—that the Incarnation takes the stuff of material existence, the physical world God made to delight and nourish and reveal Himself to us, and redeems it back from just stuff to an embodiment of God's love, His uninhibited generosity.

In the beginning, the world itself was home for human beings. We were exiled at the Fall, left lost, broken, and homesick by sin. But when Jesus came in human flesh, home became possible on an eternal scale once more. Every day in each inch of space, each rhythm of time, each practice of love, we have the chance to join God in coming home, in living so that we make a home of this broken and beautiful world all over again. Love is enfleshed in the meals we make, the rooms we fill, the spaces in which we live and breathe and have our being. The Kingdom coming into the world has to have a starting point, and I think God meant the home to be one of the primary places into which His Kingdom comes afresh, His life made known again on the scale of the everyday.

Elizabeth Goudge, in one of my favorite novels, puts it this way:

> Lucilla knew always, and Nadine knew in her more domesticated moments, that it was homemaking that mattered. Every home was a brick in the great wall of decent living that man erected over and over again as a bulwark against the perpetual flooding in of evil.[1]

Goudge knew that home is not only a refuge from evil but also a place for a new beginning after evil has done its worst, a place where hope breaks once more into human existence—not just as an idea, but as a refuge. In her novel *Pilgrim's Inn* (from which the above quote is taken), she presented a story about the Eliots, a family shattered and shaken by World War II, who leave London after the war to begin afresh in a big old "maison-dieu," an inn for travelers—pilgrims—turned into a country home. In that house, a place cultivated by each generation who lived there to be a refuge for the spirit and soul, the Eliots encounter the redemptive presence of beauty and the healing reality of belonging. Through the fireside spaces, the kitchen table, the gardens, the rhythms and shelter of the place, they are restored.

The Struggle and the Story

I was blessed to grow up in just such a home. It's not that my family had a particular house that belonged to us for generations. In fact, we moved more than anyone else I knew. But my parents understood that the world they made within the walls of our house was what constituted home. So I grew up in spaces framed by art and color, filled with candlelight, marked by beauty. I grew up within a rhythm of time made sacred by family devotions in the morning and long conversations in the evening. I grew up with the sense of our daily life as a feast and delight; a soup-and-bread dinner by the fire, Celtic music lilting in the shadows, and the laughter of my siblings gave me a sense of the blessedness of love, of God's life made tangible in the food and touch and air of our home.

It was a fight for my parents, I know. Every day was a battle to bring order to mess, peace to stressful situations, beauty to the chaos wrought by four young children. But that's the reality of incarnation as it invades a fallen world. My parents struggled, and I watched them. I saw the days when a homemade meal was an almost Herculean task. I saw the evenings when we didn't quite manage to get the house in order. I knew the effort it took my mom to bring a sparkle, once more, to the eyes of all those hungry, restless little people round the dinner table, particularly when sorrow was in her own heart.

When someone once asked me just what it was that my parents did that made me believe in God, without even thinking I said, "I think it was French toast on Saturday mornings and coffee and Celtic music and discussions and candlelight in the evenings . . ." Because in those moments I tasted and saw the goodness of God in a way I couldn't ignore.

What my parents—bless them—knew, what Elizabeth Goudge understood, is that to make a home right in the midst of the fallen world is to craft out a space of human flesh and existence in which eternity rises up in time, in which the Kingdom comes, in which we may taste and see the goodness of God.

Home is not merely a dwelling. It's not merely a state of existence. It's a story, a narrative spun out day by day, a story molded by the walls and hours and tasks and feasts with which we fill our time, reflecting the reality of the God whose love animates every aspect of our being.

The story is always possible. The narrative of home, the new creation of belonging, is one we can always begin anew, wherever we dwell. We don't have to have a perfect family, a healthy background. We don't have to have lived in one place. We don't have to own a mansion or even a house. Nothing is required for the making of home except a heart that loves God, an imagination fired by His Spirit, and hands ready to create. And, well, a bit of courage, too. It takes grit to confront those fallen realms of loneliness, those empty spaces, and fill them. But when we do, the Kingdom comes in the homes we make as the love of God becomes flesh in our lives once more.

This is what I tell myself each time I arrive, lonely and homesick once again, in the void spaces of a new life. I write to you out of my own long battle to find and make the kind of home that shaped me. I'm still holding out for a cottage with a garden someday, but until then, I know that each new little student room is my space of possible creation.

It's why, after that moment of panic or fear or loneliness on that first new morning, I will shove my jet-lagged or car-weary limbs out of bed and survey the mound of boxes or suitcases. I will look around me at the bags I haven't unpacked and the clothes I haven't folded. I will stare down every inch of my foreign little room until it meets my gaze. I will sigh, very deeply. And then I will rise with an exertion of will that feels like the lifting of a massive weight, and I will do what I have done with every adventure before. I will begin to build a life, and that means I will begin to make a home.

I will open the window and let the stale air of the night seep away. I'll brew some coffee and find a way to play music, strong and sweet, into the quiet spaces, the old Celtic melodies I love or the throaty songs of the artists I have hummed along with since childhood. Amidst the melody, I will begin to order the spaces of my new existence. I will unpack, fold, and stack. I will e-mail my mother and battle that black, hot darkness of loneliness with every atom of order and loveliness I can muster. I will pile books on the old shelves, set out a few family photos, cram flowers into whatever random jug I can find.

Then I'll foray out in search of tea and bread and find a charity shop where I can garner a poster or two for those gray walls—or, even better, some vividly illustrated cards or woodcuts. I'll seek out a vase for the flowers, an old scarf to drape over the sagging student desk. I'll gather them all together and head back to my tiny room. And when it is all finished, when I've christened my work with a first cup of tea, I'll sigh again and begin the next adventure of finding a few lonely souls to invite into my tiny, makeshift home.

As I do all of this, I am aware of the Kingdom coming. As I order and hope, fill and form, the Holy Spirit is renewing one more corner of the world. Here, in my room, the fallen stuff of the broken earth is being formed back into love, into home.

There's no place like it.

3

A SYMPHONY OF GRACE

(SALLY)

Home is where the heart sings.

SCARLETT DEVA ANTALOCZY

"Just left the freeway. Home in minutes."

Nathan's text set off a familiar flurry of activity as I hurried through the house, eager to complete every preparation before the car headlights bounced off the front windows.

Candles lit.

Check.

Favorite acoustic music playing.

Check.

House straightened.

Check.

Dinner on the stove, cookies in the oven.

Check. (It smelled wonderful!)

Joy, our youngest, was coming home from a semester abroad, her first stint to be overseas by herself for four months. Joel and Nate had been dispatched to travel the familiar hour of highway to the Denver airport and had sent the text as soon as they exited on County Line Road, two miles from our home. I had just enough time to light the lantern at the front door and write "Welcome Home, Joy!" on the small slate board in chalk colors of red and blue.

Standing just inside the door, I paused and looked behind me at the waiting house, my appreciation refreshed by seeing it through the eyes of someone who has been away. I so love this place that my family calls home, that embodies so much of what we have come to think of as "the Clarkson ways."

Each piece of furniture, each architectural detail, each tradition and ritual sings to us of beauty, safety, and growth—and of the vision, planning, thought, and artistry that went into fleshing out the vision of home that captivated me from the very beginning.

The Director of Life Art

Even as an orchestra needs a conductor to choose the music, lead rehearsals, and unite all of the instruments into a harmonious sound, so every home needs someone who conducts what I call the life music of a home—its atmosphere. The one who conducts is responsible for bringing out the swelling themes, the steady bass notes, the drama of percussion kept in its place, the soaring melodies and intricate counterparts—all the instruments sounding together in a symphony of grace.

In our home, for the most point, the conductor of life within its walls is me. This is the role I have chosen, the role that suits me best, though my husband, Clay, adds his own unique rhythms and melodies and the whole family helps perform the ultimate creation of our shared life. And even as an orchestra must practice the music—with mistakes and interruptions scattered along the way—so our home building has been a process that will take a lifetime to perfect.

From the beginning, the vision Clay and I had for our home was to reflect the reality of the living God—to embody His sparkle, pleasure, artistry, fun, and intimacy. God's truth was to be taught, cherished, obeyed daily within the boundaries of our home. His love was to be the oxygen that each one of us breathed. Observing the words and life of Christ, I began to understand that a servant's heart would be required to adequately meet the needs of those who stepped through our doors—whether those needs involved friendship, a place to rest, forgiveness and grace, guidance and instruction, a safe haven from the stresses of the world, or just a place to retreat from the mundane or the burdens of life. And this task began with a heart commitment to make home a holding place for all that is sacred, beautiful, valuable, and reflective of His reality.

As the one conducting the life-music in this home, I would be the one who established the atmosphere, the relational standard. But the music was not original to me. The heart of our home was to be inspired by spiritual connection to the One who called Himself the Light of the World; the Bread of Life; the Good Shepherd; the Way, the Truth, and the Life. To me, He is also the great Composer. He wrote the music of home and lives out His reality here.

What does the music of home "sound" like? Each home is different and will have a unique melody that defines its atmosphere, but to me there are particular themes and voices that belong in every home. These are the elements that transform a mere space into a haven of refuge, a resource of growth, and a transmitter of grace. Allow me to point out a few with my baton.

The Music of Welcome

Offer hospitality to one another without grumbling.
1 PETER 4:9, NIV

A little plaque that sits atop our piano reminds me of our core value for all who enter our home:

> *To invite someone into your home*
> *Is to take charge of their happiness*
> *For as long as they are under your roof.*
> J. BRILLAT-SAVARIN

This saying has become the commitment I seek to follow when people enter my home. I learned it from my mother.

As a college student out of state, I used to love the way my mama welcomed me home. She would plaster sticky notes all over the house so that everywhere I turned I would spy another little message:

"We are glad Sally is home!"
"Hurrah, our little girl is back again!"
"Welcome home. We missed you!"

That's the impetus for the little chalkboard that graces our porch. It's our welcome board. We always try to write the name of those we know will be entering our home. ("Welcome, Smith family! We are so glad you are here.")

Adopting the attitude that every arrival at my door is a divine appointment for me to care for others, to understand and listen to them and to serve them a cup of cold water in Jesus' name, changes the way I see both my home and those who come into it. When I see my home as a source of life to be extended to all who enter, I will put aside my own responsibilities in favor of doing the ministry of home. I will be committed to the well-being of all those who enter.

A home that says welcome opens hearts to real relationships. We want all who enter our little kingdom—family, friends, and guests—to know that they are welcome and cherished in this sacred place we call home.

The Music of Safety

The Lord will guard your going out and your coming in
From this time forth and forever.
PSALM 121:8

Everyone who enters my home must come through some kind of door. Doors are wonderful inventions. They open in welcome, but they can also close to provide barriers against insects, storms, thieves, and other dangers. Doors help protect everyone inside from harm.

As a Christ follower and doorkeeper of my home, I try to ensure that wisdom, truth, and the reality of God's grace are kept within and that my home is a haven from the destructive voices of the outside world.

Clay and I and our children have experienced our share of heartbreak, sadness, and depression. Having a place where we can shut the door to the rest of the world—where we can be ourselves, wail together, make mistakes, and live through seasons of growth—has been a grace to us. The closed door allows us to work on our inadequacies, our limitations, our personal struggles without the eyes of the public viewing our personal lives. Since much of my life as a writer and speaker is public, making sure the door to home is closed to the judgment and influences of the world has been a profound commitment I make on behalf of my family.

There is a broader sense of the need for protection in a home behind the closed door. If someone knocked at my door and said, "I would like to molest your mind and heart—and by the way, could I molest and harm your children as well?" I would keep the door locked and never intentionally allow such a person to come inside. Home is to be a safe place, a refuge for all who enter, a protection from the harm and storms of the world. Yet often or even daily we open our doors—usually via television or the Internet—to ideas and images that can damage our faith, abuse our hearts and minds, scar our psyches, and tear apart our peace.

Home should be a place where, behind its doors, one should expect to find protection and safety from all the harms of life, including voices that do not speak truth or wisdom. Only the foolish would invite just anyone to enter the door of their home.

In order to protect ourselves and others from finding menacing influences, as much as possible, we must purpose ways to keep our homes as havens of all that is good, pure, innocent, and excellent. If the Lord guards our own coming and going, so we should be guards over what is allowed into our homes.

The Music of Knowledge and Wisdom

By wisdom a house is built . . .
And by knowledge the rooms are filled
With all precious and pleasant riches.
PROVERBS 24:3-4

A treasure chest is full of sparkly jewels, shiny gold coins, valuable booty of every kind. As a young woman, I began to picture my children's hearts as treasure chests of a different sort, and I vowed to fill them with intrinsic treasures: the best stories, memorized Scripture, priceless images of classical art, excellent books, memories from great feasts enjoyed together and special days celebrated, great Bible stories and wisdom passages, plus heart photographs of love given, holidays cherished, lessons learned. I hoped my children would be able to draw from this chest of internal treasures when they needed wisdom or comfort in their adult lives, that they would have soul resources that would speak to them for a lifetime.

Early in my adult life, I realized that what I had read, listened to, and stored inside my mind was what I would draw from in my daily interactions with all people. I wanted this for my children as well—to provide them with the best ideas, thoughts, and wisdom. Over time, this practice shaped my understanding of offering these resources to others as well.

That's how our whole home became a library. Every table in our house has a place underneath where magazines and books are piled for the reaching. Baskets of books sit at the end of couches for grabbing in spare moments. Literally thousands of books, magazines, audiobooks, devotional writings, and biographies, collected little by little, are scattered throughout every room in our house. Each one has been chosen as a source of inspiration and mind-filling strength.

My hope was that these resources would help everyone who passed through my home—family members and visitors alike—to have the treasure chests of their hearts stocked with what is sacred and worthwhile and be able to draw from this treasure for the rest of their lives.

The Music of Beauty

He has made everything beautiful in its time. He has also set eternity in the human heart.
ECCLESIASTES 3:11, NIV

God did not create us merely as intellectual beings, of course. He gave us senses with which to experience and enjoy what He made. We have eyes to see, ears to hear, nerve endings to feel, tongues to taste. Human beings are created to respond to beauty and to create beauty for ourselves. We honor Him when we make beauty a priority in our homes. This is another way of filling home with "precious and pleasant riches."

I have always wanted our home to be a place of interest, inspiration, education, creativity, and enjoyment—to embody the spirit of Christ in every nook and cranny. I wanted it to provide pleasure for the senses as well, to point toward the amazing beauty of God's creation, and to inspire everyone who passes through our doors.

In light of this, every wall of our home is adorned with images that remind us of what we treasure as a family. Photographs of friends, memories, children, and life events smile from every corner. Scripture verses rendered in exquisite calligraphy surround us with the beauty of God's Word. Artwork collected on our travels not only reminds us of where we have been but also reminds us of the world outside our walls. Framed prints of classic masterpieces teach as well as delight.

Beauty is more than just pictures on a wall. It is also about colors that bring pleasure, smooth and nubby textures that reward the touch, the wafting fragrance of food in the oven that keeps us sniffing appreciatively, the comfort or excitement of music on the stereo. Beauty is found in the way we light the rooms (we keep a well-stocked shelf of candles and lighters in constant use), the books we open again and again, the way we arrange the furniture and set the table. It is found in natural objects we use for decorating—potted plants, shells, autumn leaves, always fresh flowers or pine boughs brought in from our yard—and open windows that draw the eye toward the beautiful outdoors.

The Music of Relationship

Where two or three have gathered together in My name, I am there in their midst.
MATTHEW 18:20

Relationships are the core focus of celebrating life together in a place. Consequently, the desire to create spaces for friendship, companionship, and fellowship influenced many of our home choices—even the furniture we bought, where we placed it, and how we used it.

Over time, for instance, we collected four rocking chairs and a double rocker. These now sit on our front porch in view of the beautiful Rocky Mountains. Gathering on a cool summer evening almost every night, as the sunset fades into the shadows of the mountain, they set the stage for conversation and rest. We have a heritage of sitting together almost every day just to be companions sharing the moments of our days.

Grouping comfy couches and overstuffed chairs in front of the fireplace—not the television—is another relationship-based choice. In days before the television was invented, the hearth was the gathering place where community was shared and built. We have deliberately tried to re-create that dynamic in our home. We've discovered that having a media-free place to gather fosters conversation and engages people in mutual activities—games, read-aloud sessions, knitting, playing chess, discussing ideas, praying over issues of life.

The Music of Nourishment

[Jesus] was recognized by them in the breaking of the bread.
LUKE 24:35

Eating is one of the most satisfying experiences God has provided us with—and He requires us to experience it every day in order to stay alive! He has provided a wide variety of food to nourish our bodies. Fruits and vegetables; meat, fowl, and fish; grains and dairy, herbs and sweets—these too are part of the symphony of home. We have an endless variety of expression in our kitchens to both satisfy some very basic needs and provide pleasure for all who enter.

But eating is not just about filling our bellies—or at least it wasn't meant to be. There is something about preparing food and sharing it that enhances relationship, builds community, even fosters spiritual connection. No wonder Jesus' followers recognized their risen Lord when He broke bread with them.

I believe every meal should be a celebration of life itself as we break bread and enter fellowship together. And the way those meals are planned, prepared, and served enhances the connection and the celebration. Every meal, in other words, should be a feast for the senses and the spirit. (You'll hear a lot in this book about the importance of feasting.)

Collecting interesting dishware, lighting candles for atmosphere, putting together menus and trying new recipes, inviting guests to share, even doing the mundane chores of shopping for groceries, cooking, and cleaning up—all contribute to comfort and enjoyment several times each day. Even the kitchen equipment and the dining room furniture play a part.

Case in point: our sturdy oak dining room table. I saved my dollars over many years to be able to buy one big enough to hold eighteen when fully extended. We have shared literally thousands of meals around it over a variety of food, sharing in the friendship of eating, drinking, and cultivating connected minds and hearts. When necessary, we supplement the dining room chairs with folding chairs and even a piano bench—there's always room for one more.

The Music of Rest

It is useless for you to work so hard
   from early morning until late at night,
anxiously working for food to eat;
   for God gives rest to his loved ones.
PSALM 127:2, NLT

Our bodies were designed so that every day we would get a break from the burdens and demands of life by sleeping. But bedrooms are not just for sleeping! Ideally bedrooms should be special places where each family member can pull away from all the stress, escape the demands, and rest, cry, journal, and dream away from the eyes of others.

Bedrooms give sanctuary to souls and should be outfitted accordingly. For us this means, at the very least,

- *an inviting bed* with soft pillows and a comfortable spread or squishy duvet for a long, comfortable sleep;
- *a comfy chair* for reading, journaling, and praying (plus the materials to do just that);
- *a personalized space* for each occupant.

I always recognized my children's bedrooms as their own "places" to escape into their dream worlds. Here were individual color schemes, favorite posters, bookshelves holding their very own favorite stories, and practical items that spoke "safe and comfortable" to the ones living there. Even when our children have had to share bedrooms, I always looked for ways to provide them each with privacy and make sure they had at least a corner they felt was theirs alone.

Guest quarters have always been a priority for us, even when we lived in a tiny apartment. When the "guest room" is an air mattress or a pullout couch in the living room, care can still be taken to provide a comfortable and private retreat. A truly comfortable sleeping place, quality bedding, a light for reading, special towels and toiletries, perhaps a vase of flowers or writing paper—a little thoughtfulness and attention to detail assures that those who share our space for a time can hear the music of rest in our homes.

Filling the Spaces of Home

So much more will be shared in the rest of this book about ways to become creative in filling the spaces of home with meaningful opportunities to celebrate the sacraments of life. But the point is that there needs to be a conductor—someone needs to design the place and direct the usage in such a way that it meets the needs of all who dwell there and those who visit as well.

Dip into a month or season of ideas one at a time. Enjoy what you will, but never allow the ideas to burden you. I hope you will be encouraged, wherever you are, whatever your dwelling, to become an artist of life who provides a place of life for all who come to see you.

Don't forget to have fun while you're doing it. Directing the music of a home not only is essential to building an atmosphere that invites life; it is also a delightful pastime. I have found so much pleasure over many years finding ways to make my home a more interesting place to be—searching garage sales, secondhand stores, local shops, and foreign marketplaces for the treasures that now fill my rooms.

My home has been decades in the making. It did not come together all at once. At age sixty-two, I am still refining and refreshing the atmosphere to meet the needs of my husband, our now-adult children, and me. It all began with the decision to begin—to envision, plan, and build. But it didn't end there. Having a home that tells a great story happens over time as we mature, refine, create, and love.

I hope you will have that experience as well. Whatever your taste, preferences, and style, you have the freedom to create your own home art and make your dwelling a place that is distinctively yours—a place of comfort, safety, and delight for you and everyone who steps inside your door.

4

THE RHYTHMS OF INCARNATION
(SARAH)

The world cannot be discovered by a journey of miles, no matter how long, but only by a spiritual journey, a journey of one inch, very arduous and humbling and joyful, by which we arrive at the ground at our own feet, and learn to be at home.

WENDELL BERRY

LAST SUMMER, I conducted what I call my Facebook experiment. For two months I decided to deactivate my account and withdraw my attention from the busy, friendly, online world with its second-by-second excitement.

I did this because I was feeling idealistic. I had been reading Wendell Berry, one of my heroes. Berry, a literary farmer who placed high value on attentiveness to the present, famously refused to use a computer. Aware of an increasing white noise in my own head and the tendency of my attention to dart anywhere but the present, I decided it wouldn't kill me to log off for a couple of months and immerse myself instead in the color, intensity, and family presence of summer.

I expected to gain a quieter mind. A calmer mental atmosphere. I did not expect to be profoundly challenged in my understanding of original human identity. I didn't expect to emerge convicted of the vital need for a physical space in which humankind can return to God's first design. I didn't expect a break from Facebook to convict me of the spiritual significance of home and the need to fight actively to create it.

Unplugged Living

My own epiphany began with the mornings. The first days of my experiment, I woke with the impulse to check my phone. My online rules for the summer included a determination not to check the Internet at all before breakfast. With vivid clarity, I remember the physical impulse that came in those first dawns—the instinctive reach of my arm to grasp the phone, the remembrance, and the drop of my hand back onto the quilt. Then the hush as I rested in the early morning quiet—eye, thought, consciousness settling like a startled bird back into the rich present. Birdsong tapped at the window, gauzy light filtered over the foothills, and my own breath in my ear was like the subtle echo of the ocean caught in a shell.

Those mornings lengthened. I'd walk downstairs to find my mom or a sibling up in the summer quiet, out in a rocking chair on the porch. Without the online world to distract me, I'd curl in a chair next to them. We'd rock and chat. We'd read aloud a passage from the Bible or talk about something that happened the day before. I never would have expected it before the break, but everything about me slowed. I'd amble in to make breakfast or lunch and take my time about it, savoring the fruit or bread or the bright crispness of vegetables without the usual restless impulse to check a website or answer a post. I read novels aloud with my siblings. I took time to journal. I did my work with far greater clarity of focus.

As the days continued, the quiet grew. That one departure from Facebook empowered me to resist the Internet in general, and a hush grew daily within me as I rooted my consciousness once more in the world of touch, sight, sound, and breath. I found myself newly aware of the rhythms of light and dark. I felt a hush that beckoned me to look out my window and learn again the different moods of the pines in the dawn and the dark and the half light. I began to garden with my mom. I planted flowers and felt the slow, rich rhythm of the earth in my fingers. I found a silence of possibility in the evenings, in which loneliness or longing were channeled into letters written and spaces ordered and stories sketched out instead of submerged in the painkilling run of the Facebook feed.

I looked, with a fixed attention I had often lacked (to my shame), upon the faces so dear to me, and I listened to my loved ones without restlessness or distraction. In the silence that grew, I slowed, and an inner space was forged within me from which I looked out on the world, able to weigh my thoughts, consider my choices, and know my emotions before the press of the outer world provoked me to action.

A Renewed Awareness

When the two-month experiment came to its end, I logged in once. Within ten minutes I was logging off, all too aware of the anxiety that had already returned to my thoughts. I sat down to write out exactly what I had discovered in my two months away from the virtual world and back into the rhythms of earth, relationship, and physical reality.

What my absence from the online world accomplished was a renewed awareness of the forms on which my experience of time, space, and physicality was built. That summer was something of a journey, away from the physical forms and mental habits of the modern world and back into the consciousness and heartbeat of creation as it began in Genesis. The further I went, the more I became aware of the unthinking way contemporary living removes us from the holy, original rhythms of creativity, work, rest, and relationship. I realized I needed to reevaluate the structures and habits of my life if I was going to create the kind of home for myself that truly reflected the goodness of God.

I recommend such a journey of evaluation to anyone interested in making a home. If we want to embody the life of God in our homes, we need to understand what God intended human life to be, and we also need to be aware of what distracts us from that intention or diminishes it in our lives. Only within such a framework can we gain a vision for how each aspect of home communicates and reflects the ultimate spiritual realities we hope to embody.

Original Intentions

To read Genesis is to be immersed in a vivid picture of what God intended for humankind in their relationship to one another and the earth. The "creation mandate" or "cultural mandate" God gave humanity when He blessed them was to "be fruitful and multiply, and fill the earth, and subdue it" (Genesis 1:28). We were meant, in other words, to continue the work of the God whose image we bore, a God who had just completed a cycle of rich, generous, lavish creation. We were meant to be fruitful, existing within the bond of family, connected to community, united in our care for the gift of the earth.

In an age when few of us live in the country, I think it is easy to forget that to intimately know and graciously rule the earth is one of our primary charges. This may have a very different expression in a modern age rather than an ancient one, but the reality is the same. Though a dozen practical reasons for this charge could be named, including the health of human bodies and the environment, I think one of the primary reasons is that it embodies and signifies the goodness of God. It speaks of His richness and sets us amidst His thought enfleshed. "In the beginning God created" (Genesis 1:1), and every atom came from His imagination. I believe He made the world in such a way that to tend it, to touch it, would be to know His heart. He told a story into the earth, the tale of His bounteous heart. We were given the uplifted arms of pines and the vibrancy of a summer garden, the laden arms of apple trees and the dark patience of mountains, to keep us alive every day to all that God is and will continue to be.

We were also meant for rootedness. God set Adam and Eve within a garden, their "place on earth," as Wendell Berry puts it.[1] I believe this garden home was to be the model for what humans were meant to accomplish throughout the earth—claiming, ordering, and cultivating every inch of creation until the whole of it reflected the order, beauty, and goodness of its Maker. But the purpose of this work was to form and root *us* just as much as the earth. We were created for belonging, made to behold the heritage of our creative diligence in children and grandchildren and in the legacy of a home forged and tended in a specific place on earth. To abandon a human identity as communal, relational keepers of the earth and, with it, creators of home is to lose a core sense of the human self and the God who made us.

A Scrambled Consciousness

The problem, though, is that we live in an age in which the original rhythms of creation are increasingly obscured, when not only the original Fall but also the actual structures and habits of modern life draw us out of fellowship, away from connection, and toward distraction, absence, and autonomy. While there are certainly benefits to the world of technology, and while social media has in many ways increased connectedness, there are also profound ways in which the overuse of virtual reality and technological media is causing us to become mentally and emotionally absent from the present world of incarnational action.

The online world occupies a space separate from the confines of our material existence. The rhythms of earth and body require me to sleep. The limitations of my physical senses mean I can only hear so many voices, so many words, at one time. But the online world is unresting. Repose and stillness are antithetical to the nature of the Internet, which is to produce "new" information every hour of the day. Moderation and even mental limitation are concepts not applicable to online reality. I can scan an incredible amount of information in an hour on the Internet, and I need never rest on one page for long. There is always the next thing to scan, check, discover.

But whenever I dwell in that universe and submit my mind to its laws, I am trained to its swift, unresting pattern of information. Facebook and other online apps teach me to desire constant surface stimulation. Influenced by the thought patterns of machines, my own mind cranks along, unable to rest, habituated to the disembodied, unresting online atmosphere. But the constant stream of information isn't helping me to think more deeply, to contemplate, to have the long-considered knowledge that becomes wisdom. Rather, it is conditioning me simply to glean information and then move on. As author Nicholas Carr wrote, "The Internet is an interruption system. It seizes our attention only to scramble it."[2]

The Bible, once you start noticing, is filled with directions regarding where we are to direct consciousness and thought: "Pray without ceasing" (1 Thessalonians 5:17), "Be still, and know that I am God" (Psalm 46:10, NIV), "Surely I have composed and quieted my soul" (Psalm 131:2), and on it goes. The more I have studied the effect of the virtual world on what we create in the physical world, the more I am convinced that God is concerned with the direction of attention and consciousness because they directly have to do with incarnation. We can only create what we have imagined. We can only embody the life of God if we have internally known and tasted His goodness.

How do I apply a scrambled attention to the construction of home and the creation of relationships? If I am conditioned to a restless mental absence from the world around me, I will be focused on checking a Facebook feed rather than feeding a guest—or at very least, distracted from focusing on the other person's needs. If the precious, limited hours of my day are used bit by bit in scanning information, I will have less and less time for the attentive, slow, good work of creativity, conversation, and connection that real people and real homes require. If my awareness of space is concentrated on a screen, my home will reflect the absence of my attention, my creativity, and ultimately, my love. How can I pray without ceasing and bring that prayer into every aspect of making home if I cannot focus on anything for more than five seconds at a time?

Choosing My Rhythms

It was questions like these that prompted me to experiment with a Facebook break in the first place. The longer I pondered them, the more convicted I became that I cannot submit my life to the rhythms of modernity without great control and inward caution. I grew convinced that part of the holy work of homemaking is an evaluation of the forms and rhythms by which we live.

Once I realized that, I began to look at the spaces of my life and home as a kind of kingdom over which I ruled. To rule my time, to clear my mind was a choice of mental sovereignty, a reclamation of the direction, rhythm, and source of my thoughts so that I could root them in the people I loved and the life I wanted to create. I began to plan my hours of rest and work, my rhythms of fellowship and silence around what I believe to be the identity God means me to have as a lover of His people, a bringer of His Kingdom, a maker of home.

When you understand the reality of incarnation, the way that the physical trappings of our lives and our use of time and space are places where God either comes in His creative presence or remains at bay, you understand that nothing is neutral. Nothing. You can't just waste an hour on the Internet. You can't just miss one sunrise in its beauty. No room is just space. No hour is meaningless. No meal is mere sustenance. Every rhythm and atom of existence are spaces in which the Kingdom can come, in which the story of God's love can be told anew, in which the stuff of life can be turned marvelously into love.

We cannot change the world if we cannot incarnate God's love in our own most ordinary spaces and hours. Homemaking must be understood as a potent Kingdom endeavor, not merely a domestic task. Homemaking requires a willed creativity, a conscious diligence, because we are called to create new life and challenged to do it in the midst of a world that actively resists us in this endeavor.

So let me conclude, then, with a challenge. Take a day, or half a day, or even an hour away. Sit somewhere quiet with a notebook and pen. Evaluate your use of time. Identify the major places where your attention is directed on a regular basis. Consider your home and what it reflects about your beliefs. And then consider how you, filled with the same creative energy that formed the cosmos, might fill and form the spaces of your home.

Remember, the home doesn't have to be a house. It doesn't have to include a spouse or children. The tiniest flat or the biggest mansion can be home because, you know, each home is a world. It is the possible space into which the Holy Spirit, through us, calls a world of order, color, love, and life into being. We are challenged by the Incarnation to make our homes a small cosmos of God's Kingdom, one more outpost of eternity right in the midst of time.

How can Facebook compare to that?

PART TWO
Seasons of Home

January

CREATING A FRAMEWORK FOR HOME
Rhythms, Routines, and Rituals

(SALLY)

Isn't it nice to think that tomorrow is a new day with no mistakes in it yet?
LUCY MAUD MONTGOMERY

DRESSING UP IN my special violet—not purple, but violet—dress, I donned my socks with lace on them, put on my patent leather shoes, grabbed my little black purse that held a new five-dollar bill, and readied myself for one of my favorite days of the year. My mama took my brothers and me to our favorite "five-and-dime" store each year to buy new supplies for school.

My favorite part was when I got to buy the crayon box filled with sixty-four different colors. All of the crayons had sharp points, and no one had used them yet. Then came a little art journal where I would create my masterpieces and a tiny journal just for me to write down all my stories.

Sitting down to a clean piece of paper and opening the new box to use for the first time gave me great little-girl pleasure. The moment held endless possibilities, with no mistakes or smudges yet.

What a joy to be able to start out new and fresh.

The Gift of a New Year

This picture has become a paradigm for all of my Januaries—a new beginning, a new year with no mistakes in it yet (thank you, Anne of Green Gables), 365 days ahead with all sorts of possibilities and a variety of ways to invest the days. To have a new start every year is a gift to me, as I always want to do things better, clear out the old, bring in the new. January gives me that new start—the possibility of wiping the slate clean and starting all over again with a new box of crayons.

Home is your garden of life, so to speak, and you are free to order it and plant it as you will. But all great works of life must be planned in order to make them productive, useful, and flourishing. With a garden, the more ground that is planted, the more yield to the crop. Similarly, the greater care we take with planning our days and years, the more productive we will be. Great works of life art don't just happen. They must be imagined, planned, and worked on before they become a reality.

That's not to say that all of your plans will unfold the way you expect. Life happens. Things come up. Plans will need to be adjusted to fit new circumstances. (That's one reason to make planning a yearly practice—so we can make adjustments.) But I have found that having a plan and looking ahead actually makes it *easier*, not harder, to roll with the punches and still keep more or less on course.

Making plans for a home, after all, does not mean that everyone will always cooperate or follow those plans perfectly. Sometimes, in fact, I used to wonder if the work of home building and investing in my children's lives made any difference whatsoever. Quarreling, selfish moments, and daily messes challenged my confidence that I was doing anything of importance. Yet now I look back and see that the plans we followed, the rhythms we practiced day after day, eventually became the values that all of us embraced as a family. It didn't always seem like they were paying attention, but all of them breathed in the oxygen of our home ideals and have grown up to reflect the values we wanted so much to instill in them. We even all like the same brand of tea, and our favorite movies and books are what we have enjoyed together.

There is no one right way to live life in a home. No one size of routine or rules or order fits all. Homes with young children will be quite different from a single-adult home. Elderly adults will order their lives by different life rituals than will single adults, young marrieds, or university students. But the more carefully we plan our days, the better our homes will provide us with freedom and enjoyment as well as purpose and accomplishment.

I have found that my own plans work best when I live within the limitations and strengths of my own personality and make plans that suit my particular circumstances. I am not like others; my family has different parameters of need. I am quite free to do what is best for us when I plan for our family to flourish with all of our uniqueness in mind. But I do this most productively, I find, when I build in the purpose, order, and satisfying systems that will keep us moving forward.

Familiar rhythms and routines give structure that provides leadership and personal care to all who live there. When children and guests know what to expect, they also know how to ask for their personal needs to be met and understand what part they play in the life of the home.

Here, then, are some of the questions I try to ask myself each year:

- *What daily rhythms will help me accomplish what needs to be done and enhance our relationships?* How can I include meaningful expectations of the work to be accomplished and the ways we will spend our time together? Morning, noon, and night bring their own demands and practices, and a good plan will take these into consideration. Planning daily rhythms—meals, devotions, cleanup, bedtime routines—should take into consideration the abilities and personalities of everyone who lives in the home.

- *What chores need to be done each day? Who will do them, and how will I make sure they are done?* Housework, cleaning, paying bills, yard work, shopping, hosting guests, setting the table, washing dishes—all of these must be done. Establishing routines for handling these things builds an expectation for my family or roommates that will bring a constant stream of order to our lives.

- *Am I doing something now that doesn't need to be done?* How can I simplify my work to provide more time to do what I value most? I want to avoid "mile-wide and inch-deep" commitments and commit to a few activities that are central to my values.

- *What daily and weekly rituals will bring pleasure and mark important areas in which I can invest my moments?* Celebrating life on a regular basis keeps me happier and more energized in the midst of caring for my four children, my husband, and our family of friends. I have learned to provide life rituals that bring energy back to my heart, mind, and soul—Saturday night movie and pizza, Sunday afternoon tea times, going out for dinner as a family every Friday night.

Many years ago, Clay, my very organized husband, gave me an acronym to work from. He said if I made a plan for managing the following areas, life would be more centered:

Family
Information
Rest
Stuff
Time

Clay was right. I find that writing down all of my current issues under each category gives me a simple way to plan for organizing my year.

One of the most important aspects of planning, I have found, is that I must include me in the process! If I take care of my own personal needs—proper nutrition, rest, exercise, prayer and devotion, work, friendships—then my family and all who come to my home will have a full well to draw from when they encounter me. But if I do not plan for my own personal life to be satisfying and productive, I will have nothing to offer or give to those in my care.

Whatever your household or season of life, make your plans according to your needs, circumstances, life stage, and personality so that your home can thrive in sync with your own preferences. You will only find your plans sustainable if they fit you as well as those who live in your home.

——— *In Our Home* ———

Endless books and planners have been written to help organize life. You can find them in any bookstore. My goal here is not so much to provide detailed organizational help as to suggest that January is an optimum time to regroup, to put priorities back in place. In the following paragraphs I'll list some of the annual activities that have helped me get my life more centered and back to a good start for each new year.

First We Celebrate

Because moving took our family all over the United States and sometimes the world, often we would find ourselves on New Year's Eve without a lot of local friends to join for celebration. We celebrated anyway! Any friend of any child plus an odd assortment of adults—single, married, old, young—would congregate at our home every December 31.

Each person invited was to bring a favorite game and favorite snacks to share. The Clarksons always contributed *chile con queso* (cheese with green chiles) with tortilla chips, a tradition from my family of origin, and a green chile stew made of pork roast, pinto beans, green chiles, and sometimes chunks of potatoes simmered together and served with a dollop of sour cream and some grated cheese. Then we played games until the clock struck midnight, when we toasted the New Year with glasses of sparkling grape or apple juice served in real crystal from the grandmothers.

Those New Year's Eve game nights were always a wonderful way of creating new friendships and cementing others. We had people all over the house, with different games in different rooms of the house—board games, physical games like Twister, kids' games, plus traditional group participation games like charades. I was always amazed to see how close people can become when battling against each other for fun.

A Day for Planning

Planning well takes time—preferably time away from the bustle of everyday decision making. If we want to fill the year's activities with meaning and purpose and also be able to say no to activities that steal time and energy, it helps to get away and think.

For many years, on New Year's Day, Clay would make a special pancake and waffle breakfast for all the people who had stayed in our home the night before. He would send me out the door and say, "Today is your day to plan your year. Have fun and I'll see you tonight." I would then sequester myself away in the loveliest place I could find—a hotel lobby, a coffee shop, even a museum café—with a cup of tea or coffee, a journal, and a pen. This was my day to enjoy some "me" time and plan how I wanted to invest in my year ahead.

I can't tell you the difference that one day made, and I urge you to try hard to get away alone every year for a little planning time. If you and your spouse cannot hold down the fort (or if you don't have a spouse), consider springing for a babysitter or trading time with another parent. The clarity and perspective you gain from that time apart will save you time and money over the long haul.

Decluttering the Soul

I love the holidays—the meaning, the traditions, and the fun and beauty of special times spent with my children, husband, and friends. But I also love it when the holidays are over. There is something deeply satisfying to me about getting all the holiday stuff put away and getting back to normal.

Perhaps it is because my normal responsibilities of caring for my family's needs demand so much of me—cooking nutritious meals, organizing our schedules, cleaning and straightening on a daily basis, and homeschooling (in past days), as well as ministry, writing, and speaking. The holidays, as much as I love them, put an extra load on top of all that. Routines go by the wayside, and clutter slowly takes over.

I am not a person gifted in handling details—too much mail, too many catalogs, too many e-mails, too many belongings (except books!), too many options. The more stuff there is, the more I become responsible for and the more work there is to be done . . . and so the more anxious I become.

The same is true of activities. The more I commit to, the more I say yes to, the more I have to drive, the more my house gets into a mess . . . the more anxious and weary I become, and the more hurried we all feel. When I am not at peace, nothing in our home is at peace.

Too much clutter and too many piles of stuff can cause anyone to feel overwhelmed. So I have found it's necessary to declutter our home as often as I can. Clay is really the master at this. He helps me get rid of things, organize things, and put away things.

At some point in early January, for instance, Clay always cleans out our pantry. He throws away chip bags that hold little but take up space, clears out empty water bottles, tosses containers of junky Christmas candy that have been given to us but will never be eaten, picks up baskets that have fallen off their nails, and organizes groceries that had never been put away in the proper place. If someone came into my pantry after Clay finished, they would mistakenly think I am an organized person. (Thank goodness for Clay.) It always makes me feel good just to open the door and see that all is manageable again.

But decluttering isn't just a matter of stuff. I have also come to realize that my brain and heart can be the same way—cluttered with worries, responsibilities, duties, concerns over the future, finances, time constraints, expectations, disappointments, critical attitudes, resentment. All of these added together can tend to create soul piles and mind clutter. If I don't take the time to sort them out, my spirit becomes a mess, and my heart becomes overwhelmed and weary. And this kind of decluttering is something no one can do for me.

Each year, then, I make a new plan to simplify the "mind messes." This involves cleaning out my heart and thoughts, asking (and answering) questions like the following:

- Do I have any lingering feelings of guilt that I need to give to God?
- Is there any bitterness toward friends or family? Any resentment?
- Do any of my relationships need mending?
- Have I created any rifts between me and God that I need to clear up?
- Are there ways I have failed or disappointments I have carried that are draining my energy?

I also try to identify ways I have missed my goals and ways I want to strengthen my commitments in the major areas of my life—*physical* (diet and exercise), *emotional* (my relationships with Clay, the kids, my friends, and our extended family), and *spiritual* (books I want to read, when is best to have a quiet time, what I will study or read in the Bible, ways I want to grow). I choose one or two areas I will concentrate on during the following year and find a pertinent Bible verse to memorize as a support.

For instance, if I want to become more gentle, I might memorize Matthew 11:29: "Take my yoke upon you. Let me teach you, because I am humble and gentle at heart, and you will find rest for your souls" (NLT). I write this verse out and put it on my refrigerator where I will see it every day.

Next, I take time to pour out all of my heart and thoughts, feelings, and dreams to God. I end with my prayer requests for the next season ahead and make a point to leave my life and issues in His hands. This process of decluttering my soul gives me a fresh attitude for beginning a new year.

Planning for Fun!

The fun and excitement of the Christmas holidays can leave both adults and children drained, and short days and winter weather can make things worse. Making sure that life has homey pleasures gives grace to those long, cold days—so while I'm doing my serious planning, I try to dream up some recreational ones as well.

- *Play outdoors if you can.* Bundle up in your coziest winter gear and enjoy a hike in the crisp winter air or a walk on a winter beach. If you live where it's cold, take full advantage of snow forts, snowballs, ice skating, and the like.
- *Take advantage of indoor entertainment.* Cold or wet winter days often force families indoors, so always try to find some fun indoor places to go. This is a great time to attend a concert, play, or movie or to explore a museum.
- *Invite friends over for cozy hospitality.* Decide who you might have over for mugs of hot chocolate and fresh chocolate chip cookies. Or plan a Frito-pie night. Cook your favorite kind of chili and combine it with small bowls of grated cheese, corn chips, sour cream, and onions, and you have a fun dinner for sitting by the fire.
- *Bake some bread and simmer some soup.* The kitchen is a wonderful place to be on a cold day. There's nothing like a pot of potato-cheese, vegetable, or chicken-noodle soup bubbling on the stove (or in a slow cooker) and the yeasty aroma of bread baking to lift everyone's spirits.
- *Listen by the fire.* Books on tape by the fireside were popular with our crew when they were younger. We especially enjoyed the radio drama versions of C. S. Lewis's The Chronicles of Narnia (1950–1956), David and Karen Mains's *Tales of the Kingdom* (1983), and Ralph Moody's *Little Britches* (1950). For more ideas, you can access our "Lifegiving Home Resources" page at www.lifegivinghome.com.
- *Create cozy play spaces* with card table tents, closet hideaways, and such. Joy had a little part of my closet where we would hang a little lantern and put a basket of toys to create an indoor playhouse for her. She loved being in her special, cozy little place.
- *Find a way to bring outdoor games indoors.* Hiding wooden painted Easter eggs all over the house provided our children with hours of play when it was too cold to go outside.

Establishing a Devotional Routine

When my home was filled with children, and even when I lived as a single woman in an apartment, I found it helpful to establish routines and expectations that everyone in the house understood. The activities we practiced daily in our home—morning and bedtime rituals, mealtime practices, chore and cleanup assignments, reading every afternoon, and more—not only anchored our days and simplified our lives but also deepened our relationships, strengthened the rest of our commitments, and helped us develop positive lifelong habits.

Probably the most important routine for us involved morning devotions. Making the worship of God a daily habit is a foundational practice for both individuals and a household. I believe it shapes the inner foundations of the soul more powerfully than almost any other practice.

For many years now I have had my own quiet time before the rest of the household is up. This means I have to discipline myself to get out of bed! I like to brew strong English tea, light a little candle, and sit in a comfy chair—usually one in my bedroom, away from the crowd. I keep a basket of quiet time books and devotionals so that I may choose what suits me or the time I have each day. At any given time I am usually working my way through a book in the Bible, a spiritual book or Bible study guide of some sort (one half or whole chapter at a time), and a variety of devotional books.

Sometimes I have just a couple of minutes for this, while other times I have longer, but I keep my quiet time chair and reading basket at the ready so I can quickly jump into my devotions and make the best use of the time I have. After reading for a bit I end by praying for each one in my family and for friends who have asked me to pray for them.

There are days, of course, when life happens and I do not get my quiet time, but planning it as a priority and making it a habit has helped bring order to my whole life. It is the single most important and influential practice of life and has given me strength, wisdom, a sense of God's truth and direction, and a thankful heart.

When I have started my days off with God, I've found it easier to share what I have been learning with the kids. But even when I did not have time for myself, I made time to have daily morning devotions with the kids. This was the most regular routine (next to eating) that defined our days. We would read a Bible story, or study one of the "24 Ways" (values that our family has chosen to follow—see the April chapter), or read through Psalms or Proverbs for five to ten minutes, and discuss what we had learned. Then we would always pray together to give God our day.

I will explore our family's devotional practices in more detail later. The main point I want to make here is that establishing positive lifetime habits is the goal for all of the areas of work, discipline, and spiritual practice. A habit is an activity one has done so often that it has become second nature, a way of life, and requires little prior thought or voluntary effort. Good habits make it easier to live a good life, and positive routines—like regular quiet times and family devotions—are the key to developing good habits.

Mealtime Routines

Mealtimes at our house were most always media-free—no phones, computers, or iPads allowed—and set aside as a time of catching up and fellowship. This provided time every day when everyone could share their thoughts, their woes, and their stories. I think we built more ties to one another through shared meals than anything else we regularly did together.

Of course, doing this was easier in the early years when the kids were small. But even as they grew into young adults, whoever was home or could be home ate dinner together. When my boys were far away in college and in new jobs, both of them told me that what they missed the most about home were the meals—we called them the family feast time.

Setting the table was always my children's job. The first one up would set the breakfast table, and the chore then rotated for lunch and dinner, with each child assigned a different meal. The routine included clearing the table of clutter, laying out plates and utensils, and selecting appropriate glasses and napkins. Whoever drew dinner duty was also responsible for setting out the candles and lighting them. We always had candles at the dinner table, whether we were eating toast and fruit or a multicourse meal. The act of lighting the candles quieted and civilized our mealtimes.

Household Routines

Attending to daily chores and housework does not come easily or naturally to me, but it has to be done. I have found that dividing the work into bite-size chunks and spreading it throughout the day makes it seem less burdensome. And developing a habit of cleaning and straightening as I go through the day keeps the messes from overwhelming me.

When I was a homeschooling mom with four little kids, I learned—and taught my children—to clear the table immediately after each meal, rinse the dishes and put them into the dishwasher, clean the crumbs and clutter off the countertops and table, and prepare for the next meal by setting the table. After a busy morning of lessons, we would stop and put away the morning clutter in the house before lunch. Then each afternoon at around five or six o'clock, I would gather all the family members still living at home, and we would take fifteen minutes to straighten the house.

When the children were little, that fifteen-minute cleanup meant LEGOs back in their box, puzzles in zippered plastic bags, books in baskets around the room, and toys in closets. At a later stage in our lives, it meant coffee mugs and teacups collected and put in the dishwasher, books and papers and computers put away, and clutter stacked or stowed. Often I would put on soft rock music for our fifteen-minute straightening time. When three songs were over, we would go back to what we were doing before. But starting the evening with a "clean-ish" house made the evening much more pleasant for everyone.

The Routine of a Morning Blessing

"Good morning, Mr. Sunshine. You make me happy to be alive!"

"Oh, Mama, you say that every day! You don't really mean it."

"Oh, but I do! How dark my day would be without my sunshine."

Then would come the tousling of the fuzzy bed-flat hair and a big wet kiss on the cheek, and off we would go into our morning.

I began practicing this morning blessing many years ago—greeting each one I met with a "Good morning! I am so thankful for you today." Or "How are you this morning, my lovey?" or "I am so glad you are mine today. You are a blessing to me." I persisted even in those times when the ones I was blessing acted embarrassed or just too sleepy to care. Oddly enough, these words are the ones my children have told me they heard in their heads many years after they left our home. Loving words have the power to provide hope, encouragement, confidence, and energy for the tasks of every day.

If you want everyone in your home—including the family who lives there—to feel welcome, consider how you greet them into the day. Your words don't have to be the same each day (or the same as mine), and what suits your family and speaks to the heart of each person in it will differ. Gentleness, not loudness, seems to suit our family the best. But however you do it, the habit of welcoming them each morning and affirming your affection for them really does help to start the day well.

Incidentally, I found this habit of mine started to wane when I began working more on my computer. My eyes would be glued to the screen when people emerged from their rooms, and I would not look up, look into their eyes, or listen to the tone of their voices to know how they were doing. As a result, I noticed my personal connection to my "peeps" diminished. Now I try to make a point to stop doing whatever I am doing when I see someone for the first time in the morning. I try to turn in that person's direction, meet their eyes with a welcoming look, and greet them in some appropriate way.

It really isn't hard to do that, and I have found it makes a world of difference. It is much rarer now for my children to roll their eyes when they see me working.

The Reading-Hour Routine

One of the best pieces of advice I have received in regard to motherhood came from a mom I met whose children were just a little older than mine. Her advice has served me as an adult as well.

She said, "If you can create the habit of afternoon reading when your children are little, they will keep it going the rest of their lives."

I may have attempted this life habit a little too early with my little ones, but I loved the idea and was determined to put it into practice. Each afternoon, generally sometime between two and three o'clock, I would give each child a special basket of books from our home or the library and encourage them to read quietly. Each basket held one or two library books of their choice, a couple of my own choosing, and one or two delightful picture books that they had picked out. When they were older, I included a biography, something on science and nature, perhaps some whimsical poetry, an occasional puzzle book, and some kind of rousing fiction—again, one of their choice and one of my choice. I finished up with a book of historical fiction.

To encourage my kids to actually read the books, I set up a system of rewards. Sometimes there would be a basket of prizes from the dollar store or coupons for a date with Mom or Dad, frozen yogurt, stickers, or some other treat. When they read so many pages and could tell me what the book was about, I would let them either choose a prize or earn points leading up to a bigger one. Because it became the expectation of each day, everyone actually learned to enjoy it and looked forward to reading time alone.

Eventually, as the children grew older, I bought each of them a bookshelf and made sure that every Christmas or birthday they would receive something new to put on their own personal shelf. I also bought each of them a small recliner or overstuffed chair for their rooms so they would have a special place to do their reading.

I'm happy to say my friend was right. The afternoon reading routine lured my children into the world of imagination and words. Because of it, all of my children have become lovers of books and avid readers on every topic imaginable.

Routines for Closing the Day

Some years ago I was speaking at the Military Regional Women's Conference in Hawaii, and I took my youngest, Joy, as my travel companion. Someone asked Joy, then sixteen, to share how to reach the heart of your child or teenager. I had no idea what she would say in response because she and I had recently experienced some conflict in our relationship.

Joy tossed her long, red-streaked brown hair and commented without hesitation, "Every night, no matter what, I knew my mom would come to my bed and spend time with me and talk with me and pray with me before I went to bed. It was our time, when I could pour out my fears, my secrets, my confessions, and my dreams. If you want to win your teen, you need to give them time to talk to you, and bedtime is a great time to do that."

I was a little surprised to hear that out of all the things we had done together, our bedtime routines came to her mind first. But it made sense when I thought about it. Early in our marriage, Clay and I had heard someone speak about bedtime being an important moment for children, and I had taken that to heart. When each of our children was born, therefore,

I determined that I would spend an extended time with him or her every night, and I would never let them go to bed without a special word of blessing.

Blessing children each night before they go to bed gives them the gift of a peaceful, restful, loved heart. No matter what a day has held—fussing, conflict, excitement, drudgery, joy, celebration, hard work—it's a way of ending the day well. A bedtime blessing ties all those loose ends together with unconditional love and helps put to rest all the burdens of the day by placing them into the hands of God.

No matter what has transpired throughout the day, we can close it by speaking to our children's hearts with something like "I love you no matter what. Please forgive me for my impatience today" or "I forgive you for your disobedience today" or "You are very precious to me. I am blessed to have you. You may go to sleep without bearing anger or a guilty conscience or fear because I love you and God loves you, and He will be with you. Sleep in peace, my precious."

It's not always easy to manage this, of course. Bedtime can be a burden for an exhausted parent, and it's not always possible to spend extended time with each child. Sometimes it's all but impossible to keep from screaming! Please do not imagine our own family bedtimes were without struggle. But I think when one is intentional about making a bedtime blessing an anchor of the day and guiding and leading your children, friends, and guests to expect that the end of the day will be relational, bedtime can become a grace to all that has transpired throughout the day. A bedtime blessing gives children one last impression of their whole day, and it is a redeeming time of bringing and restoring and offering peace. Best of all, the same principle works with a spouse or roommate.

Clay and I had elaborate bedtime routines for our children when they were young so that they knew what was coming and more easily submitted to the routine. As Nathan had some OCD tendencies about bedtime, we knew that if he could not remember the prayer and the kiss, he would not be able to go to sleep. So often I would repeat a short prayer and say, "Now this time I want you to remember how much I love you and God loves you."

For many years in our house, baths marked the beginning of the bedtime routine. We would put the kids in our big old bathtub with every imaginable toy—whatever it took to keep them there and to give them a place to expend one last surge of energy. While they splashed, I would sit down to rest and read or have a cup of something just for me, even if the dishes were still in the sink and the house was a wreck. I would spend those few minutes restoring myself because I wanted to be available to extend a nighttime blessing to each of the kids. (If you want to try this, please remember to do it only with age-appropriate children. Babies and toddlers should never be left alone in a tub.)

Once bath time was over, Clay and I would take turns making sure pajamas were on and teeth were brushed. Finally we would gather in the living room or a child's bedroom for a short read-aloud from a children's storybook. This expected routine helped them to understand that bedtime and sleep time were coming.

After we read, we would send the kids to the bathroom one last time, then tuck them into bed personally, touch or stroke their foreheads, pray for them, and kiss them. Every night we gave an "I love you" or "I am so very blessed to have you" or other intentional words of acceptance and encouragement.

The more positive and predictable the bedtime routine, we found, the more our children went to bed willingly. "Now it is bedtime," we would say. "We have bathed, read, and prayed, and now you get such a privilege—you get to snuggle in your lovely bed with your soft, cuddly stuffed animals and go into dreamland." We always talked sweetly of their beds and tried to make them seem as delightful as possible. We also made good use of positive peer pressure—when all the children worked in routines together, the younger ones tended to follow the routine without much of a fuss. And we made a point to praise them: "You are growing so strong inside. You go to bed like a big boy or girl."

As our older children grew, the bedtime routine grew longer because it involved nighttime talks in their rooms, the sharing of hearts and secret fears, struggles, temptation. Joy, however, had an extended bedtime almost from the time she was born. With so many older children vying for my attention during the day, I knew that Joy needed some "just me" time away from the crowd. So from the very beginning, I would rock her and sing songs and cherish her at night to make up for any distractions during the day. I would lie with her on her bed and talk and pray with her, and bedtime became our own special time. No wonder she looked back on it so fondly.

This routine of ending the day with love required a commitment of heart and time. I was often exhausted and drained, desperate for some grown-up time, and a bedtime blessing was the last thing I felt like doing. But I kept the routine going every night. I acted in love even when I didn't feel particularly loving, and I believe this was foundational to my closeness with my children. Somehow they all grew up treasuring that shared time together at the end of the day. Even now it is sweet to see that when the older kids are home, they sometimes come upstairs to my bedroom—but now *they* put *me* to bed because now they stay up longer than I do.

Keep On Moving Forward

Routines are often difficult to establish and may need to change through the seasons of life, but when cultivated carefully they promote life, love, regularity, and security amidst the constantly changing stresses of contemporary life. That's not to say that our family has always followed them perfectly—or that yours will. There have been entire seasons when I neglected our routines and just tried to stay alive. But I've found that having life ideals helps keep us all moving forward and makes it easier to get back into rhythm when my careful plans fall by the wayside.

So plan your days, allow flexibility, and keep moving in the direction of your ideals a little at a time. I believe you'll see that your intentional investment of time will promote valuable habits in the lives of all those who share your home—you included.

February

A CULTURE OF LOVE
Growing Lifelong Relationships
(SALLY)

To love someone means to see him as God intended him.
FYODOR DOSTOEVSKY

As I glanced out the kitchen window, the shadows that were overtaking the mountain told me that the sun was just about to set. Clay had proposed a rare and much-needed dinner date for just the two of us. Lots of issues in our life needed our focused attention—ministry conferences, book deadlines, taxes, a possible move, new staff for our ministry, a health problem with one of our children, a relationship problem at church—plus, we just needed some time together alone.

It was ten minutes before six, the time Clay had told me to be ready. I was still in the kitchen washing dishes, trying to get the kitchen clean before we left. And eleven-year-old Nathan, my bubbling, energetic extrovert, kept running into the kitchen demanding that I come look at something.

"Mama, I have something to show you! It will take just a few minutes, but you have to come *now*."

"Not now," I almost told him. "I promise I'll spend some time with you when I get home, but I have to finish the dishes now before Daddy takes me out to dinner. This way you kids won't have to clean anything up!"

I almost said that, but I didn't. After a brief mental battle I put the greasy pan back in the sudsy water and dried my hands.

"Nathan, where are you?" I yelled. "I'm ready to see your surprise."

"I didn't think you were *ever* going to come," he moaned as he appeared from the den. "I hope we're not too late."

He led me into the narrow laundry room, then stopped, looked me in the eye, and commanded in his high-pitched boy voice, "I want you to follow me up to the mountain, but you have to hold my hand and keep your eyes closed. I promise I won't let you fall."

I obediently followed him out the back door, which opened to a tiny block of cement patio at the base of a steep hillside bordering the national forest on the slopes of the Rocky Mountains. This was my own private hill, where I ended my early morning walk on the mountains each day. Its slope was covered with large red boulders, sandy hillside, and pine trees.

Holding my hand tightly in his pudgy little one, Nathan now led me up the steep hillside. Eyes shut, I followed the best I could. Then he stopped. "Mama, there's a big rock here. If you put your hand right here, I can help you climb up on top of it, and we can sit there together. But you have to promise not to look up yet. Just look at your feet."

I submitted and finally, tentatively, eased my way on my stomach to the top of a boulder about the size of a small shed.

"Okay. Now turn around and sit without looking up, and I will tell you when to look!" Nathan insisted.

As I settled down beside his sweaty boy body, Nathan's small arm fell snugly across my shoulders in an affectionate embrace. "Just in time," he said excitedly. "Now you can look."

I looked and gasped as I beheld one of the most exquisite sunsets I had ever experienced. Soft reds, vibrant golds, shimmering orange gleamed in fire-brightness before our eyes, filling the expanse of the sky with splendor. A symphony of colors seemed to sing in the evening sky. Then, slowly, the colors began to fade. The sun gave a final flourish, and a majestic wave of dark reds and purples seemed to spill out from the mountaintop, reflecting the last rays of burnished light. It was as though God Himself was providing a sparkling celebration just for us to document the importance of the moment.

Nathan beamed at me, his smile cheek-to-cheek as he looked contentedly into my eyes. "Thanks for coming with me, Mama," he whispered almost reverently. "I wanted to show you *my secret place*. I saw the sunset here yesterday, and I *knew* you would like it, so I wanted to surprise you and bring you here. I'm glad you and I are such close friends. I'll remember sharing this sunset with you for the rest of my life."

And yes, in his little boy, dramatic way, he actually said that!

As I reflect back on all of the years of our family's life together, what I remember best is not the mountains of dirty dishes and pots and pans and socks left on the floor and piles of laundry. I reflect instead on precious times shared with Clay, the kids, and those we welcomed into our home—snuggling on the couch together, nursing babies and rocking them to sleep, sharing movies and huge bowls of popcorn, comforting children after a nightmare, and all those heartfelt kisses and cards that said "I love you!"

So many other memories come to mind. Friends piled around the dinner table, candles lit, telling stories about our lives, building bridges of love to one another's hearts. Bible studies and cups of tea shared as the light of God's goodness dawned and hearts were forged together forever because of our common bond to His love. Times of grief filled with tears but also with the sweet comfort of friendship and of not bearing burdens alone. Illnesses, some months long, that tried everyone's patience yet created some of the most indelible memories—tents built, stories read aloud, soothing music easing an ear infection, one more Winnie-the-Pooh cartoon, a hand to hold during the painful and fearful moments.

To me, all these memories of love given and loved received glue the years together into a deeply satisfying collage. I am so grateful for the opportunities we took to say to each other, "You are important to me. Making time to share love, intimacy, and memories is so much more important that any task that would steal my time from you." Yet feelings of regret also occupy my mind as I realize how quickly the years have flown. I find myself thinking, *I wish I had spent* more *time enjoying these ones I love and less time fretting about all the details that have faded in my memory.*

Created to Love

Each of us is created by God to give love and to receive love. Loving acts and words of affection and affirmation are foundational to our health in every area of life—physical, mental, emotional, spiritual. God made us to need and to experience intimate relationships. All of us long for love and the assurance that validates the worth of our lives and personalities as God designed us. The narrative we tell ourselves as adults often grows out of the messages we received as children.

Unconditional, generous, intentional love was the hallmark of the home Clay and I longed to create for our little community from the very beginning of our life together. We wanted to live together in such a way that others sensed God's presence among us. And we wanted to raise our children in an atmosphere of love that defined the people they would grow up to be.

Love is the powerful energy that opens hearts to be able to hear, know, and understand the love of God, to embrace His truth and His ways. Love mysteriously heals, gives hope, builds faith, inspires heroism and personal sacrifice. Love embodies God's personality, His character and actions toward us—His ability to teach us, guide us, provide for us, delight us, and reach our own hearts. And Jesus is the ultimate picture of that love. "Greater love has no one than this, that one lay down his life for his friends" (John 15:13).

Jesus affirmed the importance of love by summarizing the two most important commandments in the Bible as directly relating to relationships. He said that first, we are to love the Lord our God with all of our heart, soul, mind, and strength. Second, we are to love our neighbors as ourselves. The two most profound commitments we are supposed to make, according to Jesus, are bound up in loving and relating. All our life accomplishments, from God's point of view, will be summed up by how much we loved God and how much we loved other people.

Foundational to our success in fulfilling the role God designed for us as people of God is our ability to cultivate mature and loving relationships with our children, our spouses, our friends, neighbors, and community. As our children receive our unconditional acceptance and generous service, they will have a pattern in their hearts to understand the merciful and abounding grace of God's love to each of us as expressed through Jesus Christ. People in our ministry and lives who experience the thoughtfulness and kindness of unconditional, generous love in our homes will understand that loving others is the foundation for influencing our world. Relationships are the starting point for others to understand what God is like and what His purposes are for us here on earth.

In taking time to build close relationships, we learn that people are more important than things or material possessions. We come to understand that close relationships, not status or accomplishment or virtual realities, are what bring happiness and meaning to life. Our lives become what we live and model, and when we invest personally in the lives of others, we will reap personally in terms of friendship and affection. Even the way we use our time will help others know that building a relationship requires a commitment of time and sacrifice.

There is always a cost to building intimacy with others. Giving comfort to one who is ill requires time and practical labor (attending to physical needs). Listening to the feelings of a teen or young adult usually involves lost sleep because the deepest conversations take place at night. Buying groceries, cooking meals, making cups of tea, providing snacks requires the sacrifice of time and energy. Keeping house—picking up those messes one more time—is a service of worship to God as we craft a place of beauty and comfort for all who enter our sanctuary of His very presence.

Love is indeed a choice, an obedience, a service and a sacrifice, an initiation. But love is also the most powerful source of joy. And it is the means through which God would have us extend His hands, His words, His redemption to our world, within the walls of our homes.

A Month for Love

To me as a child, February was always the month of giving love. How I enjoyed choosing Valentine's Day cards for my friends, making cupcakes with thick frosting with my mother, and decorating a Valentine's box with paper doilies, glitter, and construction-paper hearts at school. Celebrating my friendships and family relationships with special cards gave my heart a sense of warmth and fulfillment.

Many years later, when I was a mama with kids, I still loved celebrating that special month of love. Some years I would cut small branches from an outside tree and place them in a vase with red carnations in the middle of our dining table. I cut out hearts from sheets of thin foam and wrote our names on them with a gel pen, then hole-punched the spongy hearts and hung them with thin ribbon from the branches of the "tree." Then I would fill a small bowl with Scriptures about love written on separate little pieces of paper. The kids took turns reading the verses throughout the month of February.

There's something so special about setting aside a month to celebrate our closeness to the people we treasure most. This can also be a month for focusing on building loving relationships, drawing close to the people around us, and making others our priority.

Let's brighten this last month of winter, as the cold snows and rains beg for the promise of spring, by drawing close to one another and making a beautiful memory. And let's honor this month when we celebrate Valentine's Day by focusing on those elements that truly make our relationships special, incarnating the reality and thoughtfulness of the love of Christ.

——— In Our Home ———

Six of us were tucked under blankets on couches in our den, mugs of hot chocolate with marshmallows in our hands while enjoying the crackling fire. On a freezing winter day, with snow falling heavily outside, we sat warm in body and soul in the fine company of one another.

Having my children home from far corners of the world and inviting two dear single friends over gave me just the gift I needed to fill my heart on this bleak afternoon.

After a heavy sigh of seemingly great relief, one of my boys said, "You know, so many of my close friends at work come from broken backgrounds, some kind of abuse or divorce or unhappiness that has scarred their hearts. Seems I understand the brokenness of the world more and more. But it is such a relief for me to be back here in our family culture of love." He added, "No matter what conflict, difficulty, or failure I experience, I know I can come home to unconditional love and have all of you here to support and accept me. I know you all will help me through any conflict or failure and celebrate every joy. What a grace to grow up expecting that! I never knew how blessed our family was until I left home. We have so very much to celebrate because we know someone will always have our backs."

A culture of love. I had never heard that term, but it spoke volumes to my mother heart. How comforting it was to know that in spite of the petty quarrels, correction as a way of life, and selfish actions that were a part of our daily lives, my son still thought of our home as healthy and strong because we always extended and practiced forgiveness, showed love, and sought peace.

All of us create a home culture of some kind. The traditions we keep, the meals we make, the routines we practice, the values we espouse and hold, the movies we like best, the church we attend, the generosity we practice, the way we invest time, the company we keep—all of these invest in crafting a home culture. We can also, inadvertently, create a negative home culture—one of anger, neglect, guilt, discord, disharmony, worldly values, and so on.

I have realized over many years that crafting a culture of love—gracious, sacrificial, validating, forgiving love—requires a loving and generous heart. It also requires planning, intention, mature responses, words of life and affirmation, patience, and the investment of endless hours. It also means choosing, again and again, to focus on what really matters in life.

So often we get caught up in the immediate things, the practical tasks—getting the housework done, doing our jobs, checking homework, paying bills, disciplining our children. Yet it is the emotional and spiritual atmosphere our children and friends breathe—the way we treat people, the foundations of grace we live by, that will attach their hearts to ours and ultimately to God.

True influence and discipleship are formed intentionally by modeling ourselves after the ultimate lover—Jesus. He who bowed His knees to wash 120 man toes, who bent to embrace wiggly children who were clamoring for attention, who touched a prostitute and gave her grace, who gave His own failing disciple (Peter) hope and affirmation even in the midst of the man's failures, and who then ultimately gave everything, out of love, for our redemption, becomes our own source and inspiration for forming a culture of love.

Often I have been asked, "How have your children held to a high standard of morality when they are living in such secular places?" God's grace is my first answer. Yet, as I have prayed about it, I've also come to think that our home culture of love—shared and cultivated together, treasuring Christ in our midst every day—spoke to their hearts and tied them to our mutual commitments of faith. A strong family culture helps create a strong sense of identity that keeps a person faithful in the days of temptation. And a strong home culture of faith and love gives strength to resist the powerful draw of a secular world. (We'll explore that idea further in the August chapter.)

The grace of our family culture of love was expressed amidst arguments, quarrels about the demands of selfish hearts, and the lessons of asking forgiveness again and again. We are a loud, opinionated sort of family who often find ourselves in some kind of conflict. Yet the grace of asking forgiveness, of extending grace to one who is tired, hormonal, or grumpy, is warp and woof to the family culture. No matter how awkward a season of life, no matter how unfair the hurt of words spoken in a moment of heat, the foundation of acceptance and grace covers a multitude of sins. Somehow we always manage to get back to our center—the foundation of a mutual commitment to love.

The Heart of Good Manners

Manners are standards of behavior, trained values for how we act toward other people. Many people think of them as persnickety little rules about who speaks first or what fork is right to use. But the true heart of good manners is treating people with respect and showing them honor through the ways we behave.

Honor is a lost value in our secularized culture today. Movies, television, and Internet posts often poke fun at marriages, parenting, babies, the elderly, teachers, politicians, leaders, Christians—everyone is fair game, and the "humor" is far from good-humored. The result of feeling freedom to lampoon every institution and every relationship is a cynical culture that targets just about every aspect of life for derision and looks with disdain on innocence and purity.

When all things are humorous, there is nothing in culture that is sacred or holy. When we equate holiness with something to be despised or mistrusted because piety is looked down upon, then there is no value for respect or honor. Without the ability to value honor and to show respect to others, there is no pattern for bowing our knees before God. How can we have a pathway in our brains for humbling ourselves under the mighty hand of God if we have never learned the value of respecting or honoring those we can see?

So as we approach manners, the heart attitude at the base of good manners is showing honor to others. This means showing them high respect, viewing them with high esteem, and honoring them as people of great value.

Because Jesus said that the world would know we were His disciples by our love for one another, practicing love and valuing others is a priority for passing on His messages and influence to others in our world. However, good manners do not happen in a vacuum. They have to be taught—or, better, caught from those who both teach and model them.

A simple way that we taught a pattern for manners in our family and in discipleship relationships was based on three simple words: *Stop! Look! Listen!* Here is how we taught these principles to our kids:

- *Stop!* When you meet someone—a friend, someone in the family, or a guest in our home—stop and take a moment to ponder him or her. This is a person created by God. It is your stewardship to honor that person as someone who has value in God's eyes. Decide in your heart to give honor to all you meet. Breathe in the reality that the person right in front of you is more important than the dutiful tasks at hand. Choose an attitude that is right for the moment.

- *Look!* Observe the person's personality, age, and needs to determine how you might make his or her life a little better. If it is a child, talk to him and offer a toy, a book, or a way to occupy his time. If it is an adult, observe her needs—does she need rest? Food? Companionship? How can you help her feel comfortable or at home? Help guests in your home feel they belong by showing them where they can find what they need—food, coffee and tea and mugs, a place to rest, a movie to watch, a shelf of books.

- *Listen!* Most people have a deep desire to be known, understood, and affirmed. Take initiative to ask them questions about themselves. Get to know their stories, listen to what they are telling you with their words, emotions, eyes, and body language. Practice responding to people by perceiving what they are communicating. Reach out in love and find a way to affirm each person who comes into your life.

Those three simple commands covered most situations our children would encounter. In addition, we had a short list of more specific manners we taught in our home.

- *Say please when you ask for something.*
- *Make a habit of verbalizing gratitude.* Say thank you for material gifts and acknowledge when someone has given you time or attention or met your need in some way.

- *Don't interrupt others when they are talking.* Wait your turn, discipline your spirit, and learn to get along with others.
- *Greet others with a smile.* Learn to ask questions that give other people the opportunity to talk about themselves.
- *Build a concept of yourself as a helper.* Help clear messes. Offer to assist with a chore or burden. Give honor to those older than you and be an initiator when you see some way you may be useful. And don't forget to clean up after yourself—all the time, every day.
- *Be a person others can depend on, and develop integrity in your life.*
- *Learn to be a peacemaker, not a contentious voice.* Avoid arguing or causing conflict.

Practical Ways to Say "I Love You" to Anyone

Many books have been written about speaking to others in their "love languages"—that is, taking their perceived needs into account and expressing love to them in ways that actually make them feel loved.[1] I have found this idea of love languages extremely helpful in learning how to love my family, friends, and even acquaintances more effectively. It's so important to study people and consider the best ways I can communicate my love to them.

At the same time, I believe most people appreciate being loved and cared for and are willing to accept almost any sincere expression of love. The following are some "love languages" that I believe will speak to almost anyone.

Kindness and Sympathy

Who doesn't respond to genuine sweetness and compassionate, encouraging words? A willingness to extend the gracious love, gentleness, and humble attitude of Christ to each person as best you can will almost always pay off in terms of relationships.

Focused Attention and Time Invested

All relationships grow in proportion to the investment of time and individual attention that has been put into them. Relationship is not primarily based on just meeting basic needs—seeing that someone is clothed and fed—but by really looking, really listening, making an honest effort to understand what an individual needs most and then making an effort to meet that need.

This means tearing your eyes away from that computer, hanging up from that phone conversation, and actually looking at your "someone" when he or she enters a room. Machines may have distracted you from those who long for your attention every day but have become accustomed to your passivity in their lives. I think one cannot be focused on social media and still meet the longing of others for personal time and attention. If we want to show real love to someone else, we must carefully consider how to limit its influence.

Words of Affirmation and Encouragement
Since none of us will ever be perfect and all of us commonly fall short of our own standards, we long to know that we are still acceptable, valued, forgiven, and worthy of someone's love. Just as a plant needs to be watered daily, affirmation and encouragement need to be communicated over and over again. This can be said in many ways:

- "I am glad you are my friend."
- "You are a gift from God to me, my precious child."
- "My life is so much more fun [richer, happier, fulfilling] because I have you in my life."
- "I believe in you [your dreams, your potential, your faith, your integrity, your potential for growth, and so on]."

It's important to speak such words often, face to face. But an e-mail, a text, or a note on a pillow can also help keep affirmation and encouragement flowing from one heart to another. And of course there's nothing wrong with spoken words *plus* other forms of communication.

Helping and Serving
Once I sat in Joy's room and packed her suitcase for a short weekend trip she would be taking with a friend. And this very independent child, who usually did everything for herself, told me, "Mama, I just love it when you provide

for my needs without my asking. It means so much to me when you do stuff I haven't even asked you to do." Cleaning a room, fixing a meal, helping with a project, shopping for clothes, writing a note—such acts of loving service have the amazing power to open hearts.

Saying "I'm Sorry"

Restoring relationships is also an important way to communicate love. All of us, and especially children, easily become petty and self-centered, harboring grudges over the most insignificant of quarrels as well as over larger issues. To counter this tendency, one of my friends introduced me to the "peacemaking couch." If her children quarreled, she would have them sit on the couch together and stay there until they could tell one another they were sorry, ask for forgiveness, and pray together. When the relationship was restored, they could get up.

Peacemaking is a foundational practice to loving well. Keeping peace in friendship and in marriage just requires one person to be humble enough to take responsibility for arguments and move in the direction of peace. Often I have seen the truth of Proverbs 15:1: "A gentle answer turns away wrath." Even when I haven't *felt* gentle, learning to practice it by extending grace to one who has offended me has brought grace back to me and taught me how easy it is to restore my relationships to health. I have also learned, in the words of James 4:6, that "God is opposed to the proud, but gives grace to the humble."

Gifts or Cards

One of my friends is a masterful gift giver. Bringing about ten gifts for each person in our family at Christmas is a common habit of hers. She gathers information about each person's hobbies, preferences, and age and takes delight in finding just the perfect presents. Not surprisingly, the recipients of these loving tokens delight in them as well.

A well-chosen gift or card has the power to touch hearts in a powerful way. It says, "I thought of you specifically, and this gift is an act of my commitment to your value in my life."

Keep in mind that neither gifts nor cards need to be expensive. Instead of spending three dollars at the Hallmark store, take a trip to the discount or dollar store—or make your own little tokens. One woman I've heard of made a regular practice of making homemade cards with crayons and construction paper for her colleagues on special occasions or "just because." She would write her own heartfelt sentiments inside and send them through interoffice mail. Everyone loved those cards, and no one minded that she spent just pennies on each one.

Respect and Honor

A couple of people in our family are driven by a desire to be known as competent and accomplished, to be sufficient in life and do work that is worthy of admiration. How do you show love to these people (or, I believe, to anyone)? By noticing how they have served us or others, giving attention to their accomplishments, and respecting what they have achieved.

The Magic of Touch

Softly scratching and tickling a child's back was one of the soothing gifts of love I learned to give my babies. To many people, love is powerfully conveyed by the right kind of touch. Rocking and swaying while holding someone close, giving a hand or foot massage with lotion to soothe frayed nerves, kissing, tousling hair, embracing with a bear hug, even just a gentle touch on the arm—any of these can be powerful expressions of caring.

Touch, of course, is one area where you need to be careful. While most people crave being touched, others don't, and unfortunately some people live with painful memories that make being touched problematic. It's important to pay attention to body language and other cues before touching someone you don't know well, and it's always appropriate to ask, "Do you mind if I give you a hug?" If touching is a problem, there are many other avenues to express love and caring.

Building Memories of Love (Birthdays)

Always bubbling around in my mind when my children were young were ideas of how to inscribe meaningful love memories deeply into the pathways of their hearts. The purpose was that they would have a sense of security, ties to the Clarksons and our heritage, a biblical sense of self, and a strong sense of loving and being loved. Consequently, each birthday at our house was planned to be memorable and full of tradition.

Breakfast was our special time of celebrating, no matter what else was planned for the rest of the day. That was the time when we knew everyone in the family could be there. And yes, we would have to get up at the crack of dawn most years before Clay left for work at eight or nine. On occasion we would wait until the weekend to celebrate, but that was rare because celebrating on the actual day was important to our children. They were usually so excited that they had no trouble getting up early. And I learned over the years that if I set the table and wrapped the presents the day before, I could throw a celebration together very quickly in the morning.

The day always began in the birthday child's room, with a cup of tea or hot chocolate personally delivered. A sibling then waited with the honoree while I put the final touches on the breakfast feast. No one was allowed to come down until all was complete.

When all was ready, the birthday child was then marched down the stairs blindfolded and presented with the table, which was set with our special china or tea dishes and piled high with cards and presents—all gift-wrapped, even if they had come from the dollar store. The menu was almost always the same: my special scrambled eggs with sour cream, cheese, and bacon, and, of course, our famous Clarkson cinnamon rolls (just a simple recipe that I developed over the years but became bigger than life from being shared in our books).

The feast was consumed. The presents were opened. And then came the best part of the celebration, the one everyone was waiting for.

When our kids were wee little people, we started the tradition of having everyone in the family give a verbal love gift—intentional words of encouragement aimed at the child's heart. Each gift began, "I really appreciate you because . . ." And then would follow a list of specific character qualities we had observed over the year—strengths that had developed, ways the child had blessed our family.

I would not have expected young children to do this well, but after a couple of times they all took it very seriously and really invested their words:

- "You are such a talented singer-songwriter, and I admire the way you have developed as a pianist."
- "You have really been an encouragement to me this year when I needed to know I had a friend."
- "I have really been inspired to walk with God more closely this year because of the thoughts and ideas you shared in our family devotions."

You could almost see the soul and heart of the birthday child being filled up, his or her confidence swelling as the words of appreciation kept coming. Then we would all hold hands and pray blessings over the child. Everyone at the table prayed—for the birthday child's future dreams, desires, marriage—and everything he or she had asked for.

Teatime Discipleship

The God of the universe showed us the best method of reaching people with His message. He came to earth as a common man and lived, ate, and developed relationships within a small community of people, loving and serving them in the normal moments of life. Because of the commitment He personally made to this motley group of folks, they were all willing to give their lives for His cause after He died.

I realized early in my years of ministry and motherhood that I could not offer up influence in the lives of people in my ministry or pass on faith to my children by having one grand message of truth and inspiration. For me, it would happen best by giving up my life over many moments of focused time that took into consideration the other person's needs, personality, and desire for relationship. I developed my own term for this focused pattern of discipleship: *teatime discipleship*.

Teatime discipleship is really just planning focused time for those God has placed in our lives to influence with His grace. It doesn't have to take long. What matters is the focus—giving these people personal attention, listening to their hearts, encouraging them with words.

Here's an example: One of my friends seemed to communicate hidden stress behind her Facebook messages and her short e-mails. Even though I was leaving for a two-week international ministry trip, God put her on my heart.

So I sent her a private Facebook message: "Have breakfast with me, and then we can go our busy ways."

Our meal was simple—scrambled eggs, English muffins with raspberry jam, some orange slices, and a steaming cup of coffee. It was all I could find in my kitchen! But I set up two chairs by the window at an old tea table I had purchased at Goodwill many years before. I lit candles, put soft acoustic music on the stereo, and welcomed my friend for a short hour.

Tears flowed almost from the moment of her arrival when I said, "God has put you on my heart. You are so very dear to me. How are you?" What came out next was a story of stress, marriage challenges, and not enough money to go around. I listened. We prayed. And for our short time my living room became a sanctuary for God's encouragement, His love, His words, His hope to be shared.

What Says Love to You?

It was a cold, snowy day—perfect for a little fruit, some muffins, and tea à la Clarkson by the fireplace. Sarah and I, in our jammies and crazy bed hair, sat close together on a couch and talked. For almost an hour we sat there sipping our hot liquid gold. Candles flickered as we talked and shared our thoughts and ideas and dreams. We looked at articles together in a magazine we both loved, admired a book Sarah had found at a secondhand book store, and felt totally at ease in the comfort of our safe and close friendship. Sometimes we giggled uncontrollably over some shared memory or story.

At one point she fetched my computer and played a favorite song for me that meant something to her, one she had listened to at midnight the night before. She also shared her devotional book with me because I couldn't find mine, and I relished her inspiring reflections about a passage in Matthew.

Teatime discipleship, you see, works with my children as well. My sixty-two-year-old self has learned to love the worlds of my children, and such times of loving fellowship have given me a window to their hearts—their precious, very different hearts.

I do not expect my children to conform to me. Instead I adjust my expectations to enjoy and really delight in who they are at every stage. Entering their worlds has brought me much pleasure, though I had to give up a little of my selfish self to do so. (So did Jesus, by the way, when He chose to live among sinful, limited human beings.)

Since each of my children responds differently to the same kind of mothering, I had to study and observe Sarah to find out what was in her heart—her personality, what spoke love to her, what put her off and what drew her near, and, most of all, how to fill her heart's cup so I could reach it with a love for Jesus.

Discipleship is always an issue of relationship. It is not about curriculum, church attendance, rules, or indoctrination, but always about reaching the heart.

I look back and see how different it was with all the kids.

I remember when Nathan was little. This was my boy who often challenged the boundaries. He was a little bit of a mystery to me because my first two had been more compliant. Silly me—I had thought that was because I was such a great mother. Then God gave me Nathan, and I realized I needed to try something different.

One night Clay took the older two to church and left Nathan home with me because he had a cold. After a few hours of matching wills with my little one, I sank wearily into an overstuffed chair and said, "Hey, you want to climb into the chair with me?"

I remember he snuggled in and then began to talk. And talk. He talked for forty-five minutes without stopping as I responded with "Really?" or "Oh?" or "How funny." And then he was finished. He said, "I love you, Mom," jumped out of the chair, and went to play. He was five years old.

I was pondering this event—his sitting still for so long and talking and talking and talking—and suddenly it dawned on me: "He is an extrovert, and he needs people and activity. He wants to talk and be heard."

So I learned the way to Nathan's heart was listening to him—his dreams, his thoughts, his ideas, his feelings. As long as I made a point to listen to him, he would listen to me and try to obey.

Joy was like that too. If she felt lost in the crowd, she would get louder, perform, call attention to herself. But if I went to her room or sat on the porch with her and sipped lemonade or made a special teatime in my room just for her, she would talk and talk and talk. And then her heart would be open.

Now Joel would just withdraw and be grumpy or get irritated if he was feeling overwhelmed. He was not a "misbehaver" by personality. But I learned that if I made personal time with him away from the group, he would bubble over talking to me. Joel is an introvert like Sarah. Neither of them would compete openly with the others for heart time. I had to assume they needed it and make it happen. This opened the windows of their hearts for us to develop a great, strong, deep friendship.

Each child responded differently to life. I had to study my kids to see what was going on with them. Then I had to figure out what each one liked and how best to communicate personal love to them. When I did that, I saw their little and big hearts open.

As it happens, I found I needed to do a little focused study and love with my husband, too. I learned that Clay did not want to have to compete with the kids for my attention. I needed to make time for just us, so I could hear him and know what was going on. If I did not create the time for us, it would never happen. And a culture of love cannot thrive in a household if the parents don't put effort into loving each other.

Men's Night Out, Girls' Club In

The importance of extending love and listening to each person's love needs shouldn't be limited to talk sessions. As our children grew older, in fact, we found that a little creativity went a long way toward building memories and enhancing our culture of love.

For instance, even though we usually loved being together as a family, we found that once in a while all the boys needed to get some "man time," and all the girls needed to enjoy some exclusively feminine company and pursuits. Especially as the kids started getting older, they needed some margin to express themselves.

Our solution to this was to have Clay take the boys on his regular Tuesday night errands run into town while the girls stayed home with me. Of course the guys didn't *just* run errands, and we girls didn't just mope around the house. Nathan and Joel have great memories of going to Fazoli's Italian fast food with Clay, eating pizza and "talking Torah," as we like to call it when the men in the family discuss everything under the sun. And we girls finally got to do the fun girly things that the guys never wanted to be around for—painting nails, having facials, eating froufrou foods, and watching rom-coms.

It was the best! Nights like those took a bit of the edge off the stress of our week and made it easier to enjoy one another when we all got back together.

The Power of Expressing Love

As I have pondered the recent death of my mom and the various relationships influenced by her death, I have realized anew that words matter. So does the lack of words. I can't tell you how often in recent years I have longed to hear my mother's voice and hear her speak to me—to sympathize with my struggles, to tell me that she loved me and that I was doing well amidst the challenges of my life.

Today is the time to invest in the lives of those we love, as there may never be another time, and then a heart can be empty for lack of initiation. Consequently I have recommitted to expressing my love, taking the initiative to let family and friends know they really mean a lot to me and have made a big difference in my life. I want to make sure they understand beyond the shadow of a doubt how much they are worth to me. I want to do it in practical ways, honoring them with my actions. And I especially want to do it with my words. Words of affirmation should be said. Words should be planted in people's souls. Words not said can leave a vacuum.

One of the wonderful consequences of years and years of building a culture of love in my family is that my children have become free in their encouragement to me and to others. I have received the most wonderful cards in which a son or daughter freely articulated my worth in his or her life, and these notes have greatly sustained me in my own times of need. My children have basically grown into my best friends, and my investment of love aimed at their hearts now is coming back to me. I do not have a lot of extended family in my life—a reality that I sometimes mourn—but I have my husband and kids, and they mean the world to me.

When I started out as a mom, I did not know the depth of gift I was giving myself by creating my own inner circle. And all of this was the result of just investing lots of love and grace and appreciation into my precious children so that they would experience a safe, lifegiving place where our friendship could bloom.

I believe the same is true of every effort I make to speak love and share love with those around me. In this lifetime I may or may not see the results. But God knows. And because He is the One who invented love in the first place, who surrounds us with love every day of our lives and inhabits every truly loving relationship, I can trust Him to transform all my efforts into the stuff of eternity.

Love wins.

Love always wins.

March
THE ART OF THE ORDINARY
Finding Beauty in Your Own Backyard
(SARAH)

Everybody needs beauty as well as bread, places to play in and pray in, where Nature may heal and cheer and give strength to body and soul alike.

JOHN MUIR

FUNNY THE WAY SOME childhood memories are etched in pinpoint clarity against the Impressionist background of the years. I've often wondered why certain scenes stay with me while others fade. But there's one whose significance I never question, its setting a blustery Sunday evening in the midst of a very dreary March. I know exactly why it remains so deeply etched in my thoughts, for in a dark, windy moment, I glimpsed the power of ordinary celebration—workaday beauty—to invade and redeem a moment of possible despair.

To set the scene: a small, brick house in Texas, my mom wrapped in a sweater at the open front door, waving to my dad as his car, headlights eerie in the light rain, pulled away from us into the night. My three younger siblings pressed against her, waving too. I stood slightly behind, reserved in my new on-the-cusp-of-adulthood self-consciousness, quiet because of the dread that unexpectedly filled my heart.

I was just old enough to perceive that this was a very difficult moment for my mom. On this, the fourth Sunday of its kind, she was waving good-bye to my dad as he left again for five days of work at a distance too far to cover each evening. We wouldn't see him again until Friday. And until then the keeping, feeding, and entertainment of four children was in her lone hands—as was the housework, the driving to lessons, the loving of friends, the making of meals. Beyond this was the fact of my baby sister's nocturnal asthma and the newly diagnosed health condition that caused Mom to become intensely dizzy at the most inopportune of moments.

I was freshly aware of the fact that life can be very hard, not in dramatic ways, but in small, daily realities. The ripening of first adulthood had stolen that blessed innocence that is the gift of childhood, and I was aware of myself as confronting something, responsible for grappling with it in a way I never had been before. But I had no idea what to do.

From behind, I surveyed my mother's shoulders, saw the momentary sag as my sister asked to be carried with sweet, clutching little hands. I couldn't see Mom's face, but I waited, sure that when she turned I would behold a set or tired or resigned face that would mean a hushed evening and an early bedtime and maybe a strained week to come.

I heard the sigh as my mother firmly closed the front door. She turned.

"I think we need a party tonight. Cookies, burgers, and a movie. We can pile on my bed and have an indoor picnic."

I think I smiled, but I was too startled for it to be much more than a wondering half smile at first. My mom certainly smiled, patting each of my brothers on the head. The boys cheered. Joy clapped her little hands. And the moment of farewell—that wistful, slightly frightening moment of watching my dad depart—was transformed by one sentence into a moment of possibility.

The group moved toward the kitchen. As she passed me, my mom put her hand on my arm. "It's going to be a good week, Sarah. Don't worry. Would you make the cookies?"

The rest of the evening passed in what can only be described as merriment. There was plenty of sibling squabbling and jostling for the prized seat next to my mom. But there were also our favorite cheeseburgers and fresh oatmeal crispies and lemonade in the gem-toned plastic sippy cups whose battered presence was constant throughout my childhood. There was an old Haley Mills movie and a raucous amount of shouted laughter and a bedtime a little too late after an evening enjoyed to the hilt. And there was a next morning—still rainy, still gray, still March at its worst, but with an atmosphere of energy that allowed my habitual daily question (which must have driven my mother mad at times) to be asked in hope rather than dread: "What are we going to do today?"

In looking back at that starkly outlined memory, I understand that it remains with me because that moment profoundly shaped the way I encounter the ordinary, particularly the difficult ordinary of life in a fallen world. Nearly twenty years later, I am deeply aware of the gift my mother gave me when the face she turned to a moment of real despair was one of hope. In her choice that night, she modeled to me what it means to look at life in a fallen world, particularly on the level of the everyday, and meet it with a creative joy born of the Holy Spirit, the same One who hovered over Creation as it was spoken into being.

It's easy to conceive of home on an epic scale—as a finished product, an ideal in the mind existing as a grand, ordered place filled with the rhythms of feasting, fellowship, and beauty. And it's easy to talk about beauty in the home in idealistic terms associated with special events and holidays. We are slow, perhaps, to conceive of homemaking and, with it, the creation of beauty within the home, on the level of the everyday and ordinary, even the mundane. How can the ordinary meals, the usual days with their ups and downs of work and school, sickness and exercise, be a place where we discover and create the transcendent beauty of our Creator God?

This chapter is an exploration of that question, a wander through the different spaces, events, and possibilities of life in very ordinary time. In this chapter, set in the month of March, a time when neither winter nor spring quite holds sway, when rain forces us indoors for many a bored hour, when ordinary life can seem to be as dull and depressing as the mud out the window, we will explore the power of beauty claimed and created to transform and reveal the presence of God.

Beauty and Home

The instant association of *beauty* and *home* is of something peripheral and perfect—a Martha Stewart home, models with coiffed hair and spotless clothes, showpiece weddings, even the more natural, but no less approachable, beauty of epic landscapes and exotic locales. But beauty in home life—beauty on the level of the kitchen table, the child's bedroom, the back porch—is something at which we often stumble. What we miss in these surface images is an understanding of beauty not as a veneer we apply to the surface of our lives or an ideal only to be attained by the extraordinary, but as the tangible, daily outgrowth of the spiritual values we hold most deeply. We miss, in other words, the reality of incarnation, the truth that God created the physical world to house and express the spiritual.

When I speak of beauty in this chapter, I don't mean the ideal. I mean the real loveliness lurking in the corners of the ordinary: a bowl of apples, a child's face, a Mason jar of wildflowers. I mean the breathtaking loveliness that comes when ordinary moments are filled and formed by hospitality, ritual, and relationship: dinner by candlelight, heart-to-hearts over hot chocolate, a shared autumn walk, a sick day in which real love is made tangible in ginger ale and chicken soup and a child's favorite quilt. On the level of home life, beauty is the order and grace we bring to the waiting hours and spaces of our lives, the celebrations we choose, the rituals we make, the gardens we plant, the care we give with as much attention as we can muster.

Such beauty speaks of our belief in a God of the details, a God aware of each sparrow, each tear, each heart. Our creativity affirms His care and presence in every aspect of our lives. Such beauty is also a shelter; it makes home one of the primary places where we can step back from the impersonal, deadening craze of life in order to encounter the life of God in the midst of a fallen world.

The atmosphere thus created by color, creativity, and celebration makes not *House Beautiful* but home beloved, where every aspect of home communicates life, color, love, order, excellence, hope. Despite, and even in, the usual round of dishes and laundry, flowers or a well-set table affirm home as a place apart from the whirlwind, a place where God's goodness is tasted and known.

Beauty amidst the Brokenness

Several years ago, I wrote a blog post about beauty with the word *idealist* in the title and was challenged by an anonymous commenter to explain the connection between ideals and beauty. "Do you think ideals are just about smelling the roses?" The commenter's question came, oddly enough, during a hectic season of winter travel, and it caused me to sit down for a whole afternoon to articulate my passionate but hitherto inarticulate convictions on the spiritual significance of beauty.

To the commenter I replied that roses are gorgeous creations, and I think taking time to actually smell them would do most of us a world of good. But a weakness for pretty things isn't what I meant by a love of beauty or a home marked by its presence. In fact, I meant the opposite.

So much of life consists of dusty, normal days often punctuated by sickness (that no doctor can diagnose), thorny relationships (especially those involving family), general struggle (flat tires, money, irritation), and loneliness. I am keenly aware that my love of beauty is equaled by my total inability to force my life to be beautiful. The world and I myself are profoundly broken. My natural impulse in the midst of this is a quick discouragement that seeps into every vein of my being. It can end in a dark numbness of heart that leaves me incapable of either seeing beauty or allowing it to teach me hope. That is what I think I instinctively feared on that long-ago March evening with my mom.

And yet, despite the grief of life in the broken places, my heart still catches glimmers of what life was meant to be, echoes from the shattered gladness of original Creation. The remnants of Eden reach out to me in the very stuff of the everyday, slivered shards of ideal beauty glittering through the daily muck. I see it in sunlight slanted on my table, the scent of coffee, the flight of song, a moment of utter quiet, and yes, sometimes in a glorious bank of roses. In those moments I am aware that beauty speaks. That loveliness tells me of something beyond the brokenness. Every experience of joy I find is the promise of a coming and complete redemption.

This is what I believe my home should communicate. This is the atmosphere I want those who come into my sphere to taste—the goodness of God made tangible in food, in pictures, in music, in the way they are served. I want my home to reflect the deepest affirmation of my heart that God is with me, that He has given me every good thing. I want my home and life to be an invitation to feast, to touch, to savor, and to know the goodness of my beautiful God.

To cultivate beauty is to act in keeping with my faith in God's goodness rather than my doubt. It means to fight tooth and nail, day by day, to keep alive my faith in a love that transforms the ordinary and, in that transformation, offers a glimpse of a one-day, ultimate redemption.

The beauty I make is the way I picture and offer my ultimate hope right smack in the middle of messy, ordinary days. I put on music when I really just want to despair. I laugh over housework instead of screaming about it (which I usually want to do). I open my eyes to God's creative presence in the earth when busyness could easily distract and rob me of wonder. I reach out to needy people and unresponsive friends one more time. I take, with God's help, the musty clay of dusty, messy days and mold it into hours of laughter, landmark feasts, music making, and memories.

Tasting, Seeing, and Hoping

When it comes right down to it, everything I believe in lies just beyond my touch. But in Christ, in the incarnate God, I have the model by which my faith can be crafted into every corner of my life. My love of Christ drives me to live in a certain way, compels me to picture my hope in my words, my actions, the set of my face as I encounter the daily world. I may not grasp the Kingdom of God on earth, but I picture its reality.

Idealism, at heart, is about hope. And so is seeking beauty.

It has almost nothing to do with Martha Stewart or *House Beautiful* or "the perfect home." Beauty is about picturing God's unchanging goodness and daring to bring it into my own small, dusty days.

There is no one right way to embody the beauty of God, and that's the wonder. I have had the good fortune to travel the world and sojourn in dozens of homes. From farmhouses to mansions, cottages to cabins, apartments in China to flats in Warsaw, I've experienced countless living spaces, schemes of decor, mealtime traditions, and family rhythms. The variety of human experience and culture never ceases to startle and challenge my ideas about the scope of God's creativity. But there is a certain quality of grace present in some of those homes that has the same deep root regardless of cultural distance or difference. The quality is in the atmosphere of order and care with which it was crafted. I've eaten "stinky tofu" (fermented, deep-fried tofu) in China, borscht in Poland, and pizza in America, and each of those meals was something close to sacramental because the people who prepared it offered the love of God in every aspect of what they cooked and created in their lives.

Each one of us, every day, has the stuff of great incarnational creativity at our fingertips in the ordinary substances of home life. In the image of God, in the strength of the incarnate Christ, we can fill our home life with beauty.

We can craft our spaces with color, art, and order, fill them with music, mark them with rhythms of meals eaten by candlelight and laughter.

"Taste and see," said David in his psalm, "that the Lord is good" (Psalm 34:8). That's the challenge of this chapter, to discover God's creative presence in the stuff of the messy everyday. To craft from sick days and bored hours a home and life in which the eternal springs up in time, made touchable in hugs, feasts, cups of tea, and bowls of soup.

God literally "with us" in the humblest corners of home.

Awakening Wonder

I vividly remember the first time I heard my mom read aloud from Lucy Maud Montgomery's *Anne of Green Gables* (1908), because the next time I went outdoors, the world presented a different face to me. Always I had sensed a great and present goodness in the scent of new grass; in the arc of our little patch of backyard sky with its smattering of stars; in the rough, knobby tree just outside my second-story window; and in the black-capped chickadee who sang me awake in the mornings. But Montgomery's heroine, Anne, put words to it all. She spoke of trees that made a cathedral and wind that was the breath of God and orchards that smiled amidst their apple gems and autumn fields that brooded and fretted until the mist of their thoughts rose above them in the dawn. Anne's words inspired me to see the world around me as an active, almost sentient presence—not merely "nature" but *creation*.

There would be many other experiences in which reading shaped my experience of the world. I had a rich literary childhood immersed in books of all sorts—*The Wind in the Willows* (1908), *A Girl of the Limberlost* (1909), *The Lord of the Rings* (1954–55), *Winnie-the-Pooh* (1926), and so many more. Each of those stories introduced me to the world anew and challenged me to stop in my tracks and look more closely at that tree outside my window, the sky and changing seasons, or the face of the beloved person I tended to take for granted. But that reading of *Anne of Green Gables* marked my first awareness of the way that the words in a book, words used to sketch an imaginative world, could reawaken me to the mystery of my own.

As an adult, the word I would give to that reawakening is *wonder*. Wonder is a state of mind in which the sight and senses are wholly engaged in what is before them. Wonder reveals the world as the miracle it is because it intensely focuses our eyes on what is before us—the veined crimson of an autumn leaf, the play of sunlight in summer trees, the ripple of light over water. We may "see" these things every day, but our eyes are often restless, our minds preoccupied; we seldom truly look. Wonder helps us to notice with quiet, focused attention that helps us perceive the inherent, unique beauty of the people and the world around us.

For young children, wonder is a natural state because every single thing they encounter is something new. They encounter grass in the backyard and snow and thunderstorms in the same way an adult might encounter the sight of a shooting star or a double rainbow—with awe and amazement. The wonder natural to childhood is precious, something many adults spend a lifetime trying to protect and reclaim, because wonder is the fundamental condition of education.

Have you ever considered what it means to be a lifelong learner? Have you ever considered the role that cultivating wonder might play in helping you or your children tune in to the beauty of the world and the reality it communicates?

How will children encounter nature? Will they be distracted by technologies set in their hands since birth, or will they have learned to look, to love, to hold the world around them as holy?

How will children encounter other people? Will they see others as mere extra bodies that stand in their way or as treasures, each one a masterpiece of beauty to be met with love?

How will they perceive faith? Will they learn to pay attention only to what is right before them, or will they have been taught to listen with heart and soul, to look at the beauty around them, and to reach toward the mystery that lies at its heart?

In the earliest years of childhood, parents have the chance to train their little ones to the habit of focused sight that is the beginning of wonder. They can help their children develop and nurture a curious mind and innocent delight in every new thing. Distraction (whether by screen time, constant activity, or ceaseless entertainment), boredom (often caused by overstimulation), and fear are the natural enemies of wonder, forces all too common in childhood today. But if children are given time away from all the noise of the world, time to be alone, if they are loved and affirmed and given time to explore nature or listen to music or read a book, they will have the chance to be filled with wonder once again.

But beyond even these, one of the primary ways in which the eyes and ears and the very brain of a child can be cultivated toward wonder is through the powerful force of language. In other words, *words*! Language shapes consciousness. The words we learn when we are little, the ones we are given to describe the world around us, often dictate what we actually *see* in that world. Owen Barfield, a philosopher whose thinking about language and consciousness greatly influenced C. S. Lewis, pointed out the following about the way we humans experience and *know* the world:

> I do not perceive any *thing* with my sense-organs alone, but with a great part of my whole human being. Thus, I may say, loosely, that I "hear a thrush singing." But in strict truth all that I ever merely "hear"—all that I ever hear simply by virtue of having ears—is sound. When I "hear a thrush singing," I am hearing, not with my ears alone, but with all sorts of other things like mental habits, memory, imagination, feeling and (to the extent at least that the act of attention involves it) will.[1]

In other words, before you can "hear a thrush singing," someone had to teach you what singing was. Someone had to show you a certain bird and teach you its name. Someone even had to tell you that you should use your will to stop and listen to the song of a bird because it is something beautiful. Words played a central role in helping you identify and name the experience of hearing a thrush singing and made it more likely that you would even notice the song. In the same way, with each new name children learn, with each description they hear of the world, language is teaching them *what* to pay attention to, *how* to perceive it, and what *value* to place upon it.

This is why literature is such a powerful force in shaping the consciousness and cultivating the wonder of young children, directing them to gaze upon the good, true, and beautiful. To read a book by Lucy Maud Montgomery— not just *Anne of Green Gables* but also *The Story Girl* (1911), *Jane of Lantern*

Hill (1937), and more—is to become aware of the natural world as a story in which every day is a fascinating page, with each sunrise revealing a fresh glory. With her words in your mind, it is all but impossible to look out the window with indifference. George MacDonald's stories—such as *At the Back of the North Wind* (1871) or *The Princess and the Goblin* (1872)—challenge readers to consider what mystery lies in the voice of the wind or the depths of the mountains. Louisa May Alcott's *Little Women* (1868) and *Little Men* (1871) invite their readers to enter into a round of sibling-inspired plays and feasts, troubles and triumphs, picnics and forest explorations driven by a delight in the world and other people that causes readers to desire such fun for themselves. Reading about Winnie-the-Pooh, with his slow but oh-so-wise observations of his fellow creatures, his love for Christopher Robin, and his revelry in the golden goodness of honey ushers a reader into a simple, but rich world of innocent hearts and fast friendships.

Each of the stories above describes the world to its child readers in terms of beauty, friendship, and joy. The rich but simple language of such children's classics shapes the minds and hearts of their readers by helping them notice what is lovely, love what is beautiful, and value what is loyal and true. A mind filled with the homey images of A. A. Milne and stocked with the wondering words of Lucy Maud Montgomery will look on the real world not with indifference but with interest, curiosity, and even affection.

It will look, in other words, with wonder.

In Our Home

Finding Beauty by Whetting Aesthetic Appetites

You can call it "the good, true, and beautiful," in keeping with the ancient philosophers. You can call it "whatever is lovely," in keeping with Philippians 4:8—"Whatever is true, whatever is honorable, whatever is right, whatever is pure, whatever is lovely, whatever is of good repute . . . dwell on these things." Whatever name you give your standard of aesthetic and moral excellence, the idea of assigning value to what is ultimately excellent remains.

The aesthetic atmosphere you create around you and your family has a profound impact on the aesthetic appetites you form. In a pop-culture, fast-food world, the only way to cultivate a love for the truly beautiful, the excellently crafted, the pure and true is exposure to art, music, literature, and words that embody excellence. As you outfit your home, as you fill your bookshelves and pick the images that will fill your walls, consider the habits of thought and desire they will kindle in those who behold them.

Our parents decided to fill our walls with the artwork of a calligrapher they discovered early in their marriage, Jonathan Blocher. Our home atmosphere was marked by his "Manuscriptures," Bible verses illuminated and illustrated in intricate, medieval style and illustration. But it was also formed by the etchings brought home from Austria—village pictures of peasants or drawings of the Viennese skyline—or classic art prints by Renoir, Monet, and Rembrandt dear to certain members of the family.

Pictures books in our house were a special area of aesthetic opinion. We had very few of the cartoonishly illustrated ones I always seem to encounter in mainstream bookstores. My parents believed (and I now concur) that picture books provide the first taste of art and literature to which a child is exposed. If you want children to love Rembrandt, don't give them stick figures. Give them Barbara Cooney or Thomas Locker, with prose by Cynthia Rylant. Try some Jerry Pinkney—*The Patchwork Quilt* (1985) is a favorite—Patricia Polacco, or Tomie dePaola. Give them pictures and words that evoke the complex beauty of the world in its myriad personalities and places.

The point in all this isn't to create elitists or to have a home of pretentious taste. It isn't even to fill your home with art and books that appeal to us Clarksons! You may prefer other books, other styles of art, different music than we do. But choose your aesthetic atmosphere with the awareness that every encounter shapes the heart. If you want your children to grow up loving what is true, beautiful, and good, your whole home should reflect that wholeness.

Finding Beauty in Family Rituals

Come Sunday afternoon when I was growing up, there was always a heightened buzz in the kitchen right around four o'clock. As the teakettle worked itself to a merry boil, someone would pull something hot and sweet from the oven—fresh scones, a blackberry crisp, or maybe an apple cake in autumn—and summon the family to the table for what we always called "high tea." While a true English high tea is a feast of a meal with savories, scones, sweets, and cakes, our tea was simpler, just dessert and Yorkshire Gold tea with milk and sugar. But we set the table as if for the queen, with green-rimmed Gmundner Keramik pottery from the family sojourn in Austria, our biggest teapot, and the crystal milk jug and sugar bowl carefully kept unbroken since my mother's single days in Poland.

For half an hour then, in the unrushed ease of a Sunday afternoon at home, we gathered round for tea and a feast. The food was delicious, but the real point was fellowship, a space of beauty and civility forged in the midst of busyness, a claimed hour of joy as a way to begin the new week together with grace.

We sat up a little straighter than usual in our chairs, sipping tea from real china cups and saucers, manners imposed by my mother's uplifted eyebrow or gentle hand. Often, when my father had finished his scone or crisp, he'd don his glasses and read aloud an episode from James Herriot's tales of animals in the Yorkshire countryside or perhaps a chapter in our current cycle of The Chronicles of Narnia. By the time we finished, a few evening shadows might be lengthening out in the yard, the hurry of Monday just ahead. But our Sundays, our rest days, were marked throughout the years of my childhood by this ritual of tea, civility, and fellowship. The tradition is something we grown-up children still, when we're home on a Sunday, look forward to savoring. Several of us have continued in our own single lives as well, inviting friends over on a Sunday afternoon, late in the quiet day, for tea in a real cup and something fresh from the oven. The charm of a little formality and a good dose of friendship is a significant gift in a hurried, impersonal age.

Intimidated by the intricacies of English high tea? Don't be. You can use any jumble of your favorite teacups or mugs to set a lovely table. Hot chocolate is an easy substitute for those who don't like the favorite brew of the Brits. Use whatever dishes and favorite foods you like. The point is not a perfectly laid table but one that delights the heart of those who gather. Sunday teatime is a space to gather and celebrate those we jostle through life with during the week, to be a bit more formal, a bit more present to each other through the ritual of feasting.

If you do, however, want to try your hand at a real English "cream tea," it's actually pretty easy. All you need is a good scone recipe, a jar of your favorite jam, and some sort of cream. For real authenticity, you can hunt down a jar of Devon cream from a specialty store, but to save time and money, we usually just whip up some heavy cream with a touch of honey and vanilla. Serve the scones split down the middle with a good slathering of cream as the first layer and jam drizzled on top. If you like, you can add a variety of sandwiches—cucumber and butter, egg salad, ham and cheese—all cut up into bite sizes with the crusts removed. Miniature quiches, cheese and nuts, a cake or trifle, or even a bit of chocolate will round things out.

If, on the other hand, you have no real interest in teatime, consider instituting other little family rituals that serve the same purpose in your family. One family I know always made a ceremony of buying, chilling, and carefully cutting the first watermelon of the season together. Another family always made waffles on Sunday before church. The point is to carve out time and make it special—different, set apart, beautiful. Carve out a time for a little formality, a little warm fellowship, something you can all remember and repeat for years to come.

Finding Beauty in Convalescence

Have you ever thought of illness as an opportunity for cultivating beauty and wonder and establishing a loving atmosphere? Beauty is about aesthetic creation, yes, but it is also about the creation of relational and spiritual spaces in which those who are weary can be comforted in "taste and see" ways. Beauty can be created in the sense of care—both physical and spiritual—offered to one who is lonely, sick, or suffering.

In our hurried age, we have little time for frailty of body or soul. Sickness is an inconvenience we resist with the popping of pills and the forcing of will, or something we fret about inordinately as we google symptoms, afraid of the thousand dire diseases we might have. What we rarely consider is the value of convalescence, the gentleness we sometimes need to offer ourselves and those who are weary and worn around us. Sickness is a space in which the uneasiness (dis-ease) of the body alerts us to the need for margin, rest, and special quiet.

For an adult, convalescence can provide a space in which to restore strength and wholeness. I list convalescence under the idea of beauty in the ordinary because it is a forced space of time that requires physical and spiritual shaping. If you have the flexibility, listen to your body and allow yourself some time to come back to the center, spiritually and physically. Even if you have a busy, intense life and cannot step back, try to give yourself as much grace as you can. Be gentle with your body and let sleep be the healer it is. Consider stepping back from the mental frenzy of modern life on a sick day, distancing yourself from technology and noise when you have the freedom to disconnect. As much as possible, allow your mind to quiet, your breath to deepen. If you are restless, choose music, books, or magazines that allow your mind a space of beauty, and don't forget to pray for healing. Nourishing, vitamin-rich foods like whole grains, vegetables, broths, and fresh juice will help your body do its work of restoration.

For sick children, convalescence can be a time of great tenderness, when despite their discomfort they know themselves to be highly valued and cared for. That was true for us growing up in the Clarkson home. Sick days, despite their misery, were oddly enjoyable.

We didn't really have them unless the sickness was genuine, of course. A few sniffles or sneezes never halted an afternoon outdoors. But for a truly sick child, there was always a ritual of convalescence. First, a "pallet" on the couch, which really just meant an old blanket draped over the cushions and tucked round the sufferer, who was propped up on pillows of all sorts and sizes. Then a special drink or two, perhaps the rare Sprite with some potato chips or crackers. Quiet activities—a pile of books, a favorite movie, some music by a favorite artist, a few crafts—helped us pass the time. The sufferer was excused from chores and allowed to sleep, to sip, to rest. We sometimes wondered at the end of such a day if the energy that surged anew had as much to do with rejuvenation of the heart as with healing of the body.

Finding Beauty (and Fun) on Rainy Days

However lovely a home may be, however rich the life within its walls, some days you will feel stuck inside. Blustery March wind and rain—not to mention late-season snowstorms—can easily spawn an epidemic of cabin fever that draws the worst from everyone involved. If you are in a new or lonely place, those hours of boredom can be the ones when loneliness becomes a greater presence than usual. Learning to fill the void hours with creativity, comfort, and possibility can make all the difference.

Because of this, our family has always practiced keeping our homes stocked with resources for these empty hours. With a little ingenuity and grit, the restless days sometimes become the best ones, when boredom or angst is dispelled by immersing ourselves in beautiful diversions.

For instance, Mom and I both have collected *Victoria* magazines for years. These rich, beautiful collections of literary, travel, artistic, and historic explorations are stacked on a bookshelf along with books by Tasha Tudor and other favorite artists. They are a resource for the soul, something reserved for savoring on those special "stuck" days. We've also found that some cookbooks are fun to read even without cooking. We've built up a merry pile of favorites over the years. And whether our browsing just passes the time or launches a marathon rainy-day baking session just depends on our mood at the moment.

Nothing beats a marathon TV-watching session on a rainy day when we don't feel like reading. There are countless fun series and miniseries to watch, especially the historical or literary tales that provide stories in which to immerse the imagination. And a craft box is a rich resource for rainy days, sick days, or bored hours. We always kept a few boxes of supplies in a corner downstairs and brought them out whenever creativity or restlessness struck. (For recommendations on books, miniseries, and craft supplies to keep on hand, see our resource pages at www.lifegivinghome.com.)

Finding Beauty through Walks, Wanders, and Hikes

When Joel and I spent a summer on an internship in England, one of our English friends mentioned that their children were trained early in the joys of country walking. "We try to get them to be able to walk three miles by the time they're three, even if we have to carry them at first; then we add a mile per year after." While the Clarksons were never quite so stringent in their requirements, the delight of a long walk, an afternoon hike, or a ramble through the countryside filled many family days. The pleasures and profits of walking, together or alone, are myriad.

First, to walk outdoors is to step into the larger beauty of creation, to enter the house of God Himself. Away from walls, screens, and work, we are reawakened to the wonder of the universe and the presence of its Creator in the countless levels of creaturely existence we encounter just in walking down a country road. Seasons at work in the color of the leaves, flowers and herbs ever changing by the road, insects and animals, wind and storm—to be immersed in the splendor of creation is to be reminded of our place within the world, to have our eyes freshened so that we are able to "taste and see" God's present work with renewed capacity.

Second, the physical rewards of walking are well documented. Any health book or website will tell you that a good walk can strengthen your body and quicken the flow of blood, but there are other benefits too. One of the gifts of a good ramble is a stretched ease that comes to both muscles and spirit. In our hurried, stress-burdened age, the rhythm of walking regularizes breath and thought. Detached from frenzy, the mind calms.

Did you know that countless artists, scientists, writers, and thinkers throughout history swore by walking as a way of working out the knots of their inmost thoughts? Charles Dickens walked up to twenty miles a night through the back streets of London, collecting inspiration and character ideas for his novels. J. R. R. Tolkien and C. S. Lewis had their famous discussion of myth during a midnight stroll down Addison's Walk in Oxford. There's just nothing like a brisk walk or a meditative amble to get the mental juices flowing.

Walking with others gives an additional benefit. The camaraderie of a joint ramble allows for sharing thoughts and secrets, old memories and new experiences. As a family, we have walked and talked together all over the world, and those walks have become a special rhythm of connection and consciousness. When we gather together from our disparate lives, we always ramble out sometime in the first days we're home, a good long walk our way of centering ourselves, sharing our experiences, seeing the world and one another afresh.

Here are just a few of the walking possibilities we've enjoyed:

- *After-dinner stroll.* In each house we've lived in, we found a nearby walking path, hiking trail, country road, or favorite street, and when the weather and season permitted, we rambled for half an hour in the evenings. We've walked red dirt roads in Colorado, leafy asphalt streets in Texas, winding roads in Tennessee, and age-old cobblestones in Vienna.

- *Saturday hike.* When we kids were little, our dad often took us for Saturday morning excursions along a park road or on a mountain trail. He always packed granola bars and water for each of us. As we grew older, we went for longer adventures. We packed sandwiches and trail mix, threw in cameras and notebooks for the artistically inclined, and spent half or even a whole day exploring. If we drove up to our favorite mountain trail, we always stopped for coffee on the way home.

- *Nature walk.* We loved to do this as children, too. These were not hikes, but opportunities to wander slowly through a beautiful outdoor space and see what we could notice. Girded with cameras, sketchbooks, and colored pencils, we would let our senses come to the fore, honing our sight to notice, then stop awhile and document. We would sketch a fallen leaf, draw a weary butterfly, notice the shift of sunlight through spring or autumn foliage. Such walks provide a matchless way to help children learn the art of attention, to train them in the art of wondering so that they learn to meet the world as a miracle.

- *Early morning with child or friend.* Practically every morning throughout my childhood, my mom slipped out early for a sunrise walk. When I was about twelve, I began to join her on these walks, and they became a source of deep friendship, discipleship, and comfort for both of us. Walking can create a space away from the busyness of home life in which to hear and care for the heart of another. Those mother-daughter walks shaped the close, kindred friendship that we share to this day.

Finding Beauty through Impromptu Adventures

Some days just call for escape. When restlessness or loneliness or just the stickiness of life in a fallen world makes the walls of your home feel a bit close, the remedy may just be an adventure. Some days it's entirely all right to be Bilbo Baggins and follow the road to whatever adventure you can find. When we kids were small and everyone was restless, one of the best things my parents ever did was simply to throw a picnic in a basket, pile us all into the car, and chase the rainbow down the road.

The destination? Any number of places. Our favorite adventures often ended up just being a picnic by a river or a hike down a random mountain trail. Sometimes we just drove down country roads, stopping for hot chocolate at whatever local café we could find. Sometimes we'd try a new restaurant—a Polish café on a back highway, a diner in a mountain town, a hole-in-the-wall Mexican place in rural Texas. The only requirement was that we would end up somewhere that diverted and delighted us. And beauty, we quickly learned from these impromptu forays, was almost always right around the corner.

Finding Beauty through Local Events and Attractions

Glee spread over the faces of all four of us Clarkson children at the sight of a Scottish-Irish festival right in our Colorado mountains. It's been almost fifteen years, but we all still remember the fun we had that day. We followed kilted men and tartan-swathed women through the festival grounds, darting in and out of the booths, eyes wide at the Irish and Scottish dancing, mouths full of fish-and-chips, toes tapping to the pipes and drums and the pulse-quickening fiddle of ceilidh (Gaelic dance party) music.

One of the best ways you can widen and enrich your own life and those of the people near you, whether children, friends, or family, is to seek out the opportunities for education, celebration, or artistic experience happening in your area. Identifying them takes only the littlest bit of work, and the experiences and conversation they provide are rich gifts.

There is much more going on around you than you probably know. You can use the occasion of hosting out-of-town guests to find the sights and places unique to your corner of the world. But you really don't have to wait for guests in order to explore your own backyard. Check your local newspaper, watch for signs and bulletin boards, or google the name of your town and see what comes up. A visit to a nearby visitor center or chamber of commerce office can also give you ideas. We've even found racks of brochures at interstate rest stops.

Here are just a few ideas to try:

- *Festivals.* Renaissance, Bach, crafts, food, antiques—you can find festivals celebrating almost anything. Within Colorado alone we discovered a Shakespeare festival in the summer, a Beethoven mountain festival in the fall, an apple festival complete with pick-your-own orchards, a craft and historic foods festival in late summer, and several other fascinating possibilities each year, including the wonderful Longs Peak Scottish-Irish Highland Festival in Estes Park.

- *Museums.* Almost every major city—and many smaller ones—will have at least a small museum of art, history, or science. Make a point to visit. One of the best things we did as a family was to regularly visit the art museum in our area. We kids liked to visit—and sketch—their favorite paintings, which we then researched at home. Old Masters, Impressionists, black-and-white photography, modern art—we tasted it all and talked about it all the way home. We also learned to look for special events, lecture series, and children's activities too.

- *Local businesses and attractions.* In Colorado we have the Celestial Seasonings tea factory within an hour's drive. In Texas, we had the original Dr. Pepper facility in Dublin. Both made for fascinating field trips for the kids. Find out what is unique or located specifically in your area and explore.

- *Farmers' markets and open-air markets.* These are great sources of locally grown fruits and vegetables, but typically they offer much more—from homemade jams and goodies to handcrafted treasures to entertainment. Mom always attends a local wholesale plant extravaganza in the spring.

- *Music.* Most large cities have a symphony or concert hall, and many have smaller folk, acoustic, or indie outlets. So find out what's playing, and keep an eye out for free or low-cost concerts. Even in the western reaches of Colorado Springs we enjoyed *Les Misérables,* folksinger Loreena McKennitt, special performances of Beethoven and Elgar, and Josh Groban. And we often attended meetings of the Black Rose Society, a local folk music organization that brought in all sorts of local and acoustic musicians.

Finding Beauty through Gardening

Every springtime in Colorado, as the snow begins to melt and the sky gets that bright, golden tinge of returning warmth and the leaves on the aspens begin to unfurl, we begin to dream about what we will plant in the beds by the front door or in the big pots on the back porch. As soon as it is warm enough, my mom takes whatever child happens to be at home—these days it's usually Joy—and makes her yearly foray to our nearby mountain nursery. Colorado may not be known for moist or fertile soil, but a bit of coaxing can produce a tumbled, vivid garden in even a high and very dry climate.

Browsing the rows of tiny new flowers and seedling tomato and pepper plants, they will choose a few boxes of flowers and vegetables to plant in the slim beds in front of our Colorado home, knowing that their choices will enliven and color every single day of our summer. One year Joy planted an apple tree. Another, they tried Russian sage bushes along the driveway. Once they managed a few beds of fresh mint. But the lilacs are always the best, returning year after year. To open the summer season with this ritual of readying and ordering the yard for the heat of summer is a way of marking the gracious return of warmth and the gift of color, taste, and refreshed life that comes with spring.

However we view vocation and occupation in this modern world, the fact remains that in the beginning, one of the primary human cares was that of the earth. To grow, tend, and, we believe, simply to behold the splendor of what comes forth from seeds planted in the ground was part of the original human identity given by God in the opening glory of a new creation.

Planting a garden is a way of returning to an awareness of essentials. It is, first, a way to remember our dependence on the earth to produce the food that nourishes and heals our bodies. It helps us learn what good work looks like and gives us a taste of practical, literally "down to earth" skills so increasingly rare in modern life. To garden is to immerse oneself in the richness of physical creation, aware of its capacity to produce both food and beauty, the gifts God gave for the nourishment of the human body and soul.

You don't have to have a country estate or an English cottage in order to have a garden. Even if a burgeoning vegetable garden and trellises of roses seem out of your reach, a window box, a patch of tilled earth in a little backyard, a pot of herbs on a windowsill, or even a single potted flower in a child's room can also give access to the gift of growing things, the splendor of a garden. Consider these easy possibilities:

- *Raised beds.* Do you have a corner of yard in which to build a simple structure? Consider filling it with soil and planting a vegetable garden. Even a few rows of good producers like cherry tomatoes, green beans, zucchini, or peas can yield an amazing summer harvest.
- *Herb pots.* A tiered planter or simply a row of clay pots on the back porch can yield a rich harvest of herbs—rosemary, basil, thyme, oregano, or marjoram—for cooking, drying, and scented delight.
- *Perennials and bulbs.* If you don't have much time to garden, consider investing in plants that bloom year after year without much tending. A lilac bush, iris bed, or scattering of daffodils can provide years of enjoyment with a minimum investment of time and care.
- *Forced bulbs.* These are delightful in winter. Hyacinths, daffodils, and tulips are easily coaxed into sprouting after a season of chilling. Just place the bulb in a glass that cradles it so that its roots can reach down into water and the flower can grow out the top. Lovely on a winter windowsill.
- *Child's garden.* Children love the ownership of a small plot of earth all their own. Just read Frances Hodgson Burnett's classic, *The Secret Garden*, and see if you can escape the delight of Mary and Dickon in their hidden corner of earth. Give your children a square of the backyard or a terra-cotta pot all their own. Help them choose flowers, herbs, or vegetables for their tiny plots and offer advice if asked, but give them the free rein of creativity and ownership.
- *Outdoor planters.* A huge copper pot passed down through my dad's family has sat by the front door of every home we've ever owned. Whatever the season, that pot brings a touch of nature's grace to the entrance of our home: magenta geraniums in summer, maroon chrysanthemums in autumn, a tiny fir tree in winter. Similarly, we choose

several potted plants—impatiens, roses, geraniums—to place around the porch and deck on our springtime trip to the nursery. With faithful deadheading and water, those plants grace and brighten the outdoor spaces of our home all summer.

The Promise of the Everyday

The wet, formless mud of March is the ground in which summer begins. In the damp days and gray days, amidst the wind and cold, the seeds of spring burrow deep into the wet, malleable earth to begin the growth that guarantees a season of trees and flowers, meadows and forests, and whole gardens of rich, lasting beauty.

May your ordinary time and spaces be the same. No moment is useless, no day void when shaped by the creative power of love. May your mundane March realities be the ground in which you plant the seeds of faith, beauty, and hope that sprout into a life marked by the goodness of God.

April

A HERITAGE OF FAITH
Engaging with God's Story
(SARAH)

Keep on walking along the way.
Keep on trusting Him every day.
We walk by faith and not by sight,
Following the path of light.
Keep on walking until we see
Jesus calling out to you and me
To join us in our heavenly home.
Keep on walking along.

CLAY CLARKSON

"Keep on walking..."

Our Pied Piper father strummed loudly on his guitar and began a merry march round the room, crooning the simple chorus. We marched behind him giggling, stamping, marching with knees high and singing the now-familiar tune at the top of our lungs. Immersed in the melody and words, we had no idea we were gaining spiritual instruction in the process. Morning devotions with music by my dad were always a delightful affair.

In a sense, Dad's music formed the soundtrack of my childhood. He hummed in the garage, wrote songs for family events and holidays, and shared favorite new releases with my siblings and me in the car. The pluck and strum of musical creation often sounded faintly and mysteriously behind the door of his orderly, sequestered office. His early recordings were the music by which my siblings and I fell asleep for many years, his clear tenor crooning Scripture and peace into our anxious little heads. Throughout his life, and particularly in his days as a pastor, he often performed his music in and for the churches we attended.

His "Keep On Walking" song came about during the Vacation Bible School week when the children in our little church explored John Bunyan's *The Pilgrim's Progress.* The whole group sang the song at the opening of each talk. I think Dad deliberately wrote a song that would etch itself into little ones' minds and memories. He wanted us to think over and sing and follow that "path of light" every day, all our lives, right into the presence of Jesus.

It worked. "Keep On Walking" became a kind of family theme song for faith, I think, because in its simple lyrics and straightforward, marching melody it reveals a truth about how spirituality is passed along from one person to another. Someone walking on a godly path draws another person to walk alongside, to sing as they march, and together they press on, hand in hand, toward the light. That song embodies, in a way accessible even to a little child, the pilgrim nature of faith, the shared journey, the notion of love for God as it grows in the human heart and drives the believer forward.

That we learned that song in the circle of family and marched to it first with siblings and friends through the landscape of the living room is a gift indeed. For what better place to begin that shared journey, that onward quest of faith, than in the first fellowship of home?

The Pilgrimage of Faith

According to the great medieval poet Geoffrey Chaucer, April is the month when "folk long to go on pilgrimages."[1] Sap quickens in the trees, warmth burgeons in the air, desire stirs our blood. We sense we are called forward into new life, new love, new growth. In April I feel an almost irresistible invitation to set out on one of the damp mountain trails near my family's home in Colorado, to taste the returning warmth in the wind and find the first flowers bravely breaking the snow-hardened earth.

We speak of "spring fever" so carelessly, but in some sense there is a real, seasonal restlessness whose energy is part of the profound renewal of the earth. I think there is an equal and needed quickening at times in the life of faith, and it often coincides with the outer life of spring. For April is (usually) the month of Easter, a time of profound spiritual renewal if we take the time to make it so.

Easter is the season in which we mark the climax of God's journey in human flesh, the long pilgrim road that led Jesus to the cross and the resurrection that was the marvelous, world-altering homecoming at the end of that journey. But Jesus' finished pilgrimage is simply the beginning of ours. His completed journey is our promise of eternal home, a promise that puts us on our spiritual feet and calls us forward through the time and days of this life.

We do not travel alone. Christ is the first and ultimate guide for our journey, but each faithful person since has left a trail of footprints showing us how to walk and which paths to follow. None of us practices our faith in a vacuum. We watch the ones who go before. We mark their endurance, catch their passion, learn from their wisdom. And the first pilgrims we meet in this world have a profound influence on how we journey. Ideally, these first companions on our spiritual journey will be members of the family household into which we are born. And the first stumbling baby steps of faith we manage will be taken in the confines of home.

In this April season of restless pilgrimage, it may seem strange to speak of home because it often signifies the completion of a journey. *Keep on walking.* We see home as the end point, the resting place to which our physical wanderings lead. But in the spiritual realm, home is also, paradoxically, the starting place. Home is—or should be—the shelter in which we taste a love or beauty that ultimately drives us out in spirit, searching for its source. Home is the haven in which the desire for the eternal is nurtured, in which we are strengthened, companioned, and equipped to begin the journey toward Christ that can become the quest of a whole life. Home is the place in which the great journey of faith begins.

The Training Center for Faith

No pilgrim just walks out the door one spring morning and manages to make a successful quest. Real pilgrims have already spent months in prayer and practice, gathering the needed supplies to keep them walking when the way is long, building the courage to keep them going when the way is dark. In the pilgrimage of faith, those supplies are the practices and rhythms of the Christian life, the habits of kindness, the cadence of devotion, the gathered resources of Scripture. Because both of my parents came to know Christ in student movements, they both experienced intense "discipleship," being mentored in Scripture and prayer by someone just ahead of them. Their concept and experience of faith was to daily practice the rhythms of devotion and then to teach them again to others.

This is, inherently, a pilgrim model, and my parents practiced it in our home almost from the day of our birth. To them, preparing us for the great adventure of faith was one of the primary gifts our home could give us.

In the Clarkson home, I learned firsthand that spirituality can be as natural as the air a child breathes if parents are willing to be creative, flexible, and intentional. Breakfast table devotions were a daily practice, as were nighttime blessings. We memorized Scripture with little prizes for incentives. We washed dishes (and danced while we did it) to the music of singer-songwriters my dad loved, and the spiritual poetry of those lyrics echoes in our ears to this day. We read irresistible faith-based allegories together. We made baskets for the elderly. We prayed as a family, the littlest child snuggled on my dad's lap, when a friend was diagnosed with cancer.

In all these ways, the thought of God—that awareness of the eternal in which our home life was rooted—was a constant presence, a wider reality we both acknowledged and learned to desire. Faith wasn't just something we were taught in church. It was the air we breathed.

On a more practical level, my parents involved us in their ministry. We took part in every aspect of prayer, preparation, and giving in both their church and discipleship work. My parents took time to explain their vision and drive, drawing us into what they saw as "the Kingdom life," the practice of love given and service offered that brings God's Kingdom to earth. Instead of feeling obligated by religious practice, we were drawn into a world in which God was present, active, and deeply engaged with those who turned toward Him.

Not that we were perfect—in our faith or our behavior. We fought. We squabbled. Our parents lost their tempers. Sometimes we enjoyed helping with ministry; sometimes we bewailed our fate. Sometimes we loved our siblings; sometimes our actions were done in anything but love. Some days the whole family forgot to pray because there was just too much going on.

The truth of the matter is that no matter how far along the path of faith we walk, the reality of fallen human nature will always get in the way of perfection. We lived that, too, in the Clarkson household. But because the habits of faith had been established early on, we were usually able to return to prayer, to love, to song, after the stressful day, the fight, the meltdown. We learned to take ourselves lightly because grace removed the burden of guilt, even as we worked toward a spiritual environment of maturity and forgiveness. In that sense, our parents were wise, influential guides in the way of faith, showing us how to seek, walk, and constantly return to the path of life. Home was the safe, sacred space where we learned those rhythms of struggle, faith, and return that would mark the spiritual journeys of our coming independence.

As each of us has reached adulthood and ventured out into the world, we have found that the rhythms of faith begun in childhood have given us the rhythm by which we now "keep on walking along the way." Our devotional practices may be different, but the words of Scripture haunt our thoughts, the cadence of morning devotion continually calls to us, the habits of prayer and ministry remain.

Most important, the identity of a pilgrim called to follow after God shapes our deepest sense of self. It was an identity learned at my mom's elbow, in my dad's simple song. And it's one that remains deep within us, a core strength that keeps us walking "by faith, not by sight" every day of our lives.

—— *In Our Home* ——

When a group of musicians prepares to play a piece, the first things they look for on the page are the time signature, the key signature, and the tempo. The first tells them what rhythm the piece is based on—the sequence of stronger and weaker beats that determine whether it's a waltz, a sturdy march, or a syncopated jazz piece. The second conveys the tone and feel of the piece and the sequence of musical steps and half steps that determines its distinctive flavor. The third prescribes the pace of the music—how fast or slow it should be played. Each notification is vital to playing the piece correctly. Without them there would be no music, just discordant cacophony.

So it is with the home. Each home environment has different parameters that require different spiritual time signatures, key signatures, and tempos, and how we go about spirituality in our varying worlds will be affected by how we set the music of that spirituality. Will it be a lilting dance of faith or a stately march of sanctification—or one after the other? Is it a bright and expressive faith like a Vivaldi piece in a major key, or is it a more reflective, mystery-infused spirituality in a minor mode, a requiem by Brahms or a ballad by Andrew Peterson? Does it move forward at breathtaking speed or progress at a slower and steady pace so that we can savor each melody and note along the way?

There is no right or wrong answer. Every home has its own musical framework, its own marvelous cadence and distinctive tonality that keeps the music of its spirituality in play. But the music must be chosen, cultivated, and practiced. No home can realize its spiritual potential without finding the rhythm, tone, and tempo of faith fitted to the particular men, women, and children who inhabit it at any given time.

In our home we learned the art of creating a set of regular family practices and environmental elements that helped us write the music of our family, moving us forward in our shared pilgrimage of faith.

Starting the Day Off Right with God

One of my earliest memories—one that would recur in a thousand slight variations throughout my childhood—is of my mom, legs tucked under her in a corner of a couch or armchair, with a cup of coffee in one hand and an open Bible on her lap. (Dad had his own devotions in the order and quiet of his home office before we kids awoke.)

When I was small I'd curl up beside Mom, begging a sip and listening to her read aloud. She would share with me something she had learned that morning or read to me from a devotional Bible for kids. Thus I came by my love of both coffee and Scripture early. And the intensity with which she earnestly taught us in such moments to love God and His Word gave my siblings and me a smile when we were older and talked about our common memories.

As I grew older, my mom began to train me and the other kids in the art of having our own morning devotional moments. As soon as I could read, I was given a simply worded children's Bible. By the time I was a teenager, my "quiet time" half hour was a staple of my day, a habit of devotion that remained, and steadied me, through deep seasons of questioning, sorrow, and doubt.

The same is true for my siblings, who also learned from my parents to start their days with a quiet time. The actual way we approached this morning practice varied with the person and with the day. In fact, one of the things that so ingrained this habit in us was our freedom to express our individuality. We each had our little corner, our journal or devotional. Sometimes we would read our Bibles and reflect on a portion of Scripture. Sometimes we would read a devotional or faith-themed book. Sometimes we would simply pray quietly. The point was to seek God's presence before doing anything else in a given day.

In addition, we tried to start our mornings off with a shared breakfast before going off to our respective worlds. A nice warm meal most days along with tea or coffee helped get us all in a good mood. Devotions followed breakfast.

They didn't usually last long. Someone would read a passage from Scripture, and we would discuss it for a few minutes, or my dad would read aloud a chapter from a daily devotional. Sometimes, as we grew older, we were given the chance to share what we had learned from our quiet times that morning. We shared our prayer requests and our prayer commitments and prayed together. Then we would quickly disperse to begin our busy days.

Again, we were far from perfectly disciplined in this. Sometimes one or more of us would miss (or deliberately skip) either our personal quiet time or the devotional at breakfast. And our devotional times were rarely serene and serious, especially when we were little. Someone was always squirming or spilling a glass of juice, playing with the dog on the floor in front of us, or competing for a place on the couch. Our parents learned to make allowances for short attention spans, to keep prayers short and to the point and focus more on regular practice than lengthy sessions. I suspect there were times when they thought their attempts at discipleship were getting nowhere. But the habit of both personal and family devotions first thing in the morning ensured that we rarely missed the opportunity to seek God before the day began in earnest.

Our "24 Family Ways"

Early in our life as a family, our parents, both being planners, developed a list of values they wanted to develop as part of our family culture. This was eventually codified into a collection of specific stated "ways" we would follow as a family. Basically a series of value statements rooted in Scripture, our "24 Family Ways" were conceived as a way to guide our choices day to day. They functioned as teaching tools, devotional aids, and a kind of family contract. When we were little, especially, that list helped reinforce expectations for the way we were to behave and our sense of who we were as a family.

The list was divided up into six areas of life—authorities, relationships, possessions, work, attitudes, and choices—and each area included four statements about what "we" did to live a well-formed life in that area. For example,

- "We love one another, treating others with kindness, gentleness, and respect."
- "We are diligent to complete a task promptly and thoroughly when asked."
- "We choose to be joyful, even when we feel like complaining."

The entire list was written on a chart and posted where we could all see it throughout the day, and we would collectively discuss one of the "ways" each day during our family breakfasts.

The 24 Ways thus became part of the rhythm of our lives, with most of them being memorized and repeated (and sometimes copied out numerous times when my parents felt we were not sufficiently convinced of their truth). A Scripture verse accompanied each one, and we memorized those as well. The system was eventually developed into a published book, and many other families have integrated it into their homes.

As a child growing up with the 24 Ways, I can testify that they took root in my heart and my life, particularly in shaping my interaction with my siblings. I think much of our friendship as adults is due to the fact that the Family Ways regulated and shaped our speech, reining in the rash teenage tongues that can create years of division between siblings. To this day, when I am angry, I can still hear the statements about forgiveness, compromise, or peace echoing in my mind, forming my reactions. The 24 Ways have also expanded into my adult life, so that the values of kindness, responsibility, and grace are now expressed in my friendships, work, and ministry. In a deep and personal way, they are still a mental guide on my pilgrimage of faith.

Prayer Times

Of all the different spiritual rhythms, prayer is the one that pervades all of life. It takes many different forms, from quiet, unspoken prayers on the spur of the moment, to prayers spoken in community, to the shared language of liturgical prayer.

In our family, prayer has always been the regular punctuation in our lives. As with many families, prayer before meals was a natural daily event, but we also often incorporated a practice of morning and evening prayer into our lives.

Beginning and ending our day with prayer brought us near to God and, in a way, taught us to mark all the beginnings and endings of our lives with conversation with God. Each prayer time usually consisted of sharing requests and thanksgivings and perhaps reflecting on a passage of Scripture or an aspect of God's character, followed by a time of talking to God together. Sometimes for the sake of brevity, a couple of people would be chosen to pray aloud. At other times, everyone would take the time to participate in the prayer process. There were no hard-and-fast rules, except that we did our best to make it happen every day. In the process, we lived out the reality of Christ's promise that "where two or three have gathered together in My name, I am there in their midst" (Matthew 18:20).

We also learned very early from watching my parents that part of faith was the practice of coming to God on our own, seeking Him in the secret and sheltered places of solitude. Sometimes, we found, such prayer is the only way to face deep problems and dark moments of doubt or disappointment.

I remember the curiosity I felt in watching my mom seclude herself for half an hour. I wondered what exactly she found in speaking to God that allowed her to emerge in calm. I also remember the first time I consciously tried it myself, pouring my childish woes out to God and feeling a sense of care that honestly startled me. One of the fundamental truths I learned in my home growing up was that God is ever available, ready to meet with those who seek Him. This is one of the most vital truths of my faith, one that shapes the deepest moments of my life to this day. I have made a priority of passing it on to the girls I mentor in student ministry.

Scripture Memorization

Scripture is the vocabulary of the Holy Spirit. The Spirit speaks to us through the words of Christ, the psalms of David, the stories told and retold over centuries. And Scripture, like prayer, has always been a cornerstone of our family's spiritual life. Our prayers and devotions were nearly always accompanied by a reading of Scripture. And from the time we were very small, we were encouraged to memorize the words of Scripture, hiding it in our hearts and minds, allowing it to become the voice that narrated our reactions, decisions, and hope.

Often we would take a passage such as Psalm 23, Matthew 5, or Romans 8 and memorize it together as a family, returning to it throughout a given week. Sometimes we would choose a weekly theme—living in the power of the Holy Spirit, being conformed to Christ, loving one another—and each theme would provide context for memorizing several verses. Sometimes we kids would take on the challenge of memorizing passages independently. See the resource section of www.lifegivinghome.com for a list of passages that are worth hiding in every young person's heart.

As my siblings and I have grown up and gone out into the world, we have often had discussions about how verses from Scripture would suddenly appear in our minds in challenging situations. We learned firsthand that memorized Scripture is a gift that can accompany someone through all the different seasons of life.

The Music of Faith

No matter where you find any one of us on a given day, music will likely be playing in the background. It was always a constant presence in our home when we were growing up, and we all caught the bug. Music can be used in amazing ways to "set the scene" of the home; it provides aesthetic context without intruding into the conscious happenings of the day. Beautiful music enhances the spiritual life in the home. Beauty is an intrinsic aspect of God's character, and listening to beautiful music trains the channels of our minds to desire that which is good, true, and beautiful.

In our family, we often listened to classical music by composers like Bach or Mozart. Much of their music was set to sacred texts, and we loved those pieces, but even their beautiful instrumentals helped set the atmosphere of our home toward that which is true, honorable, right, pure, lovely, admirable, excellent, and praiseworthy (see Philippians 4:8). And of course we also listened to more contemporary music that we believed met those standards.

Music can also be used to build a bridge between an intellectual understanding of God's character and a gut-deep, emotionally satisfying understanding. We may have a mental comprehension of God's desire for us to be joyful, but when we hear vibrant music and we are filled with exuberance, it becomes real for us. Some of my earliest memories are of our entire family dancing and romping around the living room to an energetic praise and worship song, even when we were washing dishes or straightening the house. It is in that catalytic connection between knowing and experiencing that we begin to encounter God in a meaningful way.

Making music, too, was integral to the experience and expression of faith in our home. We were even called the "von Clarksons," after the von Trapp family in *The Sound of Music*, because we sang so often and all had some bent toward music. One of the great gifts of our home was the opportunity to interact with and create music as a way of communicating the deepest emotions and desires of our hearts.

My parents made it a priority to give each of us at least a bit of musical training in childhood because they knew it could be a way of expressing and affirming the deepest things we knew to be true. And their efforts took root. For Joel, music is now both a vocation and a call. In his classical, choral, and film-score compositions, he understands himself to be narrating his faith in a language without words. Nate and Joy are both singers and songwriters, recording and performing songs that express the challenges and grace to be found in the journey of life. I am more inclined to play accompaniment, although I compose an occasional instrumental piece. For all of us, the language of music is like the language of nature as described in Psalm 19—a voice that goes out into all the world and can be understood by anyone.

Music, of course, is supremely a matter of taste, and different forms of music will speak to different people. Our family particularly loves the creations of contemporary artists Fernando Ortega, Rich Mullins, Andrew Peterson, Michael Card, and Chris Rice, whose music basically made up the soundtrack of our life together. For an annotated list of our favorites from these superb Christian musicians, see our resource page on www.lifegivinghome.com.

The Art of Faith

If music experientially manifests God's truth to us, the visual arts can have a similar effect. Filling a home with beautiful artwork creates an environment of beauty so that the knowing—through prayer, devotion, and Scripture—is cemented in reality by experience.

In our home we had a number of original works by various fine artists. More than just a nice way to fill blank space on a wall, such artwork introduced us to excellence and attention to beauty. We were encouraged to reflect on the intricate brushstrokes and penmanship present in each piece and were reminded that they reflected the perfect mind of our God, the master Artist, who crafted the world with a mind toward beauty, order, and imagination.

As I mentioned in the previous chapter, the art of Jonathan Blocher was an important part of our home atmosphere. The work of this master calligrapher, who creates exquisite artistic renditions of various verses from Scripture, added beauty to our home and created a constant Scripture narrative. But our experience of beautiful art and faith-filled art was not limited to the pictures on our walls. We also visited art museums and even took our sketchbooks to copy the pictures—a time-honored way of learning by doing. And back at home we often pored through the full-color art books on our coffee tables and our shelves. (See www.lifegivinghome.com for some of our favorites.)

Though we tend to be a more word-and-music-oriented family, we kids were always encouraged to express our faith and vision creatively through the visual arts as well. One practice our parents always followed in our Family Day tradition (see the August chapter) was to give each child a blank piece of paper and allow him or her to draw something to commemorate God's goodness during the previous year. We've collected all those sketches in a notebook that we consider quite the treasure after all these years. Another individual expression of art and faith was the chance for each child to choose a few posters or framed prints to set the tone and atmosphere of his or her room. And as we've grown older, all of us have explored other forms of artistic expression. I have tried my hand at calligraphy inspired by the Celtic illumination of the *Book of Kells*. Nathan once painted a mural in his room. Joy likes creating portraits. And Joel has shown distinct gifting in more technical design.

Reading and Writing Faith

If anything quintessentially characterizes the Clarkson home, it is our dedication to faith as a family and our voracious appetite for reading. From independently sitting in our respective rooms with a cup of tea and devouring a great novel to gathering in the living room for a read-aloud session, books were a reliable cornerstone of our family life. Not surprisingly, books were an important part of our faith heritage too. There were always spiritually focused books on hand to teach, inspire, and challenge us. Our parents made sure of that.

When we were small, our reading baskets contained Bible story picture books and child-sized prayers. As we grew older we read inspiring devotional works and books on theology and then passed them on to our brothers and sisters and often our parents. Our high school and college reading drew us deep into the philosophies and worldviews of classic works of literature, allowing us to explore and discuss the spiritual challenges they raised. Our individual quiet times often included books of classic spirituality or devotion such as Oswald Chambers's *My Utmost for His Highest,* Dietrich Bonhoeffer's *The Cost of Discipleship,* and Dallas Willard's *The Divine Conspiracy.* (See www.lifegivinghome.com for other standouts.) We also read Scripture aloud with one another, considering the "Good Book" integral to our literary lives.

Not surprisingly, our immersion in the life of books inevitably made writers of us all. The language of faith was a daily delight and challenge for us as we were taught to express in our journals what we learned in Scripture and to articulate our values for other people in written words. Writing our faith was a form of prayer, a way to narrate and clarify our spiritual journey and hone our convictions. Out of this private practice—and, no doubt, from observing our parents' literary efforts—grew the writing of books, blogs, poetry, songs, and stories expressing and exploring the life of faith. For some of us, the craft of weaving faith into words has become a vocation.

Feasting with Faith

The story of faith ends with a feast. What an alluring, celebratory promise. I love the vivid adjectives used in the book of Revelation to describe the end of time, when all things are made right and God invites us to His table for a wedding feast. Meals are more than just a way to satisfy our bodies; they are an opportunity to nourish our souls. We may "know" intellectually that God is our portion and sustains us with good things, but when we eat a delicious and satisfying meal, that truth becomes real to us. It incarnates the mental truth into the world.

Jesus Himself gave His own life for us—His body as bread and His blood as wine, a spiritual food to nourish us in our need. When we eat with one another and break bread together, we are in a way reflecting the beauty of that sacrifice. Enjoying a wonderful feast with friends and family can be a way to reflect on God's giving of Himself to us as a nourishing meal.

As you might have already gathered (and you'll hear a lot more about this in later chapters), feasting was a major theme in our home. Even the most ordinary of dinners signaled a special time to be enjoyed together, and the simplest meals were usually accompanied by music and candlelight. Special occasions brought special feasts, with menu items that only appeared on those special days and the whole family working to prepare and serve.

The point of feasting was not merely to consume good food or make a bit of random fun. For us, to feast was to affirm the essential abundance of God, to recognize and celebrate His gratuitous goodness. With every bite and every sip, we praised Him—and built a heritage of delicious, incarnated faith.

Celebrating the Rhythms of Faith

At the heart of the strongest homes, I believe, is a rhythm of celebration—the marking out of time, family, and faith as something in its essence that requires us to rejoice. At the heart of such homes is the recognition that every aspect of our lives here on earth gestures toward or embodies the ultimate realities of God's love. This means there is heaven in the ordinary, in the simple goodness of the everyday and the ordinary rhythms of work and prayer. But sometimes we need to step aside from the mundane and remember the source of all the life and love we see. We need to take the time to remember our origin, our purpose, the eternal Love toward which all work and wonder direct us.

At such moments we affirm the reality of God's momentous involvement with His people and our hope that all the world will one day be wholly joyous, wholly beautiful, wholly good. And the heart of that hope, of course, is the Resurrection. Easter is Resurrection Sunday. Celebrating the day and retelling the story of the events that surrounded it must be a vital part of a family faith experience.

No matter their tradition, nearly all Christians celebrate some form of Holy Week, the time between Palm Sunday and Easter Sunday each year. As a family, both at home and at church, we often participated in several different events in the week prior to Easter, remembering and even reenacting the story of Christ's passion and His glorious resurrection. This, we realized, was the true, epic story—as strange and glorious as anything Tolkien or Lewis ever conjured—of which our own small stories were part. To live Holy Week was to reenact and claim the holy drama of heaven as it invaded our own particular days, drawing our individual lives into its own.

Christian Seder Dinner

This beautiful event, often held at our home or at the home of one of our friends, was always a staple in our family's observance of Holy Week. Based on the traditional Jewish feast during Passover (the original Seder), it incorporated common aspects of the Jewish Passover but linked them to the prophecies of the Old Testament fulfilled in Christ, especially the correlation between the original Passover described in Exodus 12 and Christ's sacrifice on the cross.

With various Scripture readings, each step of the meal reminded us of the intricate and beautiful narrative of God's redemption of the world. We children asked questions about the meaning of the night, and the answers we heard told us the story of Israel's slavery in Egypt and God's miraculous deliverance. We tasted bitter herbs, and the taste evoked the pain and yearning of God's people, longing to be free from oppression. Lamb, served as a main dish, brought to mind the lambs whose blood told the angel of death to "pass over" the Israelites, the lambs sacrificed to God in the Temple, and of course, the ultimate Lamb sacrificed for us on the cross.

Filled with meaning and dramatic narrative, this exquisite dinner was always a poignant punctuation of Holy Week not to be missed.

Good Friday

Observed by many churches around the world, Good Friday commemorates the day of Christ's crucifixion, the darkest day in Christianity. The church services and Scripture readings associated with this day are typically solemn and sad, and many people observe the day with fasting instead of feasting.

So why is this day called "good"? Some linguists point out that the word *good* used to mean "holy," so the original meaning was "holy Friday." Others believe *good* derives from God—"God's Friday." Either explanation fits. But I have always liked the explanation that we call this Friday good because through Christ's sacrifice, God's enduring goodness overcame the evil of the world.

We usually went to church to observe this special day. There, we would listen to a Gospel reading that outlined the turning of the people, who only a few days previous had proclaimed "hosanna" and now shouted for Jesus' crucifixion. The service painfully reminded us that we, like the people of Jerusalem, were destined to turn away from good and fall into sin. That, we were told, is why we needed redemption.

The entire Good Friday service centered on Jesus' great work on the cross and often included an opportunity to participate in prayers of repentance. It helped us understand that Christ's sacrifice would seek us out in even the darkest corners of our lives and bring us back to redemption. No matter how lost we might become, God would find us. And that news, even to small children, was good indeed.

Easter Sunday

One of our most celebrated holidays throughout the year, Easter is filled with community, feasting, fun, and of course, joyous celebration of Christ's resurrection. For the Clarkson kids, it was a day to be celebrated both with our home family and with our church family.

For many years we would start the morning with Kinder eggs[2] for everyone around the table at breakfast. We could say that these little hollowed-out Italian chocolates added a touch of whimsical surprise that reminded us of the surprise of resurrection. But to be honest, we just considered them fun and delicious. So I'll just mention them here as part of the joy of Easter and let you draw your own conclusions—and confess that we all still enjoy a touch of chocolate at Easter breakfast.

Of course, attending an Easter service at church formalized our understanding of the beauty of the resurrected Christ in the world and gave us an opportunity to celebrate that truth with brothers and sisters in the wider body of Christ. While in Oxford, I attended the Great Vigil of Easter, a Saturday evening service that commenced with the relighting of the Paschal (Easter) candle in the darkness, a powerfully visual act that made the proclamation of Christ's resurrection a viscerally joyous experience. As a family, we now seek out this service as well.

Following our Easter service, we always had a grand feast, replete with deviled eggs, vegetable casseroles, salads, desserts, delicious drinks, and a special main course, often a baked ham. And we always made a point of bringing guests into our home to share the celebration. Easter, we believed, was for the whole community of faith.

After lunch we invariably held an Easter egg hunt. Each participant would be assigned a different color of egg and be directed to search out only that specific hue of egg. Each egg contained some sort of fun prize—a small amount of money, some candy, a gift card—with one special egg containing a bigger prize.

Of course, in the margins of the day, we enjoyed wonderful fellowship with our friends and sometimes rousing discussions as well. It was an exciting, full holiday filled with the joy of Jesus alive in the world—an annual high point in the rhythm of our faith.

Keep On Walking

"The Road goes ever on and on," said Bilbo the hobbit in the first book of Tolkien's classic *The Lord of the Rings*.[3] It does, indeed, particularly the pilgrim road of spiritual growth. No one escapes the summons to journey; we all walk toward Christ . . . or something else. But when the journey is begun in the profound fellowship of home, with those who are farther ahead standing beside us, equipping us, whispering their wisdom in our ears as we fare forth, our journey becomes not an individual quest but a shared pilgrimage. We are drawn forth by the stories of those who have gone before into a living story of our own.

Home is the shelter in which those quests of soul begin, in which we are strengthened for our adventure, equipped for the long road of faith that lies ahead. Home is the refuge whose peace allows us a glimpse of the ultimate good we will journey to find.

Said Bilbo of the road, "I must follow, if I can."[4] May we follow the road of faith all our days.

— May —
DAYS TO COMMEMORATE
Marking Growth with Celebration
(SALLY)

The man of our time is losing the power of celebration.
Instead of celebrating, he seeks to be amused or entertained.
Celebration is an active state, an act of expressing reverence or appreciation. . . .
Celebration is . . . giving attention to the transcendent meaning of one's actions.

ABRAHAM JOSHUA HESCHEL

GIGGLES, CHATTERING, AND melodious voices young and old filled the room as people munched fresh strawberries slathered in whipped cream, tasted sumptuous slices of quiche Lorraine, and consumed countless bite-sized cinnamon rolls.

My boys, fourteen and twelve, noisily dragged two folding chairs apiece to complete the circle of furniture gathered in our living room by the piano. Sarah, our sixteen-year-old daughter, flushed pink with excitement. Today she was to be honored in our home ceremony before we graduated her to an adult world from our own home.

After all had been satisfied with Sarah's favorite brunch food, each guest and family member found a place to sit as we gathered to commemorate her precious life.

Clay cleared his voice and tapped on a coffee cup to gather the attention of all who were settling in and clearing their throats and whispering last antics to friends nearby. Then he began his speech.

"We are here today to celebrate and commemorate the graduation and commencement of Sarah Elizabeth Clarkson as she concludes her formal studies during the elementary and high school years, to honor her for the many skills she has developed and the honors she has completed, and to remind her of the great ways God has worked in her life up to this point. We also want her community of friends to join with us in blessing her together as she begins to seek God's direction and call on her life as a Christian and as a woman of God."

So began the first Clarkson home graduation ceremony for our first and oldest child, our celebration of her completing high school and venturing out into the world. Some friends have hosted similar ceremonies when their children reached "teenagehood" at age thirteen. Scripture is full of celebrations, commissions, and formal feasts that God called His children to celebrate every year. Having the Israelites take time to commemorate special milestone events—to remember acts of God's lovingkindness and faithfulness or to herald His saving them in the midst of a battle—was God's way of holding them accountable to their commitment to remember Him. These journey markers reminded them to walk in His ways and to be faithful to His role in their lives.

Stopping our normal activities of life to commemorate a special day or person can play the same role in our lives. It brings honor to the person or event and highlights significant accomplishments. It also reminds us of the many ways God has guided and helped us and of our responsibility to both live for Him and uphold others as they try to do the same.

In Our Home

For many of us, May is a month of celebrating special people and special milestones. We celebrate graduations and accomplishments at school—all the way from kindergarten to college. We honor mothers on their special day. Piano and choir recitals often showcase the accomplishments of music students—the results of all those hours of practice—and we attend wedding and baby showers to mark the beginning of new life commitments. In the paragraphs to come I've listed just a few of the special ceremonies and activities that have been a part of our lives.

Our Home Commencement Ceremony

Each of our four children had different graduation experiences when he or she completed high school. Some, like Sarah, had just the home ceremony. Others walked the stage with other friends who were graduating but had a personal home ceremony, too, celebrating their entry into the adult world. For us, it was a time of personally commissioning our children to go into the world, a coming-of-age ceremony to remind them of the values we held and the faith we cherished and to challenge them to take those ideals into their adult worlds. We wanted our home to be a keeping place for sacred days, sacred commitments, and sacred moments, and this gathering of friends helped all of us remember what our days had held.

When we first began to plan the ceremony for our children, we knew we wanted to include several elements:

- *Accountability.* Commencement—the formal affirmation of a person's life, vows, commitments, and accomplishments—does more than just celebrate that person. It also helps hold him or her accountable for continuing to live well for the glory of God. In a day of informality, where churches and schools require little accountability for life commitments and stewardship, we wanted to include that element in our home commencement ceremony.

- *Community.* It was important to us that the ceremony take place within a community of love, a home where they could always find acceptance, comfort, and help when needed, a stable home base for sending them into a less-than-stable world.

- *Identity.* We wanted to stress their security in God's love for them, their indelible value to our own community, and God's call on their lives to serve Him and to invest their lives in His Kingdom ways.

- *Remembrance and responsibility.* We especially wanted to remind them of their roots—the faith, traditions, values, beliefs they had been exposed to in our home—and of their responsibility to steward their lives well, remaining faithful to their priorities by passing these values on to their children and friends in their lifetimes and to generations to come.

With all this in mind, we created our first home commencement ceremony for Sarah, our firstborn. We would repeat it in more or less the same form for each of our children.

Though my description of this ritual may seem a bit long, it never really felt that way to us. Our children enjoyed having different friends participate by reading Scriptures or even making presentations. Having a company of witnesses, so to speak, surrounding them and believing in them was deeply meaningful. All of our children have considered this special day a rite of passage and wouldn't have missed it for anything.

Here's a summary of the ceremony as we developed it for Sarah and adapted it for each of our children:

- *Opening Scripture and remarks.* Our ceremony always opened with a reading from the book of Jeremiah: "'I know the plans that I have for you,' declares the LORD, 'plans for welfare and not for calamity to give you a future and a hope'" (29:11). We then specifically reminded Sarah that God had created her uniquely (see Psalm 139), that He would always be with her wherever she went (see Deuteronomy 31:8), that God had uniquely prepared her for good works to do in her lifetime according to her personality, design, and skills (see Ephesians 2:10).

- *Speech from the graduate.* Next came a little speech from Sarah in which she told about her hopes, dreams, and ideas for the future.

- *Special music.* Because each of our children learned an instrument to play or practiced their skills at songwriting (after their dad, who is a songwriter), we always had a solo or musical presentation. Sarah played a warm, Celtic-flavored piano piece she had composed. (Clay used to love listening to Sarah play the piano and called it his "Sarapy"—or Sarah therapy.)

- *Sharing memories.* Each person in the group was asked to share a memory or a blessing for the child being celebrated.

- *Presentation of commencement gifts and comments.* Extending gifts to remind them of our values, traditions, love, and unique heritage as Clarksons was a fun part of our celebrations—each gift wrapped up with paper and bows and presented with appropriate Scriptures and an explanation of its symbolism. (For instance, a small oil lamp would be a reminder for them to keep the light of Christ burning and to take it out into a dark world.) Clay and I always had a wonderful time picking these gifts out. For a list of the ones we used, please see the resource section at www.lifegivinghome.com.

- *Prayers for the graduate.* Each person who had come to share this time with us was encouraged to offer a brief prayer for Sarah as she entered a new and exciting season of life with the Lord.

- *Closing song and benediction.* For graduations, we liked to sing David "Beaker" Strasser's wonderful song, "Step by Step."

Gifts for the Recital Season

Clay and I entered parenthood unprepared. I was the only girl and the youngest in my family. When I gave birth to Sarah, I had never changed a diaper and had babysat only a handful of times in my whole life. Clay had been exposed to children even less than I had. And so we entered the world of being parents with no practical knowledge or experience.

That's not to say we had no idea what we wanted for our children. We decided we would do everything possible to give them some intangible gifts that would prepare them for adult life in ways that a conventional education might not. We hoped these gifts would bring them joy and confidence through their adult lives. I'm happy to say we haven't been disappointed.

The Gift of Music

As you may have picked up on by now, a love of music was important to both Clay and me. From the beginning we planned that each of our children would have at least one year of music lessons of some kind. Over the years this included piano, guitar, and violin, as well as songwriting, jazz, and worship training. Participation in choirs, musical plays, and bands was encouraged to give a taste for being engaged in musical performance. To enhance this love of music in our home, we collected and played music every night at the dinner table, often throughout the day in our home, and almost always when we were in the car. The selections varied widely from classical to acoustic, Christian to secular, Celtic to choral—all as part of helping our children develop a taste for all sorts of music.

Attending recitals and performances and celebrating each child's efforts were mandatory in our house. Usually we would enjoy a special dinner or go out to eat after the performance. And Clay and I always made sure to place personal notes on their pillowcases, telling them how excited we were to see them growing or attending to these interests.

The Gift of Speaking and Drama

Majoring in speech communications in college, I became aware that for many people, speaking in front of a group was among their greatest fears. We didn't want that to be true for our family, so Clay and I made it a goal to incorporate verbal arts into our home atmosphere. Reading aloud with dramatic voices set the stage. Eventually we would all take turns reading stories and poems as well.

Having multiple places to speak, share what they were learning, or be involved in a local performance group of some kind was a sort of life requirement for our children before they left our home. Because we held our own ministry conferences for women for twenty years, we would often have our children emcee or share a story, a Scripture verse, or something they had been learning. We wanted each of them to develop the habit of speaking without fear.

When Joy was in high school, she entered national competitive speech and debate, so almost our whole family gained experience in traveling with her on the competitive circuit. Becoming judges at tournaments added some fun experiences to our lives.

Running dramatically across a stage, crooning harmony with a guitar and a small band, humming a background melody in a chorus—all these experiences were familiar to our children in certain seasons of life. They learned to communicate—and love doing it—through Easter pageants, dramatic plays or musicals, speaking competitions, speech classes, and church performances. For three years in a row our whole family was part of a seasonal, professional musical production in Texas. Consequently, all of us—even the introverts—are more or less comfortable speaking or presenting in front of crowds. This habit has helped our now-adult children in their professions.

The Gift of Hospitality Skills

Hospitality has always held a special place among my heart's values. Growing up in a home where a cup of tea or a meal was always available to visitors on short notice, I had always found that welcoming and serving others came naturally. After becoming a Christian, though, I realized that hospitality contained a deeper dimension. It was a way to open the hearts of those I met to God's love and ways. And it was a practice I wanted to pass along to my children.

From toddlerhood, the kids were offering a bowl of nuts or chocolates to guests. As they grew a little older they learned how to serve tea and coffee and talk to guests. Making meals, cutting flowers, putting on soft music, and straightening the house eventually became second nature to all of them—boys included.

Our children especially enjoyed hosting their friends for parties and get-togethers. Giving them ownership over their own preparations—shopping for food, cleaning the house, preparing and organizing it, and seeing to guests' needs after they arrived helped make hospitality a lifelong value and habit for all the Clarksons.

The Gift of Travel and Missions

Beginning our family life as missionaries overseas, Clay and I wanted our children to be familiar with and comfortable in the world at large, experiencing different languages and foods and the beautiful variety of believers in Christ around the globe. Hosting missionaries in our home over the years exposed them to the exciting stories of those who were doing God's work abroad. But I wanted even more for my kids. I wanted to give them the opportunity to experience missions firsthand.

Living as a young single woman in Communist Eastern Europe had given me a special love for Poland and other countries where I had traveled and worked. So when each child turned fifteen, I took him or her on a special trip to visit my old missionary stomping grounds and then either attend or work in local ministry.

Being alone with Mom, receiving all my attention and focus for a change, made this a life-changing time for each of them. And having a great international experience to tuck into their grid of understanding was a wonderful bonus. It's no accident that all of our children have traveled internationally since then.

Celebrating Weddings and Families

Springtime in general and May in particular is a time to celebrate (or look forward to) weddings. Hosting wedding showers was a special delight to me and my girls. As I view the landscape of marriage and divorce in this time of history, it seems more important than ever to affirm biblical, traditional values at showers or parties when the couples are celebrated.

Whatever your religious background, strong and healthy family relationships are something to cherish and celebrate and teach. Each year around our anniversary or on Family Day (see the August chapter for more on this special Clarkson celebration), we typically read Scripture passages that describe how God created marriage and the family as the structures through which all of life should be organized. And whenever I am called upon to host a bridal show or celebration, I always include some of this biblical instruction and inspiration for the bride-to-be:

- *"Then the Lord God said, 'It is not good for the man to be alone; I will make a helper suitable for him'" (Genesis 2:18)*. I talk about the fact that God made us, at the beginning of time, for companionship, to be a family, to have a place to belong. I discuss how important it is to cherish marriage, family, and our commitments to one another and to build and protect these relationships by investing in them.

- *"God blessed them; and God said to them, 'Be fruitful and multiply, and fill the earth, and subdue it'" (Genesis 1:28)*. Reading these verses together every year helps us remember that before the Fall, when everything was perfect, God had families in mind. He said having children and seeking as a family to govern and rule over the world to make it a better place would bring meaning and purpose to the sanctity of living, belonging, and working together.

- *"God saw all that He had made, and behold, it was very good"* (Genesis 1:31). Finally, God said that all He had created up to this point, family included, was good—worthwhile, wonderful, a blessing!

I have been surprised at how well prospective brides and grooms respond to this message. In the midst of all the craziness that comes with wedding preparations, it helps to be reminded of what it's really all about. Not dresses, photographers, and flowers, but God and family.

Babies, Babies, Babies

Because I have held many a baby shower in my home in May, I thought this might be the chapter where I at least mention something about the importance of valuing babies in a home—any home, both the homes where little ones live and the ones where they visit.

In a culture that often views a child in terms of the expense in time and money he will cost in his lifetime, how important it is to intentionally recognize the infinite value of a tiny human being, created with the very imprint and image of God on his life, and to understand that this little one's life will have consequences for eternity.

Jesus whispered this into my heart when I was a young mama: *This child, whom I created, has special significance to Me. Will you take this child for My sake and show her the touch of the love of God, whisper the messages and truth of Scripture, teach her to have the character of Christ in living and serving with integrity, and show her how to give her life to a world that is longing for redemption? Will you raise this precious gift I have given you for Me, as an act of worship?*

I understood that no matter what other work I would accomplish, part of my service of worship to God was to serve the child He had given me. Children are the adults of the next generation, and so our love, education, training, and modeling of all that is valuable in life will indeed shape the history of the next adult generation.

And the opposite is true as well. Our failures to live up to God's call can do incalculable harm both to our children and to our future. How many children's accomplishments or scars can be traced back to their childhood years?

I'm not saying that every mistake you make with a child will result in catastrophe! Thank God there is abundant grace available for those of us who accept the challenge of raising babies to adulthood. His love really does cover a multitude of sins. At the same time, I believe we need to take to heart the importance of our challenge.

The way we touch a child's life matters both in the long term and the short term. And this very important life work takes place primarily inside the walls of home. But as Clay and I found when we embarked on our own path of parenthood, the reverse is also true. Over the years, our little ones have shaped our lives as well.

Babies in a home bring it to life.

Cherishing Babies as Gifts

The beginning of a lifegiving home for a baby is to be welcomed into its space. Touching a child often and softly, singing into her ear, rubbing her fuzzy head, responding to her needs, smiling, serving—all of these acts help you attach to her very being and write patterns upon her little brain about the truth of God. I am convinced that a child who breathes the oxygen of acceptance and love is predisposed to believe in the love of God when the concept is later introduced.

Giving Babies Time to Be Babies

Love to all little ones is spelled T-I-M-E. All babies are created by God to need time and attention. Growing from a nursing, totally dependent infant into an independent human being takes lots of time. Every baby throughout all the centuries has taken a while to grow up. If we shun that realization, we'll just find ourselves impatient and frustrated.

I've seen so many parents who spend their time and effort trying to control their baby's behavior to make life easier. It doesn't work! Life will go much better if we learn to watch the growth, notice the beauty, understand the process, enjoy a time that will never come again. In the process, as we sacrifice our own needs for the little ones placed in our lives, we'll catch a glimpse into the secret places of God's father-love for us.

I have found that there is some mysterious value that stretches our own ability to become mature and loving by accepting the limitations babies bring into our lives. When you fight against the duties that come with the arrival of a child in your life, you may find yourself fighting with God. It is His plan to give us precious, fragile, crying, loving little human beings who need a mama and daddy—and lots and lots of time—in order to flourish.

Preparing Babies to Comfort Themselves

Nine hours of sitting next to a screaming toddler on the plane home from London to Denver recently gave me hours to consider how I might help parents comfort their babies—or, more important, teach those babies to comfort themselves. The poor, exhausted parents were frazzled and angry by the time we landed, and they seemed to have no idea how to handle their sweet baby.

I do know plane trips with little ones can be exhausting. I once made a twenty-five-hour journey from Vienna to Dallas, Texas, with six-month-old Joel in my lap and two-and-a-half-year-old Sarah as my seatmate. That said, I have picked up a few tricks over the years for keeping the chaos to a minimum:

- *Recognize that each baby has a personality and specific needs.* Some need more attention and input, some will be gentler and quieter, some will move all the time, some will be more placid, and some will be whinier. Trying to make individual babies conform to a formula is a vain exercise. All four of mine were quite different. Learning to observe them, know them, and respond to them as individuals helped me acquire the ability to calm them and meet their needs most of the time.

- *Give babies comfort objects the moment they come out of the womb.* (Well, maybe not the moment—but soon after.) We gave each of our children a soft "blankie" with silk ribbon trim. Each time we rocked them, we would put the blankets against their little cheeks with the silky part between their fingers; babies love texture and love to rub something. When our babes cried, we immediately gave them their blankies to help them begin to comfort themselves.

- *Don't be afraid of a pacifier.* Though I know I will probably get some letters about this, I am a firm believer in pacifiers or the like. I nursed all four of my babies for a very long time, but I also gave each of them a "paci" after I had nursed them to give them a way to calm themselves when I was not able to nurse on demand. I've heard all the arguments about it ruining their teeth. But only one of our children needed braces, and that was because she fell twice when young and knocked her teeth in toward the back of her mouth.

- *Bring a "bag of tricks" wherever you go!* I always had a little packed bag that we used only when we went out and another little box of items inside the house. The contents varied according to the ages of my children, but they included rattles, hand toys, little books, soft puppets and stuffed animals, toy cars, stickers, bubbles, sidewalk chalk, and other little bits of entertainment that would engage them and keep them occupied.

- *Keep food and drink on hand.* No matter your opinion about water, juice, or mom's milk, babies who have drink available at a moment's notice and some small bits of something to munch or suck will be easier to get along with. I always carried a little container of organic O-shaped cereal for mine. I learned that these melted in a baby's mouth and would not choke them and would stave off hunger when I needed to buy a few moments.

Establish Predictable Rhythms at Home

Babies thrive on routine and repetition, and they need a predictable schedule and environment—mealtimes, time outside, bedtime and wake-up routines, cleanup times. Little ones don't come into this world knowing what to expect. Everything is new and, from their perspective, more or less random. They need to know that their needs will be met, their hunger will be satisfied, and their desire for comfort will be fulfilled. Once they understand that, they'll be happier. And we all know a happy baby makes for happier parents.

Set Up Your Home to Welcome Babies and Children

It's now been quite a while since we had a baby of our own in our house, and grandchildren aren't on the immediate horizon. But baby guests are common in our household—for overnight stays and for the moms' Bible studies I lead at home. So we make a point of being baby friendly so the moms and dads who come here can enjoy our hospitality. We keep a crib, several soft blankets, toys, nibbles, sippy cups, rocking chairs, colorful baby books, CDs with lullabies, and Winnie-the-Pooh videos ready for any who might need them.

For slightly older children, we've held on to LEGOs, puzzles, coloring books, colored pencils, stuffed animals and puppets, and a variety of games that might be played when a visiting parent longs for adult attention from us. By being prepared to meet the needs of our little visitors, we've found that many moments of frustration can be avoided.

Celebrate It All

There is no end to the possibilities of celebration in May, when warmer weather is returning (or already here!), when gardens are beginning to grow and spring fever is in full bloom. I hope you'll take full advantage of this lovely month—with May baskets, Cinco de Mayo celebrations, Mother's Day observances, Memorial Day picnics, end-of-school scavenger hunts, or just enjoying the outdoors together with your family.

But whatever else you do, remember to celebrate the joy of each day and the wonderful people in your life.

Remember to take the time to enjoy.

June
TIMES OF DELIGHT
Creating a Value for Play
(SALLY)

It is a happy talent to know how to play.
RALPH WALDO EMERSON

IN THE MIDDLE OF the most hectic, demanding period of our family's life, we made a crazy, stereotypically Clarkson decision: We moved in with my mother-in-law.

Our kids were young, Clay and I were idealistic but penniless, and we were trying to find a way to make our way in the world. We wanted to start our own ministry but didn't have the resources to do this while living on our own since Clay had recently lost a job. We saw few options but to take our three kids (Joy had not yet been born) and hunker down with Clay's mother while we figured things out, wrote a few books that were on our heart, and started our ministry in Walnut Springs, Texas, a virtual ghost town with just over seven hundred residents.

It was undoubtedly one of the hardest years of my life. Though Clay's mother was a good sport, the inevitable adjustment to living with a mother-in-law hit me hard. When we arrived in Texas, the weather was over a hundred degrees and humid as all get-out. Within months all three of our kids had contracted chicken pox, burst eardrums, possible encephalitis, and pneumonia—yes, each child had all four maladies! I also had my second miscarriage in less than a year. I was overwhelmed and underslept, and I could barely get up in the mornings, much less be available for three kids. There were no coffee shops, cafés, or even large grocery stores within thirty-five miles.

Needless to say, that was not the high point of my life. But when my older children look back on those first few months, they have very different memories. While for me it was a constraining, difficult period, for them it was a time of wild joy. Whereas before we had lived in suburban Nashville, in a home with a regular suburban-sized backyard, now we suddenly had two hundred acres of Texas countryside for the taking.

For my three innocent adventurers, a whole new world of excitement opened up. They marched all over "the land," as we called it. They climbed trees and waded in streams. They built forts and playacted at being everything from Scottish warlords to cowboys in the Wild West. Collecting fossils, catching snakes, and creating a butterfly collection provided hours of discovering nature up front and close. They explored and imagined in a world far outstretching their scope for curiosity. That time at my mother-in-law's home helped establish a love for creativity, imagination, nature, and adventure in my children's hearts.

Painful as some of my memories are from that time, I'm so grateful they had this fabulous opportunity to play, and many stories from those days bring a smile to my mama heart.

The Importance of Play

Play is the way children learn. By setting the narrative of life in the relatively safe world of play, they discover how to interact in real-life situations and embody character qualities fitting of great people. In the process, they expand their palettes of imagination, curiosity, and intuition. Heroes become real when a child can become one in his or her own backyard. Play is a way for children to see their lives as stories, to inhabit a creative, imaginative space that exists alongside normal life. It allows them to practice the kinds of great lives they will live in reality when they grow up.

So often I have read my children a story or observed them reading one to themselves, then watched as they would try to reenact that story in their recreational time. After reading Robert Louis Stevenson's classic work *Kidnapped*, the kids would dress up and pretend to be pirates, gallivanting all over a pretend Scotland, mimicking the book. Several of my children read Tolkien's *The Hobbit* when we first moved to Colorado. Suddenly, the nearby mountains were no longer the Rockies; they were the Misty Mountains that Bilbo traveled through with the wizard Gandalf and thirteen dwarves from the lonely mountain, and the thick trees behind our home became Mirkwood, the dark, mysterious forest where elves lived.

At play, my children quested for great treasures, fought off evil beings, and saved one another from peril. In doing so they learned the value in pursuing great quests, joining a fellowship of their own making, pursuing goodness in the face of a corrupted world, and looking out for the least among us. Now all are young adults, but they have each had to face their own enemies, walk through their own kinds of peril—and still choose to be righteous. Their playful pursuits as children have found a rooting in their real narratives. They practiced nobility, bravery, and goodness in their play as children so that they could practice it for real as adults.

These days, such child's play has too often been replaced by time on machines. Children easily become dependent on the immediate and constant interaction and the instant gratification that comes from interacting with gaming toys, computers, and tablets. And I suppose this kind of play in moderation can provide certain limited benefits, such as hand-eye coordination and certain kinds of problem-solving skills. But few online games I have seen involve the kinds of problem solving, imagination, physical exercise, and cooperative pretending that old-fashioned play requires. They limit whole areas of brain growth. And because they tend to be addictive, they limit the time available for healthier pursuits.

When I was a young mom, I read an article that said geniuses are often born out of boredom. To develop to their potential, I believe children need time to be bored so they will be motivated to create their own fun. They need time to dream and imagine and time with adults and family without lots of outside distraction.

Such play makes for happier and more creative children. It also encourages healthy moral development. If children can learn to embrace and love concepts of truth, goodness, and beauty in their games and playacting, living by those values will eventually become an ingrained practice, an instinct as natural as breathing or walking. Acting out positive morality creates mental and emotional pathways that children will continue to walk in their whole lives.

Play also has another important role in development: It helps expand a child's ability to learn. As they play, children learn how to solve problems intuitively rather than according to set rules. Because they enjoy the experience, they are motivated to use these problem-solving skills to process any later knowledge they acquire. That's a good thing. After all, we don't want our children to simply gain some sort of database of knowledge through education, and we don't want to simply indoctrinate them with our platitudes. We want them to *understand* the information they take in—to actively engage in it, not just compile the information. Enjoyment is a catalyst for owning what one is learning.

Childhood play, especially outdoor play, encourages physical development. Children at play will run and jump and climb and dance. In the process they develop strength, flexibility, balance, and endurance. Even the inevitable scrapes and bruises help encourage resilience. And again, enjoyment is the key. Children who are having fun will be motivated to move more and get up when they fall because they want to play some more.

And childhood play is an invaluable way of learning relationship skills. Playing with other children tends to be a constant series of negotiations—"You be Gandalf and I'll be Legolas" or "You be the daddy and I'll be the mommy" or "Now let's be horses." In the process they learn (I hope) to communicate, to support one another, to give and take and compete in healthy ways, to handle disagreements, to assert their needs but also watch out for the needs of others, and to not take themselves too seriously. Even solitary play is good practice in self-reliance and helps kids become comfortable with their own company.

Have you ever considered that play might be good preparation for faith? Ultimately, we want our children to encounter Jesus and become like Him. When their imaginations develop strong mental muscles from engaging in stories of goodness and bravery, they will be predisposed to engage in the great Story of life—the vibrant, exciting, rousing tale of God invading the world, living among fishermen, prostitutes, children, and demon-possessed people, throwing over tables in the Temple, kneeling to wash feet, and giving up His life for us all. We want them to have an experience of faith that becomes personal and sustaining for them, and imaginative play helps them develop the capacity to experience this.

Not Just for Children

Ultimately, play is a process that, though most commonly practiced in childhood, can be enacted throughout the entirety of life. It is no doubt common that the slow desensitization of growing older, along with peer pressure and a desire to conform, steal a sense of play from our lives as adults, but I don't believe it was meant to be that way.

There is no reason that imagination and a playful spirit should be suppressed in either childhood or adulthood. As adults, our capacity to play is only hindered by our fear of looking silly, our busyness and constant activity, or our own involvement with screens. Cynicism has replaced innocence as a cultural value. But without innocence and childlike belief, we may miss the fingerprints of God.

There is a reason that Jesus said, "Unless you are converted and become like children, you will not enter the kingdom of heaven" (Matthew 18:3). Children aren't afraid of experiencing excitement, joy, curiosity, and wonder to the fullest extent. They laugh, point in excitement, ask unusual questions, and stand openmouthed in new and exciting encounters. They approach life without preconceptions; they are open to possibilities. And so must we be, if we want to know God.

God is active and present in every moment of our lives, but too often we are so caught up in how we ought to be rather than allowing ourselves to be swept up into the whirlwind of the Spirit. God desires that we learn to play again, to experience Him like little children do, open in wonder to the vastness and endless wonder of Him.

The genius nineteenth-century poet Gerard Manley Hopkins once wrote that "Christ plays in ten thousand places."[1] Jesus Himself is waiting to play with us, to shape us and overwhelm our imaginations, if only we would once again learn the movement of His dance of joy.

—— In Our Home ——

June, the month when school typically goes on hiatus, is cemented in most children's minds as a time to get really serious about playing. Days are longer. The weather is often good. A vacation or road trip may be on the horizon. Even parents are prone to that "get out of school" urge to go out and have some fun—even while they're wondering how in the world they'll keep their kids occupied during those long summer days.

It's important to realize that play—or a spirit of playfulness—can extend far beyond the boundaries of what we usually think of as fun and games. It can include all that we cherish, practice, participate in together—anything that brings joy and delight. Some of the things my children remember as their most fun experiences are things others might not think of as play—concerts we saved for and attended, trips we took together, the dramas and plays we participated in, the gatherings we hosted as a family. All these brought great enjoyment and enhanced our shared life values—and they provided great ways to fill up those bright June days and long summer evenings. The rest of this chapter lists just a few of the activities the Clarkson family worked and played at together. You can find more of these ideas in other chapters and on our website because fun as a family truly knows no season.

Building Blocks of Fun

In our desire to make our whole home a learning, an experimenting, and yes, a playful environment, we started collecting LEGOs early on in our marriage. Initially Clay and I bought two enormous bucketsful of assorted LEGOs at a garage sale, and over time, we added to that collection by purchasing specific sets for birthdays and Christmas. Eventually, we collected three crates of LEGOs.

For our kids, these toys provided endless hours of fun. They designed everything from castles and knights to race cars and jets. Sometimes they would follow instructions included in a given set, but more often they would just rely on imagination and experimentation. At one point, the boys took two three-by-five-foot craft tables and created an elaborate complex of buildings and structures, well populated by cars, planes, and helicopters.

LEGOs and other building-block toys (including Duplos for young children, old-fashioned Lincoln Logs, and Playmobil toys) are ideal ways to unlock your children's creativity. There are no set rules for what can be designed; the only limit is what the imagination can conceive. Building-block toys have been shown to improve spatial reasoning, mathematical understanding, critical thinking, and other areas of intelligence in children. One study even suggests that children who play with LEGOs regularly develop better language skills. So they're a no-brainer for providing endless hours of play. Look for them at yard sales and discount stores as well as toy stores.

Puzzles

We love puzzles in our family. Working together to create a picture out of a jumbled pile of pieces can be a fun and immensely satisfying rainy day activity for all ages. Because we lived in Austria, Ravensburger puzzles—exquisitely designed German puzzles for everyone from preschoolers up to adults—were favorites with us, and we gradually amassed quite a collection.

Keeping the puzzle pieces together can be a struggle for busy families, and there's nothing more frustrating than *finally* finishing a puzzle, only to find out a piece is missing. We solved that by ordering some oversize zippered plastic bags, and each puzzle had a bag of its own to go back into when the kids finished with it. This way, most of the pieces stayed with their own puzzles. Only one puzzle per child was allowed at a time so that the pieces did not get mixed up.

As the kids got older, we started to get larger and larger puzzles. For one birthday, Joel received a thousand-piece puzzle of a map of C. S. Lewis's fantasy land, Narnia. Working on that monster puzzle together became a way to encourage the kids to focus on details so as to learn the bigger picture.

Make-Believe

For children, play and pretend inevitably go together. My children loved to act out the stories they had read, the movies they had seen, and whole scenarios from their imaginations. As their mom, I found a number of ways to support their play and, in the process, join in their fun. Here are just a few of the ideas that worked for me:

- *A box of dress up clothes* can provide years of costumes for our children's playacting. Thrift stores, secondhand stores, and yard sales are inexpensive sources of boots, long dresses, scarves, boys' army jackets, Halloween costumes (animals, angels, superheroes), and all sorts of costume jewelry and trinkets. After holidays, you can often find items such as bunny ears, top hats, and Santa beards on clearance at discount and party-supply stores.

- *Keep plastic or Nerf swords on hand* so whoever wants to defend someone in a rousing tale has a weapon to act out being brave. (Be sure to talk about safety, even with fake weapons.)

- *One yard of bright, silky material* is easily transformed into a versatile costume accessory. Just add an inch-wide hem on one side (I sewed mine by hand, but you could also use narrow iron-on tape) and thread a length of ribbon through the resulting "tunnel," and you've got a cape. All of my children used their capes to play superheroes, and the girls also used theirs as princess capes or tied the ribbon at the waist to make long prairie skirts. I was constantly amazed at the creative ways all four used the contents of their dress-up box for creative play.

Game Nights

It's a natural temptation for many families to revert to TV at night. We all get tired from our busy lives, and most of us—parents included, or maybe parents especially—just want to relax at the end of a long day. As a family, we've found there are a lot of different ways to mitigate against that habit without putting undue strain on anyone. One of our favorites is playing board games or card games together. It's a way to get everyone in a circle, making eye contact with one another, laughing, and enjoying the companionship of family.

It's also a great way to spend an evening with friends. We long ago began a tradition of inviting over a group of families we felt closest to for a monthly potluck and game night. This evolved into close friendships through many stages of life. We all still love to gather and not only compete to the hilt but also pray together, share holiday dinners, and stay open to "I need a friend; let's plan another evening together."

When we invite people over, our go-to plan is to order out pizza and soft drinks and ask each family attending to bring their own favorite games—board games, commercial offerings like Pictionary or Balderdash, or ideas for "party games" like charades. We've discovered some really fun games this way. If we're really feeling ambitious, we will make a tournament out of the evening and have a prize for the family or individual who wins the night. Some of our game-night staples are listed at www.lifegivinghome.com. Most of the commercial ones are available for a reasonable price, but check out thrift stores and yard sales for used versions.

It is amazing how many games can be played with a single deck of cards. Some of our favorites are hearts, spades, cash, gin rummy, spoons, and golf.

(If you don't know the rules, they're easy to find online.) Even this week, on breaks from editing, Joel, Clay, and I played an ongoing game of golf. Our running competition was punctuated with guffaws and good-natured trash talk: "I'm definitely gonna win this one" and "I can't believe you got the wild card again." (I won, by the way.)

The Great Outdoors

After three of our children were diagnosed with asthma and we had to acquire our own emergency equipment for treating midnight bouts of gasping for air, Clay and I decided to relocate. We moved our family from the heat and humidity of Texas, which heightened the symptoms, to the relatively cool and arid climate of Colorado. Through God's grace we were made aware of an unusual unbuilt lot backing up to Pike National Forest, just north of Colorado Springs, where we were able to build a wonderful home suited to our values and preferences. Suddenly we had a mountain wonderland to explore, with limitless acres of preserved forestland to discover. Although all of us had loved exploring around our Texas home in the country, when summer rolled around with its oppressive heat, I had sometimes found it difficult to get everyone to go and play. Now in the cool of the Colorado mountains, my children began to love being outside more than ever.

Studies have shown that children benefit in body, mind, and spirit from being outdoors. Benefits range from strengthening muscles and bone mass to limiting stress. Being outdoors, in fact, is one of the greatest gifts to give to a child. I saw this worked out in real time during our sojourn in our Colorado home. As a family, our stress levels actually began to decline as we spent more time in the great outdoors. We took hikes together to a beautiful outcropping near our home, known by the locals as "inspiration point" because of its stunning views. We toted picnics with us while walking on the many trails behind our home and ate sandwiches while we felt the cool Colorado breeze on our faces. We slept out on our large wooden deck in the summer, listening to tranquil mountain sounds and looking up at an endless expanse of stars, far from city lights.

Clay and I also made a concerted effort to encourage outdoor life by cultivating our property, just barely over an acre. All of us, with no experience, spent a whole day planting strips of sod all over our yard, providing a lush, thick blanket of soft lawn for the kids to play on. We built a playground and a sandbox at the end of the yard, both of which quickly became the setting for any number of different playacted adventures. We even planted a grove of aspen trees near our driveway, which have now grown into their full height. Our children learned to love the outdoors because it was one of the rhythms of our home life together, and gradually they, too, took up the stewardship of cultivating the earth.

Our children did more outdoors than yard work, of course. Swimming, hiking, and biking were daily outdoor activities. Our kids eventually all acquired mountain bikes over the years and rode for miles on trails and on streets near our neighborhood. They organized or attended large-scale outdoor games such as Capture the Flag, water-balloon battles, even laser tag and paintball. It's a whole load of fun to get a bunch of people together, find a great terrain, and make a day of it.

We found our community was full of places where children and parents alike can have fun outdoors—parks, nature centers, botanical gardens, zoos, and community centers for outdoor sports such as tennis or basketball (many offer lessons and competitive leagues). In every home where we lived, we found a community pool nearby, and I took the kids there from the time they were young—to help them improve their swimming skills and also to fill up long summer days. Each week we organized pool days so our kids could join in with other friends, playing water games, learning how to use a diving board, and having a lot of splashy fun.

Travel Fun

From the time our family became a family, we were on the road. Travel was not only something we enjoyed; our ministry vocation made it a necessity. We traveled constantly for speaking engagements and often took the kids with us. We saw the majority of the United States by car, and we had lots of fun doing it—usually.

But as exciting as this was for us as a young family, it was simply unrealistic to expect four young children to sit quietly in a car for eight hours of travel without getting bored, restless, or anxious—and driving Clay and me batty. To mitigate the long hours, we developed several strategies to help the time pass.

Activity "Briefcases"

Whenever we traveled, each child was given his or her own "briefcase," a special tote full of items to play with along the way. The items could be used individually or as a group, but only when we were away from home so they remained novel. Clay and I had great fun assembling the kits, adding new items from time to time, and the kids really looked forward to delving into their personal stash of fun. Often all the kids would draw at the same time, or sometimes they would play a game together.

One of the most favored games in the Clarkson car was the license plate game. We found an interactive book with pictures of each state license plate in the United States, plus Guam and Puerto Rico. Especially when traveling through urban areas, the kids would keep their eyes peeled for new license plates. Any time a rare plate was spotted, such as Alaska or Hawaii, there would be a moment of triumphant jubilation for that particular child, and everyone else would strain to see the unique find.

Here are some ideas for packing a kid's briefcase for the road—all have been hits in our family. (You can keep these around the house, too, for rainy days or sick days.)

- *Paper* (graph paper, sketch paper, folding paper for origami and paper airplanes)
- *Colored pen and pencil sets*
- *Coloring books* (architectural masterpieces, scenes from history, and so on)
- *Stickers*
- *Snacks* (little bags of gummy candy, nuts, healthy munchies)
- *Activity books* (puzzles, paper airplanes, brain games, origami, mystery and quiz books)
- *Books* (picture books and a variety of touch, pull, and feel books for little ones, plus age-appropriate fiction and nonfiction for older kids)
- *String games* (yarn tied in a circle for playing "cat's cradle" and such)
- *Car games* (such as car bingo) and playing cards
- *Story starters and Mad Libs* (little books that had to be filled in using the child's own imagination)

- *Bubble wands and solution* for the rest stops along the way
- *Toys* (little cars, small stuffed animals—Beanie Babies being the favorites)

Pit Stops for Play

One of the most important things to remember for keeping travel time fun is to stop often and give everyone a chance to burn off excess energy. Sitting still for long periods of time can be very hard on little ones. So we always made full use of parks, rest stops, and welcome centers. Sometimes we carried a few outdoor toys (balls, Frisbees, beanbags) and organized games to encourage our kids to *move*. Or we would stop and take a walk in a town we'd never visited before, combining fun, learning, and exercise. Our trips were always more fun as a result of considering everyone's needs.

Looking for great historical museums along our journey was a wonderful way to combine a needed pit stop with a chance to learn something new. Once while driving through Missouri, for instance, we discovered a gem of a museum dedicated to the life and work of George Washington Carver. That was a truly inspirational stop.

Our Road Trip Soundtracks

A Clarkson road trip would usually include music chosen for that particular trip. We did this especially at the beginning and end of a journey. There is something about listening to music when leaving on an adventure and getting ready to arrive that sets the tone for the trip and puts everyone in a great state of mind.

Our habit of getting on the road before dawn started when we wanted babies to sleep while we drove. The kids would slip out of bed and into their car seats and fall asleep all over again. Then, as the sun came up and everyone started to wake up, we would put on some musical favorites and sing to our hearts' content.

In the beginning we just brought along small crates of CDs. As the children grew older and technology changed, we took turns creating playlists on our computers, then either burning them to blank CDs or putting them on an mp3 player or cell phone to play on the road. These playlists turned out to be a great way for all family members to express their own tastes and share what they were excited about. We loved Celtic music, familiar albums by singer-songwriters like Rich Mullins and Chris Rice, classical favorites like Antonio Vivaldi's *The Four Seasons* and Ralph Vaughan Williams's *The Lark Ascending*, and soundtracks from our favorite films. Howard Shore's compositions for the *Lord of the Rings* films provided a stirring score for many adventures. (See www.lifegivinghome.com for music ideas.)

As a family deeply invested in words and books, we found audiobooks on the road were a natural extension of our lives at home. From *Adventures in Odyssey* and *Your Story Hour* (radio dramas for kids from an earlier time) to *Oliver Twist* and *Romeo and Juliet*—our family consumed countless hours of great "books on tape," as we called them before the advent of digital audiobooks. We learned there is nothing better than a rollicking story to fill the void of long hours inside a car—and, as a bonus, to expand our knowledge of literature. Some of our favorite family memories are of driving across the stark, flat Texas plains while listening to *Holes* or negotiating winding mountain roads in Colorado while laughing at the antics of *Jeeves and Wooster*.

Fun with Performances, Plays, and Musicals

My oldest boy, Joel, was born in Vienna, Austria, while Clay was working there as a pastor at an international church. Being the home of Mozart, Beethoven, and countless other great composers, the city hosted amazing classical performances, including public performances our family loved to attend. While there, a dear friend introduced me to an idea that we eventually copied. On Sunday afternoons she would invite a local musician—perhaps an opera singer or someone who played in the Vienna Philharmonic—to her home for a personal performance. She would make tea and sweet cakes and bring in as many people as she could to listen. She squished them all into her "largish" apartment, where all ages would engage in the music together.

What a joyful experience! We had so much fun at those miniconcerts that after we moved back to America, we decided to make them part of our lives. Clay would find young acoustic musicians and contemporary singer-songwriters who were touring the country (usually on a shoestring budget), and we would invite them to stay in our home and give a concert. Sometimes we'd have up to a hundred people sitting on the floor and up our staircase—however we could fit everyone. In return for their music the musicians would get free lodging and meals plus a small gathered payment from the crowd. We still host young musicians to this day. Some are so popular that we run out of space and have to move the concerts to our church. Occasionally we added speakers to the lineup, including a storyteller and some professors from English universities.

In addition to sponsoring musicians, we also hosted some music nights at our house where anyone who had an instrument or something to perform would come and do their thing. A shared meal or potluck dessert made the evenings a time to befriend fellow music lovers from ages five to seventy-five. Those evenings were varied, with different kinds of music and readings, and oh so fun.

Using our home as a place of celebrating arts, music, and performance was an idea that captivated the imaginations of my children, all of whom have become singer-songwriters and composers. They discovered that playing and performing can be both fun and satisfying. I did my best to reinforce that love of performance, starting them at an early age with taking music lessons and attending performances of many kinds of music. They quickly learned to appreciate the orchestra and recognize different instruments and sections.

Often before attending a classical music performance, I gave them youth biographies of the composers so that they could enjoy learning about the musicians' lives before hearing their works. We were especially fond of a collection of children's CDs called *Classical Kids*, which told the stories of the lives of the great composers through the eyes of child characters in fictionalized retellings.

Wanting our children to gain an appreciation for the art of performance, we tried to give them an outlet they could naturally enjoy so that the love for great performance would be cemented later on. As adults, my children have now introduced me to incredible works of beauty, different genres of music, and interesting artists I never knew about before, because they developed their own love and appetites for attending great performances and interesting artists.

Theater, too, was a fun part of our family life. From an early age, we encouraged each of our children to get involved in church and local theater productions and musicals, as well as speech and debate. When Clay and I first moved to Texas, we involved our whole family in a large outdoor professional theatrical production of the life of Christ, *The Promise*, at the Texas Amphitheatre in Glen Rose, Texas.[2] Every Friday and Saturday night for three seasons, six months out of the year, our entire family took part in the epic retelling of Jesus' life. Joy even played the baby Jesus!

How we cherish the memories we made during that time. The production became a big part of our lives, and we often invited the cast to our country home for seasonal potlucks and hayrides. Not only did this experience allow all of us to learn to love both theater and performance, but seeing the life of Christ acted out night after night also helped bring it alive to our family.

As our children matured, we exposed them to more theater, attending performances of Shakespeare in the Park and any other free community performances we could find. Our home became a venue for rehearsals, speech practice, even the writing and performing of impromptu skits. In the process, our kids were losing their inhibitions and becoming more confident in their ability to communicate. To inspire them even more, we sprang for tickets to see professional performances of popular musicals such as *Annie Get Your Gun*, *Hello, Dolly!*, and, most treasured by our family, *Les Misérables*.

Not surprisingly, a couple of our children caught the performing bug and sought out different ways to be onstage. For two summers, Joy served as a junior docent at a local historical home. She loved dressing up and pretending to be a girl from the pioneer era. She had so much fun convincing groups of children she was truly from a time long ago. Nathan's chosen outlet was magic. He collected simple magic tricks and had a great time entertaining children in homeless shelters by pulling nickels out of their ears and making handkerchiefs disappear. He also hosted magic-themed birthday parties for some neighbor families and even did a short gospel presentation using illusion tricks.

There are lots of fun ways to give your children opportunities to be in the public eye and gain confidence and skills in the process. Seek out children's theater performances, church dinner theaters, 4-H competitions, Toastmasters youth programs, children's choruses, and so forth. And make sure your kids know that background roles can be just as fun and satisfying as starring roles. Some kids will be happier as set builders, makeup artists, sound technicians, puppet makers, and the like—and there's always a need for these backstage skills.

Making Time to Play

Play is not frivolous! Far from it. Having fun and finding pleasure in games, make-believe, and various forms of recreation is beneficial to our brains, our bodies, and our emotional well-being—and that's true for every member of the family, moms and dads included. Playing reduces stress, enhances creativity, promotes physical fitness, teaches cooperation, and builds relationships. Families who play together, research has shown, tend to adopt one another's values more readily than those who do not invest in family friendship.

June is a perfect time to make play a priority for your family. You can start with just a few small ideas and pick activities you already enjoy, but don't be afraid to try something new as well. You will create memories that will be cherished and remembered at every family gathering—a wonderful legacy of fun, growth, and friendship.

July
A HEROIC HERITAGE
Engaging with Story and History
(SARAH)

Nurture your mind with great thoughts; to believe in the heroic makes heroes.
BENJAMIN DISRAELI

"What kind of hero do you want to be?" my brother asked one day as we walked, discussing the brave characters in our favorite stories. He asked it as if the world depended on my answer.

Nate was golden back then, hair like sunlight, eyes blue as a young summer morning. Ten good years thrummed in his steps and fifteen in mine as we strode down the gypsy ribbon of a country road, laughing in the face of a fast-setting sun and a swiftly rising June storm. The tang of coming rain was in every gust of wind. The oaks and ash and maples danced overhead in verdant grace.

"A princess, of course," I answered him. "A brave one like Éowyn in *The Lord of the Rings*, with sword at the ready."

"And a bow and arrow too?" he queried.

"Oh yes," said I.

He smiled in a fatherly way. "Good. Princesses should only sword fight if they absolutely have to."

He slipped his arm through mine then. I took it with a grin, amused by the darling presumptions and gallantries of my little brother. He was still short then; I stood a good head taller, curbing my strides to match his. The softness of childhood still rounded his face, and in moments like those, just us two in a wind-tumbled world, I could see the dreams looking out unmarred from his eyes.

"I'm going to fight the orcs like Aragorn and Legolas. I'm going to defeat enemies and fight the darkness," he said. "Do you want to hear the story I'm writing? It's about an enchanted sword . . ."

We walked that day with the loping ease of young idealists. There was magic in the air, a wind scented with a heady mix of summer's fullness and a brightness that worked like a truth potion on both of us; we thoughtlessly told each other of secrets we usually hoarded in silence.

Those secrets were stories, heroic stories. The ones we loved in books, stories that captured our vision and challenged our dreams, but also the stories we told about ourselves, the narratives we formed in imagination about who we might become and what we might accomplish. Those were the far more telling tales, and we marveled that day to hear ourselves voice our hopes to accomplish brave deeds, to live as heroes in the tales of our times.

As we strode that summer road with the energy of the high season all around us, we recalled the stories of history and fiction that had formed our dreams. We examined their respective heroes: Lucy in The Chronicles of Narnia and Aragorn in *The Lord of the Rings*. Audie Murphy (World War II hero), Corrie ten Boom, Alfred the Great, the martyred saint Perpetua, English abolitionist William Wilberforce. If they could fight and love, defeat darkness, make beauty, why couldn't we? With each step we imagined the future, each pulse of blood bringing our dreams of bravery into speech. Everything seemed possible then, and that sense of potential filled us with a breathless laughter.

When we reached the bend in the road, pausing an instant before we turned, I asked him back, "What hero will you be?"

"Superman."

The name made my lips twitch, but I didn't smile, for suddenly there was no laughter in his voice. I glanced sideways and slightly down, curious, and found him staring hard into the coming dark. Brightness was in his eyes, like light pooled in water just at dusk. He walked faster, chin up. His arm was restless in mine, and abruptly I knew that he meant it. With every ounce of his soul, my little brother intended to be the utmost of real-life heroes, and he was walking ahead as if to meet the man he would become.

Perhaps that set chin was daring me to laugh, to parry back and slough off his solemnity with a pinch of scorn. I didn't. I turned my face back to the snake of road fleeing out from under our feet and kept silent.

Imagination is the first step to creation, the instigating spark that drives the actions of a hero. As I stood on the cusp of adulthood that day, I understood the truth beneath the dreams my brother and I had shared. If we could imagine heroic stories, there was the chance, the hope, that we could live them too. The flush-faced thrill of our walk came from the hero tales we hoped to live, fancies begun in childhood now ripening into ideals and declared to each other for the first time.

To put such dreams into words is to set the soul in motion. Once we had spoken our hopes, they took on lives of their own and drew us into their possibilities. We had dared to say what heroes we aspired to be. And somehow, from that dappled minute and those spilled stories, there was no turning back.

Part of God's Story

More than fifteen years have passed between our words on that memorable day and the moment I set them forth on this page. Nate and I are both adults now, and you might assume that the difficult realities of adulthood—the work and compromise and practicality needed for life in a modern world—might have dulled the edges of our ideals. You might think the reasonable goals of being successful citizens, productive adults, contributing members to family or society would replace our youthful, wild-eyed hunger for heroism.

But oh, if you do, then I think you've never been wholly captured by a plethora of hero tales. Once the stories of a few good heroes get into your blood, you just can't rest until you've tried your best to follow them. To encounter heroism in the traditions of patriotic and communal celebration, in the memories of family, and in the stories of history, literature, and culture is to encounter an irresistible call to pursue excellence.

The doughty heroes and gracious heroines that Nate and I encountered in story and history throughout our childhood still stand guard in our minds, staring us down with a challenge to act as bravely, to give as fully, to hope as ardently in our own stories as they did in theirs. Adults though we are, adults who work and love, struggle and hope through our confusing twenty-something lives, Nate and I and Joel and Joy still believe we are called to be heroes and heroines in the story of the world.

That vision for heroism began early in our lives at home, in the rhythms, stories, and traditions we encountered in the family culture around us. (For more about family culture, see the February and August chapters.) Only in adulthood have I understood what a remarkable gift this was. We were children whose very concept of self was formed by the stories my parents surrounded us with from birth.

We heard the story of Scripture first, and we met it as an epic narrative, the great true tale of a world that began with God, the Master Artist, brooding over the formless earth and will end with the wedding of a King and a feast marvelous beyond all imagining. Every morning we woke to hear the stories of biblical heroes over breakfast, to speak of them throughout the day. We met David and Daniel, Ruth and Esther and Mary as companions and friends in a mighty quest. They invited us to be part of the adventure of God's Kingdom invading the world, and from infancy we were taught to embrace that great story as our own.

Then we had books. Countless books. A library crammed with stories old and new, baskets of picture books by the bed, and stacks of art books under the coffee table. We were children who went to bed with Narnian heroes in our dreams, woke to picture books before breakfast, and had biographies assigned for the afternoon. Our imaginations were crammed with the beauty of story, landscapes, characters, and quests, constantly expanding our concept of what was good and beautiful and possible. Every book we read, every hero encountered came with my parents' challenge for us to dream of who we might become, who we might help or save, and what we might create.

"You are part of God's story on earth," my parents whispered again and again in our ears. "You can be like Aragorn or Frodo or Sam in the battles of the world. You can bring beauty like Monet or Yo-Yo Ma or discover something new like George Washington Carver. What kind of hero do you want to be?"

Heroism Begins at Home

In creating the traditions that will form your home, you have the opportunity to put it all in a heroic framework. The holidays you celebrate, the books you read with your family, and the heroes you uphold and praise will inform your vision for your own life and story.

Heroism isn't an act that begins in a moment of crisis. It is an atmosphere, a sense of self, an identity formed through many habits of thought, memory, and experience. Because the home is the center place of life, the ground in which action begins, you have the opportunity to create an atmosphere in which the heroic is valued, rooted, and grown.

And heroism isn't just about taking your own life in your hands. It's about being taken hold of by something much bigger and more beautiful than yourself. A heroic view of life and tradition is one in which you join an ongoing story, a lived drama, following the faithful people who went before. That's why memory, history, and story are so important. By encountering the vision of the heroes before us—those who aspired and sacrificed and dedicated their own lives to noble pursuits—we gain the resources we need to rise to their challenge with fresh vision of our own.

The focus of this chapter is simply on how to cultivate that view of the world, to shape the spaces of home and tradition to further the vision, memory, and celebration that go into the forming of heroic hearts.

You Are What You Remember

When I was nine years old, we lived with my grandmother, sharing her home in rural Texas. Nana lived in an old yellow ranch house with a shadowy attic, long halls, and countless dusky corners. In the hall that led to my bedroom, she had covered every spare inch of wall space with portraits and photos of the Clarkson family. Some were of us, her grandchildren, when we were very small. Others were of my dad as a much younger man and of my mom after she had married Dad and joined the Clarkson family. But most of the pictures were of people I'd never met. And every time I passed those mysterious portraits of men in uniform and women with solemn faces or halfway smiles, a sense of awe and curiosity bubbled up in my small heart.

These were my people. Their lives had made my life. If they hadn't lived and loved and acted within the world, I would never have existed. Even at nine years old, I felt it a keen grief that most of them had passed away before I could know them because I understood at a deep level that their history made up a large part of my identity. I was born into their ongoing story. I pestered my grandmother to tell me more about them, hungry to understand my heritage, my family history, the narrative that I had inherited.

Memory is a strange and wondrous gift. In our age of instant information, in our age of youth and hurry and get-it-now satisfaction, we have turned, I think, more and more away from valuing the aged and the memories they bear. We have forgotten how deeply we need the wisdom of those older than us, how much we need to hear and remember the stories of those who made our lives possible. We need to know how those before us survived war, conflict, grief, and loss. We need to hear about the frugal feasts scraped together during the Great Depression, the parties held in bomb shelters, the grace to be found in growing a garden in a time of limited resources. We need to know the history of those who made our stories so that we can create our own histories with grace and heroism.

Wendell Berry is one of my favorite authors. His novels are all set in the same fictional Kentucky town, so that each time you read one, you go deeper into the history of that one place and its people. A major theme of his work is that of *memory*. For Berry, memory is heritage, narrative, and gift. It comprises "the long dance of men and women . . . who, choosing one another,"[1] make possible the lives that follow theirs.

Memory recognizes and joins us to those whose faithful, loving choices created the larger narrative in which the individual is rooted. It connects me to the grandfather who was known for his laughter, the uncle whose kindness my mom still remembers. Memory ties my life to the great-grandfather who prayed that one of his children would be in ministry, and also to the grandfather I never knew, alive only in the narration of those who knew him. To remember is not merely to recall past events. Rather, to remember is to return to the vision of the world held by those who have gone before.

But memory is something that can be inherited from Scripture, literature, story, and mentorship as well as family. If your family history is one that brings little grace and offers little life, if your story holds more pain than joy and more abuse than heroism, don't despair. The gift of history, the grace of narrative is that it is ongoing. Each generation is given the opportunity to tell their stories anew, to alter, shift, change, or restart the history into which they were born.

We inherit history, in other words, but we also create it. In addition to family memory or heritage, we can draw on the memory of Scripture, the identity and narrative of mentors or cultural heroes who went before us. We can act in keeping with those whose lives wrote the kinds of stories we long to live.

History, memory, heroism—they all go hand in hand.

—— In Our Home ——

Learning Character through Story Characters

Have you ever noticed that the word we use to describe a *character* in a fictional story is the same one we use to sum up the virtues and attributes of real people? The truth is, *characters* in stories can embody the *character* qualities we're seeking, the ones that will help us develop these traits in our own lived stories.

What kind of person should I be? What does it mean to be a hero? What does it mean to struggle or doubt, to endure or create? Most people, particularly children, are unable to sufficiently answer these questions on an abstract, philosophical level. We need concrete examples of what it means to be brave, good, loving, or kind. We need, in other words, great stories. We need hero tales, vivid narratives in which the qualities we are meant to embody in our own lives are revealed in the vivid imagery of a story.

This is one of the vital reasons God gave us the great story of Scripture, a book crammed full of complex characters living out good and evil, hope and regret, love and hate. We know what it means to be a "man after God's own heart" because we have imaginatively experienced the story of David—shepherd boy, musician, warrior for God, and repentant sinner—just as we have seen his opposite in the evil hearts portrayed in people like Ahab or Jezebel.

Beside and with the narrative of Scripture stands the great compendium of literature. We have the whole canon of classic stories, ancient and new, from every culture on earth—children's stories, novels, poetry and folk tales, drama, picture books, ancient epics and contemporary odysseys. Literature is humanity's ongoing conversation with itself about what it means to be human, to be good, to live with meaning.

Leo Tolstoy's *Anna Karenina* (1877), for instance, gives us two diverging histories, each following to the end the choice to live either for self or for transcendent love. C. S. Lewis's Narnia books offer us humorous, brave portrayals of children who discover what it means to be unselfish, beloved, and forgiven. Reading Kenneth Grahame's children's classic *The Wind in the Willows* is one of the best ways I know to communicate the idea of belonging and what it means to act in neighborly companionship and kindness.

Life is a story. Have you realized this? Your one life is a great tale, one facet of God's continuing narrative within the world. What better way to learn to play your part to the full than to seek out stories that have shaped generations to fight for the beautiful in their own contexts and times. Tales from Scripture and literature can fill the imagination with living images of love, courage, and sacrifice that teach us what to desire for our own lived stories.

For reading ideas and book lists galore for families, I suggest my book *Read for the Heart*, which recommends and describes hundreds and hundreds of age-appropriate books—hero tales, great novels, and children's classics—to set you on your way. You can also find great ideas in my parents' book *Educating the WholeHearted Child* and on our "Lifegiving Home Resources" page at www.lifegivinghome.com.

Memorization

This story shall the good man teach his son. . . .
From this day to the ending of the world,
But we in it shall be remember'd;
We few, we happy few, we band of brothers;
For he to-day that sheds his blood with me
Shall be my brother.[2]

The challenge above is from Shakespeare's *Henry V* and is known as the St. Crispin's Day speech. In it the English Prince Hal (who would someday be King Henry V of England) summons his weary troops to battle, promising them honor, brotherhood, and a place in memory until the end of the world. This is one of several speeches that the Clarkson kids chose to memorize in high school.

Few things can stir the mind and soul to heroic action more fully than a fitly spoken word. And few treasures are better than a mind stocked with poetry, verbal inspiration, stirring speech, and music. I strongly believe that the words a person chooses to store up in his or her heart will, in large part, help that person narrate his or her life. Words make worlds—they form an inner idea of excellence and they echo in the mind at the moments when we most need direction. The words stored in the mind and imagination through memorization create an ongoing interior conversation that inspires, challenges, and directs people in their moments of choice. In the process, they help promote excellent language skills and cognitive function in general.

While memorization can be useful at any age, it is especially important for children, whose brains are still being formed. Most children memorize more quickly and retain more than adults, and what is memorized in childhood usually stays memorized for a long time. That's why memorization was considered so important in the Clarkson household and homeschool. As I mentioned in the April chapter, we all memorized Scripture—but not just Scripture. Every one of us had to memorize Rudyard Kipling's "If" and Robert Frost's "The Road Not Taken" as well as a great variety of historical documents, speeches, poems, hymns, and folk songs.

Interested in making memorization a more integral part of your household? Check out www.lifegiving.com for lists of poetry, speeches, and Scripture that work well for memorization.

Historical Films

What could be better to inspire heroic feeling and action than an epic historical film complete with an unforgettable soundtrack? We Clarksons all have our favorites, and they cover vast swaths of history and culture. At one point in his life, Nathan became fascinated by the World War II hero Audie Murphy and watched every movie he could find about Murphy and his exploits. We all spent a summer fascinated by the Civil War and loved watching the superb 1993 film, *Gettysburg*. I was intrigued by World War II stories set in England and therefore loved the 1942 classic, *Mrs. Miniver*. I have listed more of our favorites on www.lifegivinghome.com to get you started, but ask friends and family for theirs as well. You will likely find the stories and reasons behind those favorites as fascinating as the films themselves.

Historical Travel

Several different times throughout the years, my mom and one of her best friends piled us kids into one van or SUV for a couple of weeks of historic travel.

For each trip, they chose a different area of focus—the Civil War in Virginia, colonial days in New England, Amish and immigrant culture in the Midwest, politics and presidents in Washington, DC. We always studied the general topic in advance, and then we hit the road.

Our budgets were usually tight, so we packed picnics, stayed with friends, and cut corners wherever we could, with the occasional memorable splurge, like an Amish dinner in Ohio or a seafood feast at a Boston wharf. But still we crammed in as much experience as possible. Our moms lined up museums and memorials along the way. They arranged lectures or interviews with whatever scholars, teachers, museums, artists, or politicians they could find. And while we were on the road we would listen to audiobooks chosen to fit the historic theme of the trip.

Those two moms and we kids still comment on the powerful impact those trips had on us. To actually experience the places, the houses, and the atmospheres in which history was made allowed us to engage with it on an imaginative, personal level that has piqued our interest for a lifetime.

Wherever you live and whatever your income, historical travel is a possibility. Every region of the United States—including where you live—has its own historical flavor, its own story of settlement, culture, and development. Take advantage of it and seek it out. Even a visit to a county courthouse or a local historical monument can enrich your family's appreciation of history. But go farther if you possibly can.

Most large cities have a science and history or natural history museum or one highlighting local history. Many others have specialized museums focused on the home of a famous person or an early settlement. When traveling, we always hunted ahead for the historic homes of authors, artists, scientists, or statesmen. Some of our favorites over the years are one of Frank Lloyd Wright's homes, the Missouri house of Laura Ingalls Wilder, Booker T. Washington's home, and Henry David Thoreau's Walden Pond.

If you have the good fortune to live overseas or to spend time in traveling there, by all means use your time abroad to deeply engage with the history and culture of the people who live there. Visit art museums, historical monuments, concerts, and famous markets. Seek out teachers or storytellers, read good-quality history (including historical fiction), and visit the places you have read about. (International travel was a priority to our family, so we tramped through many historical and cultural sites and tasted lots of wonderful new food along the way.)

Are you feeling the itch to get on the road? To give you an idea of what you can do, here are details from a few of our favorite trips.

Early US History and Washington, DC

For this trip, we visited George Washington's home at Mount Vernon, Thomas Jefferson's home at Monticello, the Valley Forge battleground, and Colonial Williamsburg, then spent two days of wandering in Washington, DC (where we managed to get lost in the basements of both the Senate and House wings of the Capitol). We kids collected quotes from the monuments throughout DC, sketched the grounds at Mount Vernon, and located our favorite pieces of art at the National Gallery of Art. During the long driving hours we listened to *My Brother Sam Is Dead* (1974) and *Toliver's Secret* (1976), both stirring pieces of historical fiction about young people living during the Revolutionary War.

Colonial New England

This was the classic Revolutionary War trip in which we visited Boston, stopping at Paul Revere's silver shop and the Old North Church, and made a trip to the Lexington battlefield where "the shot heard round the world"[3] was fired. We spent a day at the living history museum at Old Sturbridge Village to gain a taste of life in colonial times. And we combined our historical tour with a literary one because there was a whole movement of inspired writers who lived in Concord, Massachusetts. Bronson Alcott, his famous daughter Louisa May Alcott, Henry David Thoreau, Ralph Waldo Emerson, and Nathaniel Hawthorne all called this little town their home, and their homes are richly preserved there to this day.

The Alcotts' home, Orchard House, is one of the favorite places we visited on this trip. Kept much as the family would have known it, it included Louisa May's room, where our beloved *Little Women* was penned.

On this trip we listened to Esther Hoskins Forbes's *Johnny Tremain* (1943) and Louisa May Alcott's *Little Men* (1871) (to keep the boys happy) and had our favorite meal at a little seafood shop in Rockport on the Massachusetts coast.

Remembering as You Celebrate

With a loud clearing of his throat, our friend Jerry brought the room of thirty or so munching, chatting people to silence. Glancing around at the plates piled with hamburgers, salads, chips, watermelon—all the spoils of an excellent Fourth of July cookout—he smiled, raised his hand, and began to read: "When, in the course of human events, it becomes necessary . . ."

He read the entire Declaration of Independence with dramatic flair to a rapt audience and ended with the open question, "What did you notice this time?"

The discussion that followed centered on defining the idea of personal rights, the pursuit of happiness, and the ownership of property. It was a brief talk, but by the time dessert was served and the crowd dispersed to watch the nearby fireworks, each mind there had encountered the original idealistic fervor that led to the holiday we had celebrated with our feast.

This kind of examination combined with celebration is appropriate for any patriotic holiday. The point of such civic holidays and traditions is to enjoy ourselves but also to mark, to recall, and to honor the original events underlying the celebration.

Celebrating Independence

Amidst the summer fun of good food, of Independence Day parades down the main street of town, of fireworks and laughter, it's important to keep in mind what we're really celebrating—the ideals that founded our country. It's worth asking, at these times of patriotic celebration, how these festival days can remind us of what it means to be a citizen. What political and social ideals do we stand for as a nation? What does it mean to be free? Who are the heroes, whether original founders or current leaders, who embody our ideas of right leadership?

One of the most enjoyable ways to do this is simply to study the life and ideals of one of those who founded our nation. One summer, as a family, we focused on the life of Thomas Jefferson. We read biographies, found pictures of his remarkable home in Monticello, read excerpts of his works, discovered the many things he invented, and explored the philosophy underlying his political engagement with the founding of America. By the time the Fourth of July rolled around that year, the boys had Jefferson costumes and the girls had worked up colonial dress of their own. We all quoted Jefferson to great applause from our elders.

As we grew older, the lazy Fourth of July afternoon between lunch and fireworks offered the opportunity to talk about ideals. Our parents helped us articulate what we loved and what we disliked about current political structures, examining our own ideas about citizenship and patriotism. Some years we watched the little-known television movie *Goodbye, Miss 4th of July*—a fascinating look at American ideals through the viewpoint of a Greek immigrant family living in West Virginia just before the First World War.[4]

Celebrating Those Who Served

For many in our culture, Memorial Day has become just another long weekend, a time for cookouts and family outings and celebrating the coming of summer. Despite the name of the holiday, people seem to forget that the whole point of the day is to *remember.*

One family we know well did that in a beautiful way. Early on Memorial Day morning every single year, everyone in the family would rise very early in the morning and head down to their local cemetery. Armed with wreaths and flowers, they would solemnly decorate the graves of family members who had served in the military. As the sun rose on the freshened-up graves, they would pray together, then head back home for a breakfast feast where they celebrated the lives of "their" veterans with a merry round of memorable conversation. This family tradition and ritual deeply honored those who had gone before and deeply heartened those with stories still to live.

There's power in remembering the men and women who have died in service to our country (and those who died years after they served). In honoring their lives, their sacrifice in war, and their service to others, we recognize a little of what we strive to embody in our own lives. While we Clarksons never lived in a place where we could carry out the traditional decoration of graves, we have tried over the years to make Memorial Day (in May) and Veterans Day (in November) times in which to discover and remember family members who sacrificed, fought, or served.

My grandfather, we learned, served in the Pacific region during World War II, and a great-uncle was a prisoner in Germany. And one year I coaxed Nana to dig out the army uniform she had worn as a volunteer driver during the same war. I even tried on the uniform and imagined what bravery I could model had I lived back then.

Perhaps that's the point. These days of remembrance can give us a space to honor and maybe try to copy a bit of the bravery of those who have gone before and those who are serving now. It's worth a little extra effort to seek out military veterans, thank them for their service, and ask to hear the accounts of their experience. Don't forget to acknowledge those who are currently serving as well. A letter, card, meal, or care package can make a big difference to service men and women and their families.[5]

Hidden Heroism

One of my favorite passages out of all the novels I've read comes at the end of George Eliot's *Middlemarch*. Dorothea, the protagonist, who begins the book as a young girl with high ideals of martyrdom and sainthood, endures a series of events that tempers her yearning for outwardly heroic acts but also teaches her another, quieter form of heroism. Her heart is transformed by suffering into one whose quiet and unspectacular faithfulness sustains the lives around her. Says Eliot of her chastened heroine, "The growing good of the world is partly dependent on unhistoric acts; and that things are not so ill with you and me as they might have been, is half owing to the number who lived faithfully a hidden life."[6]

In a chapter on the cultivation of heroism, we cannot end without a consideration of the heroes whose sacrificial acts are rarely marked and often are unremembered. We must affirm the ordinary heroism of faithful people whose integrity makes them sources of grace, compassion, and strength through countless years of quiet presence. These are the people whose work keeps home running, whose presence stabilizes church or neighborhood, whose steady wisdom and good humor can usually be counted upon to save the day. They, too, are heroes worthy of our honor and our emulation.

One of my mother's favorite verses to quote to us in our youth was "He who is faithful in a very little thing is faithful also in much" (Luke 16:10). It's easy to think of heroism in terms of the spectacular—a moment of total sacrifice, an act of unmitigated bravery in the face of danger. But those are the shooting star moments of courage, the ones that flare across the sky and draw our eyes to the heavens. Behind them, around them, enduring after their briefer blaze are the long-burning, humbler flames of faithful living.

Heroism doesn't begin in the moment of crisis, and sometimes it never gets noticed at all, because its roots are in the smallest choices of the everyday. But these are the choices on which all good homes are founded.

So what kind of hero do you want to be?

We may not get to choose the story into which we are born, but we do get to choose what part we will play within it. Daily we have the creative choice to respond, to make, to give, to love. As the wizard Gandalf said to Frodo when Frodo wished he had not lived to see evil times, "All we have to decide is what to do with the time that is given us."[7]

This life, this single day, this one home is the setting in which we have the chance to remember and honor the heroes who have gone before us and allow their tales to draw us into a heroism all our own.

In the end, I believe, heroism is simply faithfulness, a moment-by-moment choice to do what is right—to love once more, to give without fear in the face of every challenge. Heroism is forged and known in such choices, whether in a blazing moment of courage or in the countless small moments of luminous, ordinary life. Let us pray for courage and grace to join the ranks of loving and brave people who have gone before us and, in so doing, take our places as part of God's story on earth.

―― *August* ――

THE STORY OF US
Shaping and Celebrating Family Culture
(SALLY)

In every conceivable manner, the family is link to our past, bridge to our future.
ALEX HALEY

It's never quite the way we imagine it will be.

We envision the warmth of the summer sun, the birds singing, the trees swaying gently in the breeze, and all of us sitting around a picnic table in a tranquil Rocky Mountains moment, with a lunch feast we have toted along with us on our trip up into the mountainous woods.

What we usually get is competitive siblings talking over one another in the car, a flock of persistent birds at the picnic area that are far too familiar with humans and expect to be fed, and rain and thunder threatening a sudden downpour that will send everyone running for cover. All that plus fun . . . and feasting . . . and love.

Our family gatherings have always been a mix of wonderful memories and misadventures. But every year in August, no matter what four corners of the world all of us have been blown to, the entire family gathers back home in Colorado for a weekend together that culminates in a Saturday morning ritual and a picnic in the mountains behind our home.

We call it Family Day.

Memorial Stones

It all started when Clay read us the story from the book of Joshua about the memorial stones the Israelites left in the Jordan River as a testimony to God's faithfulness in bringing them to the Promised Land (4:1-9). When the sons and daughters of those who had crossed the Jordan River returned to that river crossing in generations to come, they would be reminded of God's mercy in bringing their people into a good and prosperous land.

We were all intrigued by that story and wanted our family to follow suit. So we began the practice of gathering in our living room once a year to read the Joshua passage and then write down all the ways God had been faithful to us during the previous year. Those lists became our "memorial stones"—our reminders that we were part of God's narrative and that He was telling an amazing story with our lives.

We have continued the memorial stone tradition for quite a few years, even now that our kids are adults. Every year we pay for all the kids to fly in from wherever they are in the world because this ritual has become so important to us. It gives us a way of reaffirming just who the Clarksons are, reviewing our mutual biblical ideals and faith, and strengthening our bonds of love and accountability. We leave these Family Day weekends feeling the support we need to live intentionally for Christ. In the process, year by year, we are creating a history of the many ways God has worked and been faithful to our family through the challenges and blessings of life. More important, in the remembering of God's goodness, our "memorial stones" become anchors for the future.

When our children were little, we did the memorial stones ritual using actual rocks. We gave them each a little handful so that with each statement of thankfulness for what God had done, they could add a pebble to the pile in the middle of the table. As the stones piled higher and higher, the children could see the goodness of God mount as well.

Eventually our physical rocks became metaphorical ones, though we retained the practice of referring to our listed blessings as "stones." And the practice of listing them became the heart of the celebration we now call Family Day. They remind us in the best moments that God's blessings have been with us many times throughout our lives and that every moment is an opportunity to thank Him. They also remind us, when circumstances feel overwhelming, that God has been faithful in years past and will be faithful again. Thus our "memorial stones" affirm both gratitude and faith—even as the outside world seems to fight against these qualities.

Fighting the Pressure of Culture

Do you feel that pressure too? The lives of most people I know have become increasingly fast paced, and our habits are increasingly drawn into the trivial. We read less and use Facebook more. We spend more time inside than out. We have access to more information than we've ever had, and yet we understand less and less. We allow the habit of busyness to replace our habits of prayer and Scripture reading. It is only natural that in the hustle and bustle of family life, craziness easily overwhelms the calm we need so badly. In our modern, consumerist culture, sometimes it seems nearly impossible to find that center.

For our family, the memorial stones ritual helps us fight that tendency because it reminds us of the bigger picture. It takes us out of our momentary challenges and sets us in the larger narrative of God's faithful work in the lives of His people. The more memorial stones we have collected over the years, the more we have been able to see a pattern.

There have been years in our life as a family when I felt hemmed in by difficulties and insurmountable circumstances. In those years I almost dreaded our annual listing of stones because deep inside I wondered if we would be able to identify any of God's fingerprints of love that year. And yet surprisingly, as we took time to really ponder what He had accomplished through our lives, we would always see amazing provision, faithful and generous examples of mercy and grace. We always leave our time together amazed at the personal ways we can see that He has led our family.

Here is the pattern we see again and again: Challenges arise, and God comes through in time to meet them. Wilderness experiences leave us parched, and through them God teaches us patience, trust, and compassion for others. Doors eventually open, and God blesses us immensely. Taking time away to really seek God and to remember what He has done always shows us a bigger picture of Him. All of us are more trusting in His constant presence when we look back to see that He has been there for us even when we did not notice.

Certainly the patterns fluctuate from feeling like we're on top of the world to walking through the valley. But the more we practice remembering the story of God's goodness, the better we can remember that, in Him, all will eventually be well. Romans 8:28 says, "God causes all things to work together for good to those who love God, to those who are called according to His purpose."

God's purpose is to tell a story—His story—with our lives and the lives of our families, and setting down memorial stones helps remind us of that truth.

Ultimately, the little memorial stones in our lives contribute to building a larger memorial. Our lives and our families become memorials in and of themselves, something for further generations to follow after. As the Clarkson family, the way we invest our lives, the way we choose to spend them for the purposes of eternity, will be a marker for many who come after us. Just think of the incredible beauty of God's handiwork—hundreds of families and countless people, spanning the entirety of history, who have lived their lives as memorials of God's redemption of the world. We Clarksons are part of that story. Your family is part of that story too. The choices we make in faith are determining the shape of our legacies.

Of course, God's grace is abundant in the midst of that process. It has to be, because we all struggle to practice holiness day to day. Ephesians 2:10 says that we are God's "workmanship, created in Christ Jesus for good works, which God prepared beforehand so that we would walk in them." God understands our limitations because, ultimately, the completion of that work is God's responsibility, not ours. He is the master Craftsman of each of the memorials of our lives. He starts the work within us through His creative genius and then brilliantly continues to expand that work because of His desire to make us holy. As Philippians 1:6 puts it, "He who began a good work in you will perfect it until the day of Christ Jesus."

God has the long-term view. All He asks of us is to allow ourselves to be caught up in His creative narrative, in the epic story He is telling with the entirety of history. Every day, every week, every month, and every year when we practice noticing what God is doing in our lives and look back intentionally to remind ourselves, we are allowing God to shape us into beautiful and stunning tributes to His faithful work.

Family Day: How It Works

Now that I've spent some time explaining the benefits of Family Day and memorial stones for our family, are you curious about what we actually do? The following is a quick rundown of the day as we usually practice it. But keep in mind that the intention behind the day can be adapted for any family. We even have single friends who have copied the idea and celebrated such a day with their closest friends—to look back at their year and remember to look for God's fingerprints on their lives.

When we get up in the morning on Family Day, we celebrate by doing what we often do on family occasions: have a big, delicious breakfast together with—you guessed it—cheese-and-sour-cream scrambled eggs. (What can I say? My family loves those eggs.) Melt-in-your-mouth, homemade, whole wheat cinnamon rolls also make an appearance, along with hash browns, fruit salad, and tea or coffee.

After breakfast is finished, we clear the table and get ready to collect our annual memorial stones. When we were a young family, this meant passing out sketching paper, and as soon as we had made a running list of our stones, we assigned various ones to each child, who would then draw pictures of those events. We kept a notebook full of all the sketches. Even though we no longer draw our memorial stones, we do write them down and add them to the book. That notebook itself has become a living memorial of all the ways God has blessed us along the paths of our lives.

Before we make our lists of "stones," Clay always reads aloud the story from Joshua that started it all—the one about the Israelites placing memorial stones in the Jordan River. We talk about what the story means to each of us in light of each of our experiences the previous year and what we have learned through our experiences. Then, after the reading, the list making commences. Here are just a few of the events we try to record:

- *Major life changes*—anything from moving across country to graduating from college
- *New relationships*—either in personal or professional work
- *Challenges and difficulties*—from sickness to strife to struggle
- *Goals attained and milestones achieved*—losing weight, learning a new skill, gaining financial freedom
- *Travel*—a visit to a new city or state or country or a journey that brought new insight
- *Spiritual experiences*—encounters with grace, growth experiences, new awareness and understanding
- *Special serendipitous blessings*—divine encounters that especially encouraged us

Each family member lists his or her particular memorial stones. They're not all happy or triumphant; some involve what we have learned in difficult situations or ways God has provided for us in our struggles. The idea behind a memorial stone is simply to recognize a significant event or change in the previous year and put it in the context of God's work in our lives.

After we have gone through each person's events, we move on to events that have affected us as a family at large. With each entry we take time to talk out the ways we have been changed by the events the stones represent. And there's always something to talk about. Even in years when we think we won't be able to come up with anything, we're amazed to see evidence of God's faithfulness and blessing that we had hardly noticed along the way. Every year is encouraging when we take time to remember Him.

Once we have finished creating our lists of memorial stones and discussing what they have meant to our lives in the past year, we look forward toward the future. We again go person to person so that each family member can express hopes and anticipate challenges for the upcoming year. These, too, are added to our lists.

We take an extended time to pray over our "stack of stones" and align our lives again with God's plan. And then, when the last amen has been said, we turn to fun, celebration, and—of course—food!

Though most of our picnic has already been prepared and is waiting in the refrigerator, there are always a few last-minute tasks before we pack up our famous Family Day picnic of fried chicken (a rare-to-us homemade treat, with my special coating), deviled eggs, watermelon, our favorite baked beans, potato chips, and sweet tea (a holdover from our life in the South). Once everything is ready, we jump in the car and head for the hills—quite literally.

One of our favorite spots for our picnic is a beautiful Colorado wildlife reserve called Mueller State Park. Tucked behind the foothills of the Rockies, it occupies an exquisite corner between several mountains, including Pikes Peak. That's our destination of choice as we tool along the winding roads, singing along—too loudly, attempting harmony—to the music we all know by heart. The trek is timed so that we arrive at the park just about noon. We pile out of the car into the outdoors, reveling in the fresh mountain breezes and the sweet, pungent aroma of Colorado pine trees. By then our stomachs are growling and we can't wait to eat, so we unpack our picnic in no time and tuck into our feast.

When we've finished stuffing ourselves, we pull out our cameras and phones to take pictures. The park has stunning mountain vistas on all four sides, and though we have hundreds of photos from years past, we can never resist the temptation to get a few more shots. But we don't just photograph trees and mountains. Clay and I always take advantage of being together to get pictures of us—candid fun shots, individual portraits, and several of us together as a group. This annual family photo shoot has turned into an hour-long ritual. We all have new ideas of what kinds of photos we want to take for our own purposes—book covers, album covers, social media pages. The photos will also be printed out and added to our collection of Family Day documents.

The photo session is always followed by a hill-and-dale hike through shimmering aspen, swaying wildflowers, and towering pine forests standing stately in shadows. Then it's time to pack up our picnic and head for home, stopping at a favorite Starbucks location for a quick hot drink and one more traditional group shot on our way home. And thus another Family Day is added to the books, one more memorable chapter in the ongoing story of us.

——— *In Our Home* ———

Did you know a family has a culture?

I touched on this idea in the February chapter when I talked about building a culture of love. But love is just one important part of a family's culture—the rich combination of personalities, history, events, and traditions that differentiates one family from all others.

Culture sets the tone for how all of us live our lives. From the movies and music we like to the food we eat to the values that determine our behavior, the culture of a group helps define it and move it forward. Culture helps people know who they are and provides a sense of identity and belonging.

The word *culture* can be used to define any number of different groups, from large geographic regions to nations to neighborhoods and, yes, to families. Every family has a distinct flavor that governs how it operates in the world. In a family, a strong culture allows each member to feel confident and comfortable, to understand how he or she interacts in every situation that comes along.

A multitude of cultural aspects define the collective life of each family. One overarching family value for us Clarksons is that we love words. They are both fun for us and deeply meaningful. Whether we're reading by ourselves or aloud as a group, gathering around the dinner table for a lively discussion, talking one on one, or gathering for a lively game of Scrabble, words and ideas drive us. We talk incessantly and have conversations about everything in life, spanning a multitude of topics from chitchat to philosophy and theology. We build our relationships by talking to one another.

We are also all creative types. Clay is an accomplished musician, and I sang in a band for many years. He and I are both writers, and between the two of us we have produced a published author (Sarah), a composer and author (Joel), a screenwriter/actor/author (Nathan), and a writer/speaker/singer-songwriter (Joy). We have creativity coming out of our ears, even if we sometimes come up a bit short in the more practical aspects of life. For better or worse, there's not an accountant, doctor, or scientist among us.

We also have a shared strong focus on aesthetics and environment. Shaping the look and atmosphere of where we live matters to us. We care about surrounding ourselves and those we love with an atmosphere of beauty, order, and peace. From a delicious feast to beautiful music or even something as simple as lighting candles at dinner, we all are deeply invested in crafting a comforting and an uplifting environment where we can live together.

Every family is different. For another family, math or science may be a high point of shared interest—or gardening and mechanics. Instead of talking a lot, some families might focus more on building things together or remodeling a house. Others may camp or garden or study quantum physics. Who we are, by God's design, provides something unique we will pass on in our home because of personality, experience, and taste.

There are no hard-and-fast rules about how a family culture should look; it is simply an organic outgrowth of living life together. But the more distinctly a family creates cultural ties to one another, the stronger the foundations of confidence, belonging, and heritage.

A Shelter from a Disappointing World

In J. R .R. Tolkien's masterpiece *The Lord of the Rings,* the journeying hobbits find their way to the elven retreat Rivendell, a place described as "the Last

Homely House."[1] While the hobbits have been constantly in peril along their journey, pursued by evil creatures of every sort and oppressed by a wicked force, when they arrive in Rivendell, they are safe, protected from worry and cares.

Sarah and I used to love perusing *Victoria* magazines together on Sunday afternoons, dreaming of having our own Rivendell where people would come. Our goal was to collect all that had been a treasure from past generations—menus and recipes; great works of art, literature, and music; stories worth remembering; traditions worth celebrating—and find a place for these in our lives. We wanted our home to be a place where people could come to remember the greatness stored inside them, just waiting to be reawakened.

That's what Clay and I have always wanted our home to be for ourselves, for our guests, and especially for our children and our friends. Though we hope for blessing and joy in their lives as they go out into the world, we know all too well they will face challenges, frustrations, and disappointments. So we strive to make our home a refuge where those outside struggles can be left behind for a time, where all of us can come to regroup and recharge. We want home to be a haven when they are discouraged and weary of heart and soul.

So many elements of our family culture have been shaped with the element of refuge in mind. We strive to make our home a beautiful (more or less), ordered place as an antidote to the ugliness in the outside world. We stress hospitality to counter the hostility and indifference so many experience in the larger culture. We try to choose what we read, watch, or listen to with intention, surrounding ourselves with what is uplifting rather than degrading. Our emphasis on "feasting" together is meant to be an intentional contrast to the spiritual hunger that afflicts so many. And we have always stressed to our children that our story revolves around home—that no matter where everyone goes in the world, not only do they take our home and family culture with them, but they can always return back home to us.

Ecclesiastes 4:10 warns, "Woe to the one who falls when there is not another to lift him up." We need people to lift us up, of course, but we also need home to do that. The world is a scary place without a dependable refuge, and we want our home to be a strong shelter in the midst of the storms of life.

I want to stress, by the way, that making our home a shelter and a refuge has never meant retreating from the world entirely or neglecting God's call to minister to the hungry, the thirsty, the lonely—those who suffer the pain of living in the world. On the contrary, we see the refuge of home as making ministry possible. It provides us with strength, renewal, and support as we reach out to those around us. It teaches and reminds us of the abundance of God's Kingdom that we are called to share—and it helps us understand what it is we have to share in the first place. So to us, our "Homely House" and our family culture give us a necessary base camp for reaching out to a world in need.

Home Away from Home

For our family, travel is as habitual as getting out of bed in the morning. It's part of our family culture, a rhythm that is so natural we sway in and out of it constantly throughout a given year. Clay and I developed a love for travel when we were doing missions work overseas, and as our family grew we developed the habit of taking the kids with us on our adventures.

Though we Clarksons may spend more time on the road than many people, it seems that most people are getting in trains, planes, and automobiles more often. As exciting as it can be to see new places and have new experiences, travel can also be an upheaval, a disruption of comfort and regularity. As a family constantly on the go, we've learned it's possible to make home wherever we are and enjoy our family culture even while away from our natural habitat, as long as we remain intentional.

As I write this, three of us are gathered in a little hotel suite in a tiny village in France (we paid less than two hundred dollars for a whole week!). Joel and I have flown halfway around the world to meet Sarah and work on this book and its companion, *The Lifegiving Home Experience*. Since Sarah was at Oxford, this just seemed like a great place to meet.

Even though this culture and town are new to us, the first thing we did was to go to the local bakery for croissants, quiche, and cake, as well as to stock up on other food from a local grocer. When we got home, we made an impromptu teatime, lit candles, put on music, found a vase and filled it with flowers, and relished a gorgeous sunset. Our efforts to beautify our environment and make the place our own through these small details helped create a familiar retreat—a home away from home. Onto the white canvas of our little hotel suite we painted the colors of our Clarkson culture.

That's what I mean by making home as we travel. I learned to do this as a young woman doing missionary work in Eastern Europe, and my children have learned to do it as well. No matter where we go, home follows us, and we bear it forth into the world around us.

Travel can also remind us that in this world we are only sojourners, and wherever we go, we are singing the songs of strangers in a strange land. We have learned to make the words of our own songs about the grace God has provided for us in our family. Even in an unsure world, we are blessed with carrying our heritage, both in God's Kingdom and in that kingdom worked out through our family. Our family and our family culture have become lifeboats on rough seas of uncertainty and change.

Our family culture is something that must be brought with us wherever we go, into all new situations and environments. Travel is an opportunity to practice that intentionality in a broad and meaningful way, to go out into the world and take with us a little piece of home.

But it works both ways, because when we come back home, we usually bring with us a little taste of where we've been. Our home is full of mementos, photographs, books, and art from all the places we have traveled, lived, and worked—the places that have shaped us and added new chapters to our collective story. Each one represents a memory—a moment of beauty, a lesson taught, a moment of sorrow or joy. The world is therefore always on our minds and in our hearts—another aspect of our family culture.

Sharing Our Family Culture

The stronger and more vibrant a family culture, the more others will be attracted to it. Though we have moved many times as a family, we have always tried to cultivate friends as extended elements of our family culture. We see family culture as dynamic and flexible, something that matures in the interaction with others outside our immediate family. The friends and other families whom we invest in pick up the rhythms that define our culture, and we pick up theirs as well. Together with others, we learn and grow.

Wherever we have lived, Clay and I have always made a point to include others in our lives—single adults, families large and small, people of all ages. In the interactions between us, we begin to inform one another about our respective practices and perspectives on the world. We begin to integrate their traditions, and they start to integrate ours.

For us this has included a variety of shared events. Some were one-time get-togethers. Others—like the three-family progressive dinners described in the December chapter—became established traditions, part of the family culture of each participant. Our years as a family have included cookouts and potlucks, home concerts, volleyball competitions, treasure hunts, countless game nights, and rollicking, shared evenings where we bandied about big ideas and solved the problems of the world together. (Well, maybe there were still a few problems left unsolved after those memorable evenings, but we definitely made a dent.) And amidst the thoughtful discussions and the abundant laughter, we grew closer to one another and also grew together. The Clarkson family culture is so much richer for having shared with other families.

Then there are the "little lost orphans," as someone in the family once termed them. These are the people who were drifting through the world and somehow, through God's leading, ended up on our doorstep. We met them through chance encounters at grocery stores, in school activities, on the plane, through church—people who never felt the protection of a family culture and were accustomed to going it alone. They came from a variety of backgrounds and circumstances, but like anyone, they needed to know the love and support of a family and to feel they had a home culture with which to identify as they tried to figure out the world. And so we have shared our home with homeless people, missionaries, singer-songwriters, students, and a variety of people who just needed a place to stay for a while. Our home culture has become richer because of the people we have folded into it.

Embracing Jesus in our lives means recognizing that God's adoption of us into His family culture has radically changed our lives forever. Romans 8:15 says, "You have not received a spirit of slavery leading to fear again, but you have received a spirit of adoption as sons by which we cry out, 'Abba! Father!'" If God has accepted us so completely into His family, we ought to look to do the same for others.

In our home, when we consider those whom God has placed in our stewardship, we attempt to do more than simply care for those people. Our intention is to integrate them into the life and rhythms of our home so that they can learn, sometimes for the first time, what it means to be in a loving, strong, and vibrant family environment. We include guests in our special events and our everyday lives as well, drawing them into our community with others around us. We do this because we have been so graciously folded into God's amazing family.

A Word about Messy Houses

The heart of the host determines the delight of the guests. However, it can be intimidating to invite people into that culture when we are well aware of our imperfections. I have sometimes struggled to bring people in because I'm embarrassed by the state of our house.

"Without oxen a stable stays clean," Proverbs 14:4 reminds us (NLT). However, my stable has many "oxen" almost every night, so I suppose it's inevitable that it will get messy on a regular basis.

Whenever someone visits our home, I always want to put my best foot forward. I want our home to be beautiful and welcoming—and clean as well. The responsibility for making it that way has always been shared in our home, and everyone, kids included, pitched in to clean, cook, decorate, and keep our home ready to welcome guests at a moment's notice.

But if things went awry during a busy season and our house was a mess—believe me, it happened!—we never allowed our less-than-perfect house to keep us from inviting people in. Mess or not, we welcomed friends and visitors who needed a meal, fun, or fellowship—and then we often called on them to pitch in with the chores.

Most visitors, I've found, would rather come over and see that we are a normal family, with evidence of life all around us, than to be excluded until we could get our act together. The key is the welcoming attitude, "I am so happy to be with you. I love our close fellowship. I look forward to our times together."

Such an open-door policy sometimes means that the constant flow of visitors can totally overwhelm our crew. So I try to be sensitive to this, to set boundaries for my family and limits on future plans for visitors. This gives all of us a chance to refresh enough to want guests again.

Through the years, I have realized over and over that I conduct the atmosphere in my home by the way I rule over my heart. When I focus not on performance or perfection but on joy, gratitude, and service, everything seems to fall into place. Working to prepare and maintain a beautiful, welcoming atmosphere does convey that I value and welcome my guests. But allowing them to enter my world even when it isn't quite as beautiful as I want it to be communicates that, in our family, grace abounds. They learn that family culture can be both full of life and beauty and immersed in grace in moments of struggle.

Stargazing

Where we live in Colorado, we are just far enough away from major urban centers to be free of the haze of city light pollution. As a result, when we get a clear night, we can look up and see the wonder of the Milky Way—millions of stars stretched out before us with no barrier to our view. A long-held summer tradition is to go out at night and stargaze, letting the gentle mountain breeze and the smell of pine trees add to the magical, endless weave of stars. Sometimes we actually ended up sleeping out on our deck in sleeping bags, enjoying the wonder of the Colorado outdoors. For our family it became a hallmark of our story—pursuing the beauty of creation and looking up in wonder at the infinitude of expanse above us, a reminder of God's greatness and His kindness in seeing us in our smallness.

To sleep under the stars, eat outdoors in the cool night air, and ponder together the miracle of a shooting star requires a choice. Choosing to turn off the television and choosing to take the trouble to make an outdoor picnic or drag the sleeping bags and pillows outside is a choice to place ourselves into the realm of the majesty and transcendence of our Creator.

Surveying the galaxies so far above our realm invisibly lifts our spirits to the knowledge that there is more to our world than we can see, imagine, or control. His creation art reminds us that our omnipotent, all-knowing God is the One who is truly in charge of the finer details of our lives. Comfort comes in knowing that the One who holds the stars together through all the centuries is the One who holds all of us—our beloved family and everyone else in the world—within His capable, everlasting hands.

When we make that understanding the heart of family culture, we know that all will indeed be well.

────── *September* ──────

WHEN SEASONS CHANGE
Gathering In for Home and Soul
(SARAH)

Is not this a true autumn day? Just the still melancholy that I love—that makes life and nature harmonize. The birds are consulting about their migrations, the trees are putting on the hectic or the pallid hues of decay, and begin to strew the ground, that one's very footsteps may not disturb the repose of earth and air, while they give us a scent that is a perfect anodyne to the restless spirit. Delicious autumn! My very soul is wedded to it, and if I were a bird I would fly about the earth seeking the successive autumns.

GEORGE ELIOT, LETTER TO MISS LEWIS, OCTOBER 1, 1841

WHEN I GROW UP, I want to be Miss Lane.

Dorcas Lane is the lovely and inimitable mistress of the Candleford post office in the BBC miniseries *Lark Rise to Candleford*, known for the way she delights in life through many small luxuries (Banbury cakes, perfume, scented baths, gossip—each of which she refers to as her "one weakness"), but also for the world she creates at her post office, which functions not only as her place of work but also as her queendom of a home. The big kitchen and old dining table at its heart make it a place to gather, the table ever laden with teapots and cakes and crowded with the post office community.

I have loved *Lark Rise to Candleford*, with its tales of rural England, since the first episode I watched. The theme of the series is fellowship and belonging, and it centers on characters, particularly the arch and ever well-dressed Miss Lane, who live by their vision of what it means to be at home in community. Miss Lane's post office is a known shelter, a refuge to which the lonely, the sick, and the needy all flock, sure of a cup of tea and a warm dose of her wisdom.

But the post office is also thoroughly a home, made so through Miss Lane's delight in the details of home life, the fine art of making one's dwelling a space of nourishment, joy, and comfort for all who shelter within it. She is past mistress of the art of daily celebration, keeping the rhythms of cooking (her Queen Cake is legendary), preserving (her calf's foot jelly has settled feuds), cleaning (even if she has to train her maid, Minnie, in this art), and rest (she knows when to send her staff for an hour of contemplation). Miss Lane delights in crafting her shelter, in gathering all that is necessary to provide for the people she brings to her home.

For a few years now, we Clarkson girls—Mom and Joy and I—have opened our autumn months with a *Lark Rise* marathon. When the first aspen leaf flickers gold and the first stab of crimson flares in the leaves of our tiny maple, we brew a pot of tea and bake something spicy and sweet—soda bread, apple cake, perhaps some pumpkin streusel bread. We light a few candles and dim the lights, and as the sun begins its increasingly early descent down the sky, we pile on the couch with our autumn repast and watch the series all over again from the beginning.

We watch, I think, as a way of renewing our vision for home and one another. It's been several years since the three of us have been home when autumn began, but we still try to watch it at the same time wherever we are—whether at college in California or England or abroad for travel or work. We call one another right as we start, and we also gather every friend we can find, creating in our dorm or tiny English flat or hotel room the same ritual of tea, cake, and community that we first knew at home. We try to create around this story and its vision our own version of Miss Lane's kitchen, renewing our love for home and the work that makes it.

I think that this practice comes naturally in autumn because fall is the season when the world turns cooler and the heart turns homeward. In our part of Colorado, that begins in September, though having lived in Texas, I know the way that summer can linger until it seems as if the first cool day may never come. Autumn is the time in which we recognize home as a strong ship, caulked and tight, our stronghold and safe place as we sail the high oceans of winter . . . and life. Autumn is the season of endings and ingatherings as summer wanes and we stock cupboards and souls against the coming of winter.

In autumn we celebrate the gift and rhythm of home and harvest, and we turn again to the work that makes home a place of abundance. We plan just how we will provide for those who gather round us as the days grow cold, to sit at the fireside through the long nights and share the quiet hours. We revel again in the fellowship of family, the goodness of feasting together, and consider how to nourish the spaces of home in which our lives are rooted.

Our focus in this chapter and season, then, is on planning, gathering, and provision, the merry round of creativity and work that goes toward the creation of homes that shelter and delight. We revel in the small celebrations, the soup-and-bread dinners, the cooking and stocking of cupboards that make so rich a refuge for those we love.

But we also consider what it means to shelter the soul, to make provision not only for the body but also for the spirit. It's easy to gather material; it's harder to gather time, to stock the rooms of home with quiet. This frantic age that draws us out into action, distraction, hurry, and work also follows us back, invading the spaces of home, rest, meals, and sleep. Through technology we have the ever-present hurry of the unsleeping modern world, and if we do not forge strong rhythms of rest and spaces of sacred quiet, that frenzy will invade our homes and steal the life within. So to gather in can also mean to keep out what would compromise the life we want to create in the spaces of home.

Because in the end, the point of home in all its fullness—the point of good meals, full cupboards, or ordered rooms—is not just to provide creaturely comfort or to prove some sort of competence. The point of home is to be a refuge for the soul, a place where beauty can be encountered, truth told, goodness touched and known. It's why home needs hush as well as bustle, silence as well as song. The point of home is to shelter lost and weary people, draw in the lonely, cover the grieved. And the point of autumn preparation is to make a place where souls can be sheltered, grown, nourished, and healed even in the bleakest of physical or spiritual winters.

In one of my favorite *Lark Rise* episodes, Miss Lane takes in a ragtag apprentice maid named Minnie. Minnie is goodhearted but highly distractible, frivolous, and flighty; dismal at housework; and careless with the lovely things that Miss Lane treasures. She seems unable to learn the rounds of cleaning and cooking, the rhythms of housework so loved by Miss Lane. When, at the end of her trial week, Minnie accidentally spills red wine on the antique wedding dress that belonged to Miss Lane's mother, she takes one look at Miss Lane's face and says, "I'll pack my things."

But Miss Lane stops her. In a scene that still brings tears to my eyes, Miss Lane speaks to Minnie in her frustration, berating her, asking why she has no respect for the love that is in precious things, the very things that make the post office the meaningful place it is. But then she answers her own question:

"Of course you can't see. No one has ever taught you respect. No one has ever taught you love. I am not going to send you away, Minnie. I took you on, and that means you are one of us now. It is not your fault that you weren't ready for the burdens I put upon you. You need to be taught, so that is what we will do. I intend to scold you when you deserve to be scolded. I may at times be unforgiving. But I will never turn you out. The post office is your home. Do you understand that?"

"I do, ma'am," says Minnie with shocked and shining eyes.[1]

Autumn is a time to celebrate the fact that home is the place where love makes us welcome, a shelter from which we will not be expelled. In this season we celebrate the spaces in which we learn to prize and honor precious things. We celebrate shelter, belonging, and the love expressed in drawing all things into the rich, generous life of home.

——— *In Our Home* ———

A Room (or Corner) of One's Own

We had an even mix of introverts and extroverts in the Clarkson house, with differing inclinations toward silence and solitude. But the practice of withdrawing from the group to be alone, something necessary to the adult need for prayer and creativity, was nurtured early in all of us by a focus on creating a personal space for being quiet.

During the years when everyone was at home, each person had a corner to call his or her own, and for one hour in the afternoon, everyone went to their special places to read, draw, write, or dream. We worked to make these places special, tiny refuges in which we had the chance to pull away and explore the interior world of thought and imagination.

In our crowded and busy household, making both physical and scheduled room for these spaces took thought. For Mom, the space was a corner with an easy chair and pile of books, a place by the window where she could look out on nature and take a deep breath of quiet. For the kids, various corners of closets and bedrooms—or, if we were lucky, a window seat—were easily transformed into highly valued retreats by the draping of a blanket, a pile of favorite books, a basket of craft supplies, or a few favorite stuffed animals. Introvert that I am, I treasured the time in my special, quiet corner, but even my more gregarious brothers and sisters enjoyed the opportunity to create their special places.

In the autumn months, as the year draws to its close, as the days grow colder and the darkness comes earlier, the cultivation of quiet spaces allows the souls within a home to take refuge in silence. Solitude and, with it, an interior world, is something we desperately need to defend in the crazed busyness of the modern world. If you want to hear God speak, you need to have quiet time with Scripture. If you want to write a song, a novel, or a poem, you need to draw away and listen to all that echoes in your soul.

The rhythms of our ceaseless culture are set by the unsleeping Internet and the untiring world of entertainment media. We can choose to never be quiet or alone. But it is only in the hushed spaces that we can clearly hear all that echoes in quiet skies, in the eyes of children, in our own inner voices. Silence is where we dream, create, and pray, and we need it desperately.

Home is a space where such quiet can be cultivated and sacred spaces kept—even in the midst of the most talkative household. Home is the stronghold of calm to which we return; the sacred, quiet space where we may hear that still, small voice; the place we come into from our daily battles to find refuge and to draw strength afresh for the fray.

A Well-Stocked Kitchen and Pantry

If you've ever read the Brambly Hedge books by Jill Barklem, then you've glimpsed in her whimsical, old-fashioned, detailed illustrations just what a well-stocked kitchen might look like. Based on research of historic English country life, this darling series of children's books depicts the lives of a colony of mice who live in sumptuous country homes in the roots of old trees. Her drawings of tiny mice pantries piled up with preserves, dried goods, jars of jam, cans of beans, bins of rice and flour, and shelves of cooling baked goods embody the old-fashioned ideal of a well-stocked kitchen.

While we may hold a slightly simpler idea of what is necessary to an outfitted pantry—and available space may dictate the choices we make—a well-equipped kitchen is certainly central to the comfort and cultivation of home. A homemade meal, a batch of cookies for tea, a quick loaf of bread for breakfast—these are all quite easy to produce if the ingredients and equipment are right on hand.

It all comes down to preparation. A bit of planning, a strategic shopping trip, a small dose of organization, and you have a home stocked and ready for a sudden blizzard, an unexpected guest, an impromptu celebration with those you love. Half of the comfort of home comes from having what you need on hand when you need it.

So we Clarksons always set aside a stock-up day for each season—a day to make lists, to check available supplies, to shop, to envision the meals we might eat, the recipes we might try, the parties we might throw. We tried to make it a festal day as we prepared for the celebrations to come, ending a major shopping trip with a special meal or cup of hot chocolate by the fire. Our autumn stock-up day was always our favorite—the best time to gather in, to savor the shelter of home. For autumn, of all the seasons, is the one when the urge to draw back, to invite others over, to gather the ones we love close to the fireside, is strongest. (If you've never stocked up on basic ingredients before or seen your own home as a place to gather resources, you can find a list to get you started at www.lifegivinghome.com.)

The Stories We Shared

Autumn is the season for reading aloud. Well, in truth, all seasons are good for that pastime, and I wish all people would enjoy reading year round. But as autumn draws near with its cooler days and crisp evenings and I begin to ponder exactly what I want to be present in my home for the long nights ahead, I think first of books. Autumn is the perfect season in which to share stories with those you love.

During a recent gathering of my family, just minutes before half of us were leaving for the airport, my brother Joel pulled me aside. "Can I borrow *Peace Like a River*?" he asked. He didn't have to beg, because he knew I would instantly grin and agree. The mention of that book provokes a smile and glance between us that feels like the sharing of a happy secret. The story itself is plain enough, but it's the memory of how we encountered it together that makes such a knowing between us.

One autumn when Joel and I were both home on a rare autumn break, we decided to read a novel together. Our mornings were free, and we spent them in the front-porch rocking chairs. Wrapped in blankets, coffee in hand, we read aloud to each other. The tale we chose was Leif Enger's *Peace Like a River* (2001), the strange and wondrous account of a father's remarkable journey in search of his absent eldest son. The story is narrated by the asthmatic younger son, Reuben. His boon companion in the family adventures is his younger sister, Swede, whose talent as a cowboy poet makes for some of the best passages in the book.

The hours Joel and I spent experiencing that tale together created a space of imaginative fellowship that we will prize for the rest of our lives. Voicing the vivid characters, marveling at the author's wordcraft, and laughing at the fierce loves and wild creativity of Swede provided us with a unique camaraderie. We took a sort of road trip together through a land of imagination, and the reactions we observed in each other, the beauty we encountered, and the memories we made shaped our friendship in a lifelong sort of way. So when Joel asked to borrow the book, I knew he wanted to share not just the story but also the world, the truth, the joy we had discovered together. I scrambled to find my copy before we had to leave.

As I continued my travels that day, I pondered the special power, the heightened delight of shared stories. In the same way that a week's visit at a friend's home brings you closer than any number of coffee dates or brief encounters at church, the sharing of a story accelerates the comradeship of souls. When people inhabit a realm of imagination together, it's inevitable that a bit of each person's imagination and spirit is revealed to the others who sojourn in that marvelous place. I think I am especially aware of this because of the way that shared stories have helped me to be close to my siblings, shaping our history, our memories, even the language we use to talk about life to this day.

As you might have guessed from reading the earlier chapters, J. R. R. Tolkien's *The Lord of the Rings* is a particular favorite for our family. It's not uncommon in my house to hear someone refer to Frodo, the elves, or Gandalf as part of a deep spiritual observation or to make a solid point. To us, Middle Earth is almost as real as the rocks and trees behind our house. We tend to think about ourselves and our lives in terms of "fellowship" and "quest," and we talk about someday creating a Rivendell of our own.

But other stories shaped us too. We talk about loving Aslan and about God being "not a tame lion"—both references to The Chronicles of Narnia. And the minute anyone brings up the subject of grace, the name Jean Valjean is sure to follow (from *Les Misérables* [1862], another family favorite). The stories we read or listened to as a family provide our metaphors for living courageously and well because a story experienced together creates a small and vivid world of fellowship. Stories reveal the souls of those who share them and knit them together for life.

So when I think of autumn, when I consider what resources I want to gather for the winter months ahead, what riches I want to be present in my home for the nourishing of the loved ones who gather, books are foremost in my thoughts. A well-stocked kitchen is life for the body, but a library stocked with stories to share is eternal nourishment for the soul. For many long lists of our favorite books for reading aloud, go to www.lifegivinghome.com, where we have probably listed more favorites than you'll ever want to read.

But if you, like me, are keen to collect a library of your own, to make these books present friends in your home, consider the following ideas for where you might find those that will become treasures to your family. I tend to work on a budget, and I assume you know how to navigate Amazon.com, so I've listed the used-book sources that offer a little more scope for budget and choice:

- *Library sales.* Almost every city or county library will have a used-book and discard sale every few months. Check with your librarian and head down with several big bags. The prices are usually quite low.

- *Thrift stores, yard sales, and estate sales.* You'd be shocked at the excellent literary finds to be culled in a Goodwill or at your neighbor's garage sale.
- *Auction sites like eBay.* Check often for your favorite collector's titles. The deals can be startlingly good.
- *Online used booksellers.* My favorite is *abebooks.com*, an amazing compendium of bookshops from around the world.

The Art of the Schedule: Making Space to Taste and Breathe

Someone once said that the genius of music is as much in its silence as in its sound. In the rests, the quiet, the silence interwoven with active notes, a masterpiece is made. A score too crammed with notes is one in which the melody can be lost, the core motif of the musical piece obscured.

So it is with schedule. Our days are a kind of symphony whose music and meaning can be easily marred by excess activity. The fact is that our time, especially in an era of ceaseless possible action, is defined as much by what we choose not to do as by what we do. It takes a wise and present mind to discern what is necessary and right in the countless available hours of work, socialization, entertainment, Internet, and education.

Home, in this context, can easily become just an eating and sleeping space for busy people instead of a center of life and community. My parents realized this early in their marriage, and so began a seasonal practice of taking a day to plan together for the months ahead. This was in addition to the annual planning done in January. Retreating to a favorite coffee shop or hotel, they'd set out Daytimers, notebooks (no cell phones in those days), and lists of all the possibilities for the coming months. With prayer and discussion, they would select the activities that would nourish soul, vocation, and fellowship and set those on the family calendar. Some possibilities they simply said no to; some they decided to experience for a trial period. But the goal was to emerge from the end of that planning day with a schedule that would further spiritual, mental, relational, and educational growth for the entire family while still leaving space for joy and rest.

I well remember these planning days from my childhood because, at their end, my parents would return with a kind of family blueprint for the next season. On it I would discover lessons, dates, events, and friendships carefully planned to nourish and delight my little heart. Seasonal planning is a practice that most of us Clarkson children continue to this day because it is a way of stepping aside to create time, to form and choose our schedules rather than simply suffer them. Such planning allows us to glimpse the larger stories of our lives and to form our days meaningfully toward shaping those stories according to our callings and goals.

Soup and Bread

Though soup and bread is a subject that could fit any place at all in a book about home life, I feel strongly that these hearty dinners are most at home in autumn. Soup-and-bread meals were made for days when the air is tinged with frost and the wind stings the skin. Soup was made to be eaten when night comes far too soon, and fresh, buttered bread is the antidote to nighttime despair.

Note that the soup and bread don't have to be homemade to be delicious. Lovely, warming possibilities can come from a deli, a bakery, or a grocery store. But soup can be the easiest dish in the world to make—just chop and simmer or throw into a slow cooker. With a little practice, fresh homemade bread is easier to make than you think, and the practice of making it can be tremendously therapeutic. I would encourage you to develop at least a few homemade soup-and-bread combinations and turn to them often, especially when the turning seasons call for a steaming bowl of comfort.

Joys of the Harvest

Every year in late September when we kids were growing up, when the leaves had really turned and the wind was sharp and cool, we set aside a whole day or more for our yearly ritual of "applesaucing." The tradition began when we first moved to Colorado, found a pick-your-own apple orchard for a bit of autumn fun, and ended up with five bushel boxes of fruit. We had so much fun picking those bright gold and crimson apples, so firm and tart-sweet, that we all got carried away.

So we took our bushel baskets home and set up an assembly line. Nathan peeled, Sarah and Joel chopped, Mom simmered, and Joy mashed and sweetened. The result was a huge pot of cinnamon-spiced applesauce. After filling our stomachs with the delicious results of our labors, we ladled the rest into Ziploc bags in portions big enough for our family at one meal and then froze them. The delight of having fresh applesauce to accompany our soup-and-bread suppers all through that winter sent us right back to the apple farm the next year. So the tradition was born.

Now, years later, autumn still doesn't feel complete, and we certainly don't feel prepared for winter, until those of us who are living in Colorado have made the trek down to the apple farm. We wriggle into jackets, throw a picnic together, and make the drive out onto the Colorado plains to handpick our apples.

The experience of picking the apples ourselves, lugging them back, and commencing the arduous but oh-so-gratifying task of peeling and chopping them all has become a favorite memory in our family and home.

If you've never tried it, let us assure you—applesauce is unbelievably easy to make. Simply peel and core the apples, cut them into chunks, and add a little water, sugar, and seasonings. You don't need as much as you might think. For a pound of apples we use about half a cup each of water and sugar, half a teaspoon of cinnamon, and just a pinch of nutmeg. Put everything in a pan, heat to boiling, then simmer until the apples are tender and easily mashed. This makes a little more than a cup of applesauce. If you want more, just double or triple the amounts. Feel free to adjust the seasonings to your tastes. You can even substitute maple syrup, honey, brown sugar, or even agave nectar for the sugar. The taste will be slightly different, but still delicious.

If you love having a freezer stocked with good fruit, you have countless options. We also freeze big batches of peaches when they are in season, and berries aren't any harder.

Processing peaches, in fact, has become almost as beloved a practice for us as the apple adventure. Each summer we order a large box from the western slopes of the Rockies, a Colorado tradition. We dip the peaches in a large pot of boiling water for just a few seconds. This loosens the skins so that peeling is easier. We have one big bowl in which to place skins and seeds and one in which to place the peeled and sliced peaches. (For many years we would watch the *Anne of Green Gables* miniseries as we sliced and peeled away.) With the slightest bit of sweetening added, our peaches are ready to be bagged and frozen, ready to provide a touch of summer sunshine in the winter months. Of course, we always leave enough unfrozen for a right-now snack or dessert!

Autumn Centerpiece

The bounty to be found outdoors in the fields and forests as the year turns to autumn makes for marvelous decoration. The turning leaves and burnished colors of September and October are excellent resources for bringing a little natural beauty to your home.

We kids always loved making a centerpiece for the family table each year out of items we gathered on hikes or walks through the mountains—pinecones, leaves, apples, fir branches, whatever we could find. We often made an occasion of the hunt, packing a picnic and treating our foray as a quest for treasure. When we got home, we made hot chocolate and let our creativity run wild. We loved the simple beauty of our centerpiece every time we sat down to one of those autumn soup and bread dinners.

The lovely thing is how easy the process of creating the centerpiece is, how entertaining it is, and how beautiful the finished product can be. There are any number of natural items you can use and any number of containers to hold your treasures.

To make a centerpiece, simply start with a container. Almost anything will do, so look for something interesting—a vase, a basket, a copper pot, or a big bowl. (We have a golden-toned ceramic bowl that looks beautiful piled with apples and pinecones.) Then choose your fillers—apples or pears (real or quality artificial ones), pinecones, dried flowers, autumn leaves, evergreen branches, interesting seed pods, mixed whole nuts, or raffia. To hold the piece together, you might want to make use of flower-arranging supplies such as florist's wire, tape, or foam, but in our experience it's not really necessary. Just pile everything together and play with the arrangement until it looks right.

You also don't need woods to hike in; you'd be surprised what a walk around your backyard, your neighborhood, or even a city street will yield. Just keep your eyes open for interesting colors and shapes and bring them home for your own special celebration of the changing seasons.

Autumn Homecoming

Autumn always comes eventually, however long summer has lingered. The first bite of chill is in the air. Rain falls in winter steadiness or the first snowstorm sends a flurry of feathery flakes. The light wanes so early that day and night seem almost to blend. And in that moment the impulse to scurry for home becomes an ache in the stomach, a yearning in the heart. How joyous a thing it is to then arrive on the doorstep of a home whose windows are golden with waiting light, where soup is on the stove and the cupboard is stocked against any number of unexpected storms.

A home like that feels almost like a person itself, with arms open to receive the weary. In the shelter and fireside splendor it so generously offers, we taste a bit of what home, in its essence, reflects. For those rare, golden moments of homecoming allow us, through their joy, to reach beyond space and time to their source: the love whose grace is the source of all good things, the Father in whose heart we have our home.

God grant that my home be such a shelter, a refuge whose windows are alight in welcome, drawing the lonely and wandering in from the cold.

October
HOME IS BEST
Serving Life within Your Walls
(SALLY)

We shape our dwellings, and afterwards our dwellings shape us.
WINSTON CHURCHILL

CHILL AIR SWEPT INTO the room and the candles flickered as Clay walked through the front door. "Winter is on its way," he announced as he took off his coat and plopped wearily on the couch.

Having just brewed a pot of tea, I got an extra mug out of the cabinet and invited him to sit with me for a few minutes before dinner. "Tell me about your day. How did your meeting go when you shared the ministry plan with your small group?"

Clay is the unsung hero behind our ministry. Writing books to inspire parents to raise godly kids is his strong calling, the legacy he would most like to leave. But he also runs our publishing operations; organizes the contracts for our conferences; keeps the office, secretary, and accountant going; manages all of our Web operations; keeps on top of taxes; organizes the books coming and going from our office; and—well, you get the picture. And you probably can also understand how weary he gets at times—and how much he can use a listening ear.

For most of the next hour, Clay unburdened himself to me, sharing his thoughts, dreams, and frustrations. He wondered out loud about the future of our ministry and talked of the exhaustion he so often felt. And that gave me the perfect chance to encourage him—to remind him gently of the ways God had provided for us all these years and to speak forward into his future by expressing my confidence in the fruit his hard work would bring. I hoped my words would bring just the grace my husband needed as he munched on a warm cookie from the oven and finished a second cup of tea.

That's home at its best—serving, loving, and encouraging within the safe walls that contain the secrets, fears, dreams, life work, and love that knit our hearts together.

October is that wonderful season when leaves have turned golden and red and cool breezes lend a crispness to the air, creating a perfect environment to simmer savory soup and to curl up in front of the fireplace with a mug of spicy cider for an evening read. Feasting comes to mind when I remember the ways we lean into chilly nights and warm firesides . . . and eat. But I also find myself contemplating and cherishing what it means to serve—to prepare a feast for the table as a way of opening hearts and to make my home a place of comfort and refuge and beauty.

A Model for Serving

The setting sun sent shadows creeping over hills and rooftops as the crowds hurried through the streets of Jerusalem, eager to make it home before the Sabbath. Noisy tradesmen clamored to sell their last wares before the day closed. Dust flew upward as wagons pushed through the streets. Babies cried in the heat of the afternoon, longing for the comfort of home.

That day, Jesus' inner-circle friends had seen the frowns and tears of the sad and forlorn, had heard the pleas of thousands who pressed against them along the crowded pathway—the demanding, curious onlookers, those filled with hope and a seed of belief, longing for a touch from the Master. The day of serving by His side had left them almost breathless with exhaustion. How could they possibly understand what the next twenty-four hours would hold?

The aroma of strong herbs, blended with the smoke of lanterns and the fresh smell of bread baking, wafted through the home and greeted them as they made their way up the rough, sandy stairs to the upper portion of the house. Anticipating the coming Passover celebration brought a familiar comfort to the weary men who had gathered every year since childhood for this meal memorializing God's protection.

But Jesus knew this would not be just any Passover. And He had carefully planned this last night before His death, the last meal He would share with the ones He most wanted to understand His Kingdom messages. He had chosen a suitable place to imprint these profound messages into their hearts and minds forever—an upper room, a place of privacy where He could enjoy His closest trusted companions without interruption, and He had sent two disciples to prepare the feast.

From the beginning of time He had planned this night—the picture of the fulfillment of the Passover lamb, so treasured in the history, tradition, and hearts of all Jewish believers. He would fulfill Isaiah's prophecy as the true Passover Lamb in their midst.

Thinking about that evening, knowing that Jesus, too, was weary when He served most generously, has given me strength on many a demanding night. I imagine some of the elements of His preparation. A window with a view toward the crimson sunset would fill the room with a pink glow. Oil lamps would flutter as the door opened and the men filled the space with laughter and loud voices. The best cook in town had probably been called upon to prepare the bitter herbs and succulent roasted lamb, paired with the best wine, so that Jesus' profound last words would fall upon men satiated with delectable tastes in the atmosphere and beauty of a prepared place. I have to think that the God who prepared a garden of such beauty at the beginning had also put thought into preparing the place of the Last Supper with an eye for comfort, beauty, and hospitality toward those He loved most.

Jesus knew what was coming. He who had cast the stars into their place, who had existed for eternity past in the splendor of light and perfect fellowship with the Father, where myriads of angels had bowed before Him and worshiped, understood that soon He would be subjected to hysterical crowds; violent soldiers; aggressive, poisonous jeers and beatings; and finally a terrifying death.

He knew as well that His own would be bewildered by the traumatic night. So willingly, generously, intentionally, He knelt down on the rough sandy tile, girded Himself with a towel, and gently and lovingly wiped the dust off His beloved friends' dirty, stinky feet, all the while speaking in soothing tones, teaching one last bit of wisdom. In the context of this display of servant love, and in gentle consideration of the body and soul fatigue of His own dear disciples, He spoke His most ardent, lifegiving words.

- "Love one another" (John 13:34).
- "The Helper, the Holy Spirit, whom the Father will send in My

name, He will . . . bring to your remembrance all that I said to you" (John 14:26).
- "In the world you have tribulation, but take courage" (John 16:33).

Always His heart and words were focused on His beloved band of friends. Always He was thinking of how to prepare them, to strengthen them. Not even in His death did He focus on His own needs.

He did all of this for those who could not comprehend His coming sacrifice, the depth of His choice to humble Himself, or the vast generosity that was being expended from a heart overflowing with love for them. Only much later would their understanding dawn.

"Learn from Me," Jesus said, "for I am gentle and humble in heart" (Matthew 11:29).

And so, in pondering, I must ask myself, does my heart remain humble as I serve my family in our home—as I wash dishes, plan a meal, clean a toilet? Are my words lifegiving and generous, serving to strengthen those who share my home? Is my heart, like the heart of Jesus, always on those I serve? Do I bow willingly in the dust and stink of my own life because He was so willing to spend His life in giving, serving, loving without thought of Himself, even as He approached His death?

Because He has always offered a sense of place (the original garden, the land of milk and honey He promised His own wanderers, the place in heaven He is preparing for us to enjoy), I have learned to value home even more. Home is one of the places of refuge that many in our world have not valued or known in a personal way. There is no prepared place where they can come expecting to find solace, welcome, comfort, acceptance, truth, and ease. But I am determined that those I love will have such a place. And so, following Jesus' model of service and hospitality, I choose to prepare for and serve those who share my home and those who enter my doors.

It is the giving rhythms of home that provide the right atmosphere for passing on the essential heart attitudes and warm relationships in life. I reach hearts by cooking meals, by washing sheets and fluffing pillows, by reading a favorite book one more time even though I have it memorized. I do it when I clean and decorate a space to make it beautiful and comfortable and inviting. I do it when I choose to respond graciously to a question or write a note of encouragement. Both literally and metaphorically, in my home I have the privilege of washing feet every day.

The practice of hospitality, you see, is not just for strangers. Serving and welcoming spouse and children, family and friends, is an art that will truly reach their souls and give them a reason to believe in the God of love and holiness, even as it created a perfect environment for Jesus' own disciples. When body needs and emotional needs are met and minds are filled with nobility and inspiration, then souls are predisposed to want to follow the God who is revered in all of these rituals. It is not the indoctrination of theology forced down daily that crafts a soul who believes; it is the serving and loving and giving that surround the messages where souls are reached.

A truth told without love and grace is a truth that is rejected. Would Jesus' message have had the same impact without His feeding thousands and taking children into His arms and washing the feet of His friends? It is in service that God incarnate is recognized. And service begins with serving those who are closest to us, making home the very best place to be.

———— *In Our Home* ————

"It was the *food* that made me love God," Sarah pronounced as she reached for one more warm, fluffy piece of French toast, soon to be covered in hot maple syrup.

When people ask me how I influenced my children to love God and to love home, I often try to come up with something deep, spiritual, insightful, and wise. When asked how I reach the hearts of women coming in and out of my door over the years, I cannot always find an exact formula to offer. Yet over the years I have learned some principles of wisdom that have influenced hundreds of hearts that have passed through our door—and much of that wisdom has to do with the power of serving at the table.

Serving Up Sustenance—and More

A candlelit table piled high with warm rolls, pungent cheese, savory soups, fragrant cakes and pies, and colorful salads—what an alluring sight, inviting all who behold it to engage in the life spread generously there. Food is the universal language that eases hearts to open, tying secure knots of intimacy while satisfying bodily hunger, weaving tiny threads of kindred needs into friendship, camaraderie, and truth. Being served personally in an atmosphere of enticing smells, delectable tastes, dancing melodies, and affectionate emotion has opened the hearts of many people in our home.

When I ponder the amazing variety of what God has given human beings to eat—fruit, vegetables, spices, meats, fish, beans, nuts, cheeses, drinks, sweets, textures, colors, and tastes—I have to deduce that the Creator of the universe cares a great deal about sustaining us and giving us pleasure. The life Artist who crafted humans with noses to smell, skin to feel, tastes to savor, eyes to approve color and beauty, and minds to enjoy engaging with others intended to make Himself known through all of these senses and faculties. These pleasures God wanted His children to enjoy—sights, tastes, smells, sounds, warm emotions—all have the power to stir a heart alive, to inspire a soul to hope.

I am convinced that feasting can be a form of worship, an acknowledgment of God's desire to create an abundant life to be enjoyed. The table can provide pleasure for all of our senses, give comfort and rest amidst the weariness of daily life, and carve out a space where we cultivate community and draw closer to one another. When we choose to feast together—take the trouble to make each meal, however humble, an occasion for mindfulness and gratitude—we acknowledge God's artistry and provision and draw closer to Him as well.

God, you see, is not merely an idea, a philosophy, or a truth to be known; He is an artist, a lover, a comforter, a judge, a shepherd, a servant, a father, a cook, an architect, a comedian, a friend—the multifaceted One who wants us to celebrate life with Him every day. He is beyond containing, bigger than our multitude of thoughts can comprehend. And it is He who invites us to "taste and see that the Lord is good" (Psalm 34:8).

Our dining room has so often been the stage upon which our family life was played out. For us, feasting is a favorite pastime, our happiest entertainment. At least three times each day—not to mention teatimes, snacks, coffee breaks, popcorn by the fire, pizza nights, midnight snacking, holiday gorging—whoever is home will gather to share food and share our lives. Our family has logged thousands and thousands of meals where we not only ate but also talked, laughed, and rested together.

We also learned to serve one another, for mealtime provides the perfect opportunity for observing needs and meeting them. When I plan food I know will delight and nourish the bodies of family and guests, I am serving them. When the kids set the table, creating a beautiful backdrop for our time together, they are serving. When the girls and I cook and Dad and the boys clean—or vice versa—we make our home a place of service. And we all serve when we observe one another at the table, notice needs, and do what we can to fill those needs. Does someone need a refill of tea or water or mashed potatoes? Does someone need to have his or her say, to be listened to? Does someone just need to be left alone for the moment?

Practicing that kind of awareness—that kind of hospitality—is a way of washing feet as Jesus did, a practical way of obeying His commandment to love one another. I believe it, too, is a way to worship.

Serving Up Sanctuary

A few years ago, on another crisp fall evening, a blazing sunset of reds, pinks, and corals lured us all outdoors. As we sat peacefully out on the deck, admiring the beauty, the front door opened and my twenty-six-year-old, Joel, strode out with weary face and exhausted body. He had worked throughout the previous night and day.

"I just decided to come home because I need 'us' to give me some rest and peace."

Dinner still a half hour away, I quickly cut some cheese, arranged some crisp whole grain crackers on a plate, poured a bubbly drink in a glass, and gave him my offering—"Just a little something to hold you over till dinner is ready."

The furrowed brow softened and Joel said, "This is why I came home. I knew you all would fill me back up, and I wanted peace and quiet for at least one night."

One of the best powers of home is the life that comes from within that gives comfort, a "place to belong" and a place that soothes the soul, and gives everyone a sense of belonging to one another.

Living in a fallen world means that all of us will be subject to heartbreaks, illnesses, and disappointments. Our family has certainly had its share of dark passages—surgeries, car wrecks, a fire in our home, painful breakups, depression, financial struggle, and more. It was in those times that we learned the power of a home that offers refuge—a place of comfort and safety away from life's storms. Having a place and time to rest, to be encouraged, and to find hope and healing is one of the most powerful gifts of a lifegiving home. Here are just a few ways we can make a home a place of sanctuary for family and visitors alike:

- *A cozy environment.* Physical comfort helps with emotional comfort, and a cozy atmosphere creates its own sense of sanctuary. Throw blankets and pillows, candles, movies and books, and music are some of the tools I keep on hand to serve those who come to our home in need of a refuge.

- *Comforting food and drink.* Preparing favorite food and drink is one way to provide that sense of comfort and safety. Yorkshire Gold tea or some strong English breakfast tea; organic, freshly ground coffee; warm oatmeal bread; steaming homemade soups; Sunday morning feasts with maple French toast made from my homemade bread—these are some of the tastes that speak comfort to my crowd. Each family's needs and tastes will be unique based on their own favorite family traditions and recipes. Yet the cultivating of mutual appetites draws people together with invisible threads of comfort and memory.

- *Healing aromas.* Smells, I have learned, have a powerful connection to memory and a special power to bring comfort and peace. Fresh flowers and scented candles—vanilla and hazelnut are our favorites—contribute to the sense of sanctuary in our home. But there's nothing like a whiff of food on the stove to calm frayed nerves and soothe exhaustion. This was a secret I learned when I was a missionary in Eastern Europe. The yeasty scent of bread rising or the chocolaty promise of cocoa melting in butter and sugar gently invites my family and guests to partake of the goodness inside the walls of our home. And all of this speaks to those who enter of a sanctuary where all will find a haven, even for a few minutes, of life filled with pleasure and peace.

- *Privacy and protection.* Love can heal so many wounds, and that healing often happens best in a protected environment. That is the very definition of sanctuary—a place where people are safe from the outside world. There have been times when we have pulled away from our very public lives and limited ourselves to our inner circle in order to give one or more of our children a chance to heal or rest in privacy. We promised them they would not have to deal with the public, and we kept our word. Sometimes we serve best by giving those within our walls the protection they need.

- *Loyalty and commitment.* Our children have always known that they are welcome to come to us under any circumstance, that we will never turn them away. And now that all of the kids are adults, we love to see the way they always have one another's backs. No matter the tensions, flaws, or mistakes, we are all deeply committed to helping, loving, protecting, and engaging with one another through all of the circumstances of our lives. To have a secure community waiting to accept and love you is one of the supreme gifts of life found at home.

- *A listening ear.* We all need a safe place where we can express fears, failures, longings, loneliness, and bitterness without fear of judgment or rejection.

No home is a perfect sanctuary, of course. We will never be able to offer a foolproof refuge from all the storms of life or keep trouble from finding its way behind the walls of our home. God, after all, is our only sure source of safety (Psalm 4:8). But a loving home, carefully prepared, can be a powerful source of rest and healing and comfort.

Serving Up Connection

"I just can't wait to come home!" was the exact text message I received from both of my boys as they headed home for Christmas last year. I wrote them and asked why they felt so strongly about being home with us over the holidays. Both wrote almost the same answer in response: "It's the hot meals we share every evening, our favorite books read aloud, the mutual fellowship we engage in night after night—that's what we miss when we are away."

In a "connected" world where cell phones and tablets are practically extensions of the body, it's surprising how little time there is for actual connection—for conversation and face-to-face relationships. The welcome of our home, with food and conversation shared no matter what the day held, was consistent and intentional. The cups of tea and books read and all the talk went into making our home feel like the best place to be, the one place that always said, *No matter what else happens, you belong here with us.*

Every night at our house, candles are lit, music is played, and a full table is usually set, even if the cuisine is a bowl of cereal. And every night whoever is home will sit around that table and *connect*. We linger over meals, talking about every possible subject. We discuss world issues, ask hard questions, challenge thoughts, share Scripture, relate the stories of the day. Making the family table a daily habit ensures that all of us keep up with one another's lives: news, stories, victories, and disappointments.

Dinner-table discipleship is what we call it, and when our children lived at home, it happened every single night. Every child was expected to share opinions about articles they had read, Scripture passages they were pondering, inspiring stories they had heard. No comment was rejected as silly because we wanted them to practice exercising their ideas and learn to reason in a group. Today people often ask me how my children were accepted into schools like Yale, Cambridge, and Oxford. I honestly believe that to a great extent it was due to these intentional moments of discipleship—wanting our kids to learn to think both clearly and biblically and be able to defend their ideas and their faith, hoping to inspire them to care deeply about truth.

Eating together every night gave us thousands of opportunities to instruct—hours and hours of time to intentionally shape our kids' convictions, build their treasure chest of stories, and give them hundreds of Scriptures to know and remember. Even as Jesus taught His disciples over meals, so we sought to use this time of satisfying their appetites to also gratify their need for community and shape their very souls.

I remember seven-year-old Joy wiggling restlessly at the table, her furrowed eyebrows suggesting great displeasure. "Mama, do you have to talk with those teenagers every single night about big things and argue and discuss for hours? Can't we ever just eat a meal in peace?"

She was right. When our older children were teens, we discussed at the table every possible issue that would face them in challenging times, seeking to give them a moral compass for venturing out in the world. And most of it was a little beyond the comfort and interest level of a seven-year-old. But years later, when Joy won the national first-place freshman debate medal her first year of college, she quipped, "Mama, it was all of those mealtime discussions that prepared me to think clearly. I have 'those teenagers' to thank."

Mealtime isn't the only time we connect, of course—although it is a welcome constant in the Clarkson home. We're a vocal bunch, and the conversations typically continue into the living room, onto the porch, into the garden, wherever we gather. And difficult as this might be to believe, the connections we strengthen at home don't always involve talking (difficult as that might be to believe). As we play together, share chores together, take walks, or just sit quietly side by side, we are strengthening the ties that bind us together. What matters is making the time to be in one another's company and to be *present* to one another during those times, not preoccupied. In this distracted age that's not easy to do, but it makes all the difference.

Serving Up Beauty

We humans were made for beauty. As the first Artist, God crafted a stunning world of color, sounds (birds, running waterfalls, human voices), seasons, variety (giraffes, seals, penguins; mountains, deserts, rain forests), touch (freezing snow, soft grass, prickly cactus), and tastes (sweet fruit, savory salt, nuts, meat, grains, and endless ways to cook them all).

Even as God intended us to enjoy the beauty of the physical world, I believe He wants us to create beauty in the places we call home. Beautiful colors, comfortable furniture, lovely music, candlelit evenings—all these aesthetic aspects of hospitality help make family and guests alike feel a sense of belonging and joy.

Many years ago, I began to collect seasonal decorations that make it easy to sprinkle colorful, interesting touches around my home without much fuss. I keep them in boxes that have a lid attached—that way I don't lose the lid when I am pulling out my decorations. Putting big labels—"Fall Decorations," "Christmas," "Valentine's Day," "Fourth of July," and so on—on the two sides of the box helps identify which box to pull out of storage.

Over the years I have collected decorations for each occasion at garage sales, secondhand stores, and craft stores. When I find something new, I just lift the lid of the appropriate box and add the item in with the other decorations. So I never need to think about buying anything when a new season arrives. Everything I need is already in my basement storage area. I just bring out the labeled boxes, the one for the season that was just finished and the one that is upon me. I put away the old decorations and bring out the new, store the boxes, and voilà! I have brought a whole new mood to my home without much work or trouble.

In addition to my seasonal supplies, I like to keep certain items on hand for instant atmospheric touches:

- *Candles.* I buy these twelve to a pack from Ikea so I can always have candles in any room or on a tea tray or even outside on our porch at a moment's notice. I prefer the kind encased in glass because if I leave them burning, nothing will happen—I don't want to catch my house on fire! Also, candles in glass make it easier to keep children from making a mess with the wax.

- *Table coverings.* I have collected cloth, handmade doilies, tablecloths, table runners, and pashmina scarves—I got some in China for three dollars! I keep these in a little storage chest to throw on a surface with a candle or flowers for a festive touch at any time. Import and discount stores are great sources for these. And I once bought four full-length linen tablecloths with eight to ten matching napkins for ten dollars a set at a garage sale.

- *Vases of different sizes, colors, and shapes.* Garage sales are great sources of vases, and of course I keep the ones that come with flower arrangements. I keep these in storage so that when someone brings me a bouquet I always have a way to display it. I especially like ceramic and pottery vases because, when the arrangement is a couple of days old, you cannot look through and see the dingy water.

- *Themed items and collections.* I have a special story about how God used a little bird that hopped up on my windowsill when I was praying, thinking I was losing Sarah to a miscarriage. When I saw the bird, this verse immediately came to mind: "Not a single sparrow can fall to the ground without your Father knowing it" (Matthew 10:29, NLT). Since then I have purposely collected small ceramic bird figurines. I tuck them all over my home to add interest and to remind both me and my family of God's care. (I also have sheep and rabbits—my house looks like a nature center.)

- *Picture frames.* I always try to pick up picture frames of various sizes when I see them on sale. I fill them with photos of our friends, kids, parties, and events and spread these memories in every nook and cranny of the house. I always have spare frames for beautiful cards sent to me so that they look like pieces of art.

- *Baskets of books and magazines.* I place these in strategic places all around the house (the bathroom, by coffee tables, in bedrooms, on the porch). This allows something interesting to be available for all of my peeps when they have time to sit and relax for a few minutes.

Serving Up Friendships

Probably because we moved so much, I often had to find interesting ways to bring people into our home so that we could develop friendships. We did not do all these activities every year, but we always did *something*. My purpose was to serve both my family and those who visited our home by creating a space for relationships to grow.

A Mother-Daughter Monthly Gathering

When Sarah was around twelve, I invited eight other moms and daughters to our home for a meal and suggested we meet monthly for dinner and a Bible study. The mothers took turns planning and providing the meals, and each woman took responsibility to plan one fun activity each year. A visit to an art museum with lunch out afterward, a carol sing and a hot chocolate Christmas party, a day serving at the homeless shelter—we did them all and more. In the process, friendships were cultivated and the girls enjoyed that sense of belonging that they needed at their stage of life. Eventually the girls did a service project together, had a small weekend retreat, and served at our Mom Heart conferences for a couple of years.

Photo Scavenger Hunts

One of the "funnest" activities my children remember from their teen years is a car scavenger hunt I created. They divided up those who attended their party into carloads of three or four. Each group was given a list of places in our area. To win, they had to be the first group to complete specific activities at certain locations and return with proof—group pictures taken at each location with their cell phone cameras. Here are just a few of the pictures required:

- Drinking specialty coffee at our local coffee café with the barista in the picture
- Standing in front of a postal box
- Posing in front of a red car, then a blue one, and so on
- Standing with a store employee holding up a happy greeting of some sort (such as "Happy Harvest Season!") that the scavenger hunters have provided
- An address in front of a home with two of the same numbers in it
- Standing in front of a stop sign
- At Christmas—an outdoor manger scene or a short video of every "scavenger" singing a carol outside someone's home

The list was never complicated—just fun. The interaction between all of our guest "kids" was always hilarious, and the kids strengthened their friendships in the process.

Kids' Camps and Fun Money-Making Days

All sorts of kids' gatherings have happened in our home over the years, boosting friendships and occasionally making money as well. In the summer, for instance, we helped our kids host day camps for younger children—usually about ten at a time. These included a craft project, a snack, and a supervised playtime. The charge was twenty or twenty-five dollars per camper.

The camps were organized around a variety of themes. One year, for example, a group of boys watched a video about the Knights of the Round Table, made shields, and practiced "fighting" with pretend swords. We also had history camps, Mom's Day Out offerings, and camps focused solely on having fun. Though Clay and I were onsite for emergencies, the kids did the planning and the work, sometimes recruiting friends to help. Those camps provided hours of entertainment during the long days of summer. It also gave our children a creative way to make money for trips we took together and brought us some fun friends.

Inklings for Kids

C. S. Lewis met regularly for almost twenty years with a group of close friends called the Inklings. This group included Lewis, J. R. R. Tolkien, and other notable writers of his time. At their meetings they would discuss their books and projects as well as current news and life events. In the process they created a strong foundation of companionship and community.

Reading about the Inklings gave me a great idea for something I could arrange for my young teens. A friend and I conspired together to start an Inklings group for them. At each meeting we gave the kids a meal around the dining table. (I even put little bottles of sparkling apple juice at each place to replicate the ale at The Eagle and Child pub where the original Inklings met.) Then they would watch a movie and discuss it, share a song or poem they had created, talk about books they had read—whatever they wanted. These meetings forged strong friendships among the kids who attended over a couple of years. We have also had some success with this kind of gathering for men's and women's groups.

Ministry Groups and Bible Studies

As an author, a speaker, a conference leader, and a normal mama, I found I needed spiritual friends to help me sustain my life. One of my friends suggested, "You need a group around you to support you in all the ways God is expanding your borders."

I am a bit shy in some ways and so was reticent to contact women I had met, especially since I knew they were as busy as I was. But I prayed about it, then invited eight women to my home for lunch. We began meeting once a month for a meal, often a potluck. Now, eight years later, we have become a ministry team that works together at my conferences all over the world. We are also inner-circle friends who have shared many seasons and life crises together. But I had to reach out and take the initiative for this group to happen.

Mom Heart groups, an outreach of our family ministry, grew out of this idea. I wanted to challenge women to start a group like ours in their communities. And now there are hundreds of groups all over the world. Information about how to start such a group can be found at my ministry website www.momheart.com. Clay and I have also written a study guide that instructs and inspires women regarding how to start such a group. Available on Amazon.com, it's called *Taking Motherhood to Hearts* (2004).

Serving Up a Welcome

As I mentioned at the beginning of this book, I keep a little chalkboard outside my front door. When friends or even strangers come to visit, whether for a few hours or a few days, they find the word *Welcome* written in chalk along with their names. That's a little thing, but it symbolizes the kind of personal hospitality I want to extend to anyone who enters our doors.

When my children were young, we often spent time at the home of a dear friend, a single woman. She kept a mysterious little decorated box that held a treasure trove of coloring books, stickers, stuffed animals, LEGOs, and small puzzles, just waiting for a visiting child. Her practical brand of hospitality made a big impression on me, and I've tried to make a point of keeping my home ready and waiting for guests of all ages, whether they come for a few hours or a few days. See www.lifegivinghome.com for a list of the items I try to keep on hand.

In addition, I have always tried to be ready to welcome overnight guests. If possible, I like to keep a guest room (one of the kids' rooms) clean and stocked, with fresh sheets and a bowl of chocolate-covered almonds (dark chocolate!) on the bedside table, along with a couple of bottles of water. These days, with most of our kids out of the nest, I can actually manage that most of the time. But it wasn't always possible.

When we had four children at home, having overnight company usually meant one or more of them had to give up their bedrooms. But they actually loved the times they could "slumber party" together while guests took their rooms. Once we had all four of our children sleeping on our bedroom floor for a week to make room for guests.

What I learned in those days is that opening our home to visitors isn't so much about the space as it is about the willingness to carve out a place in the home (and our hearts) for those visiting. Even if overnight visitors need to occupy a sofa or an air mattress, there are still special ways to help them feel comfortable:

- Have clean sheets, towels, and necessities waiting when guests arrive.
- Fresh flowers, a candle (with matches), and a "hello" card by the bed provide a welcoming touch. So do bottles of water and some snacks.
- A lamp right by the bed is a big plus and makes reading in bed easier. (Provide something to read if possible, or point out where to find reading material.)
- Keep a stock of toiletry items a guest might have forgotten—fresh toothbrushes, travel-size toothpaste and shampoos, disposable razors, etc.
- Put out food in the kitchen—a bowl of grapes, some oranges or apples, some roasted and salted nuts. Be sure guests know where it is and that it is there for them to eat.
- Walk the guests through the house and explain the household schedule.

This last item is especially important. Coming into someone else's home can make many people feel uncertain; little gestures go a long way in providing a strong sense of comfort and belonging. As someone who travels a lot and stays in many homes, I love to be led and provided for and not left in suspense about my schedule or food and drinks. It gives me ease when someone has already thought through ways to make me comfortable in their home: "We will leave at this time, and now you are free to rest for an hour. The bathroom and your towels are here. Fruit, crackers, and cheese are right here in the fridge. Here is a place you may make coffee or tea. If I can help you in any other way, please let me know."

Having guests in the home is a great way to teach children how to serve others by welcoming them. We intentionally taught our children to be sensitive to the needs of visitors, to look for ways to make them feel a sense of belonging, and to build connections by initiating conversation.

- "So happy you can visit us. So nice to meet you."
- "Have you had a good trip? Where did you just come from?"
- "Tell me a little about yourself. Where did you grow up?"
- "Of all the places you have visited, what is your favorite place?"
- "Tell me about your work [or mission or family]."

The bonus was that our children not only learned to talk to strangers and make them feel welcome in our home but they also became comfortable starting conversations in other circumstances. Teach children to be the initiators in relationships, I have learned, and they will have friends for life.

Serving Up Rest . . . for You (A Personal Note for Those Who Serve at Home)

When you're thinking of home as a place of refuge, respite, and rest, a place to serve those in need, please remember to include yourself.

In my crowded household, I do get tired of people—often. I learned not to feel guilty about it, but to see it as a sign of my own need to take a break. I regularly collect movies that I can watch, take hot baths with my favorite music playing, go out to a favorite café by myself or with a friend, or go shopping to buy one beautiful thing for me—and while I'm doing those things, I do not answer the phone or e-mails or texts.

Burnout is always a possibility for those of us who are called to serve friends, family, and others longing for home. Take care to fill up your own soul so you can then give back to others. You matter so very much.

A Prayer for One Who Serves

Most of my life has become a habitual breath prayer to God, when the weariness of life tilts my attitude toward grumbling instead of finding joy in service. I am slowly learning to make my efforts at serving those in my home a prayer of worship to my servant King, who has given so generously to me. Practicing serving and making it a spontaneous habit of life help me to be ready to meet the needs of others I encounter.

Serving others, Jesus tells us, is the same as serving Him (see Matthew 25:31-46). He is our Model and our Teacher as we persist in making our homes a place of service. As we practice imitating Him, we not only grow to appreciate His love and kindness toward us but also make Him our welcome guest. And so we pray,

> Lord Jesus, thank You for serving crowds, washing toes, holding children gently in Your arms, and healing even old women who take from you. Let me learn from You, that I might give in the same way to those You bring into my home.
>
> Teach me to find practical ways to lighten loads that are carried through my doors. Help me to have patience with the grumbling hearts, the frustrated ones who carry their depressed moods wherever they go. Help me to remember always that "a gentle answer turns away wrath" (Proverbs 15:1).
>
> Allow me to walk in humility that others may see my failures and the grace You have given me every day. Help me remember that Your strength is made perfect through my weakness, and make me quick to ask for forgiveness. Let me remember that my home is a holy place where You do Your work. And here may the touch of Jesus, the words of Jesus, the love of Jesus, the truth of Jesus be served every day to all who hunger for Your reality.
>
> In the name of the most generous servant of all, precious Jesus, we come with grateful hearts.

November

BLESSED AND BLESSING
Grace, Gratitude, and Generosity
(SARAH)

We would worry less if we praised more.
Thanksgiving is the enemy of discontent and dissatisfaction.

H. A. IRONSIDE

THIS MIGHT SURPRISE YOU, but Thanksgiving hasn't always been a carefully planned and long-awaited festive celebration in our house. When I was growing up, in fact, the day was always a bit fraught, mostly because we never quite knew what to do when it rolled around.

For a family like mine, to whom tradition, fellowship, feasts, and holidays greatly matter, the fact that we struggled to maintain a yearly Thanksgiving tradition was puzzling and, at moments, deeply frustrating. The root cause was our knowledge that Thanksgiving would probably be lonely. For various reasons—distance, tense relationships, and practicality—we rarely spent this festive day with extended family. Our close local friends always seemed to have huge family events of their own. And often, when we stared at the calendar, the prospect of preparing just another big meal for the six of us, with nothing particularly different to mark a day that was supposed to be about the gathering of beloveds and many hands working together, seemed daunting.

To my parents' credit, my childhood memories of Thanksgiving center on cinnamon rolls in the morning and heartfelt family prayers and pumpkin pie for dessert. I clearly remember the pilgrim decorations on our table and the stories of the first Thanksgiving read aloud from the picture books piled around our home. I remember the feel of five hard, golden little kernels of corn in my warm hands as I tried very hard to think exactly which five things, of the dozens I could imagine, I was really the most thankful for, which ones I would speak aloud when my turn came in the after-dinner conversation.

So I do not associate lack or loneliness with the memory of Thanksgiving in my little years, and I think this is largely because of the narrative my parents chose to weave about the day—naming, listing, speaking, and rejoicing in the things we *had*, rather than the community we did not have. And we usually did end up doing something interesting on the day—spending time with a random friend, attending a church feast, volunteering somewhere, or occasionally (to give my mom a break) going out to eat.

But one year, as Thanksgiving drew nigh, we faced the fact that we had nothing at all planned for this day of gratitude. So my parents sat us down and asked us what we wanted to do.

As usual, a big gathering of extended family wasn't an option. Neither was spending time with our closest friends. Probably for the first time, at least collectively, we kids became fully aware of the long-term relational gaps that actually drove some of my parents' deepest convictions . . . and the deep-seated loneliness that had resulted, deep enough to make a close-knit family of six feel strangely alone.

Funny, isn't it, how holiday solitude is so much worse than ordinary loneliness?

But our grasp of that loneliness became a moment of catalyst for our own creative response. Who, we asked ourselves, could we invite to join our feast? The answer we came up with became the seed of a new tradition and, at the same time, revealed a side of home that we vitally needed to understand.

We invited everyone we could think of who didn't have homes or families of their own. We asked anyone we thought might be lonely like us. We asked a college friend of Joel's and a single friend of mine. We asked a couple of Nate's high school buddies and a family from church whose eyes had also dimmed a bit when asked what they were up to for Thanksgiving. ("Nothing special," said the mom with a sigh. "A little more cooking than usual.") We remembered an elderly couple whose children lived far away and the girl who had just moved to our area to work for my mom and the neighbor who couldn't travel that year.

As we prepared our home to receive our assortment of strangers and friends, we began to realize the way in which a home, opened and prepared, can be a place where those who are lonely or sorrowing can come to find belonging. Home isn't just about happy people making good memories.

Home is the shelter where the lonely find rest and the sorrowing come to be comforted. Home is the place where struggles may be admitted and loneliness acknowledged. It's the place where it is safe to admit how difficult, how dark, how lonely the world sometimes is. But it's also the ground in which those sorrows are sheltered and softened. Where, by the alchemy of welcome and acceptance, good food and conversation, candlelight and laughter, hope and even gratitude grow. As our own need drew others in, we learned that our reluctant generosity could become the seedbed for grace.

I think, in the beginning, the day was disorienting. It took a bit for the ice to break. We didn't know one another that well. Most of us were acutely aware of missing someone. The kitchen was stuffed with a conglomeration of dishes precious to those who had brought them, but not necessarily to the others (stewed mushrooms with water chestnuts, anyone?). Even we Clarksons, as experienced as we were in the art of hospitality, found ourselves shy, wondering what to say.

But when we gathered round the kitchen island with its piles of food and took each other's hands, the hush that descended drew us into silence and thus into a strange awareness of one another. As my dad spoke a short blessing, I remember snatching a peek at the people around me, strangers really, all of us holding hands as if we were old pals. I marveled, in my teenage shyness, at the way a prayer and a feast could knit so odd a group of people together.

The wonder only continued as we piled plates and crammed round our slightly too-small old oak table. It grew as the delicious flavors lent their verve to our tongues, as filled stomachs made talk easier and laughter began to sound a bright counterpoint to the bass hum of conversation.

When the time came to pass that basket and fill our hands with five dried corn kernels apiece and think of exactly what we wanted to say we were thankful for, the shyness had entirely ebbed away. The things listed were heartfelt and honest: God's presence in sickness, a marriage on the mend, provision in the midst of need, friendships reconciled. As we spoke our thanks and acknowledged the many and great graces of our lives, we became aware of that moment as a grace in itself. We saw, as George Herbert once put it, "heaven in ordinary."[1] We found friendship and life and beauty in people we had only just begun to know. God was at play, showing us new sides of Himself in these guests, new ways of His goodness in the kindness they showed us, new life in the food they brought and the stories they shared.

And it was a grace that grew. From that first odd bunch of Thanksgiving refugees formed a fellowship that drew a few new people in the next year and a few more people the year after that. Thanksgiving in our house has become the day when we never know who might show up, a day when we wait not in loneliness but in expectation to see what unknown friend might stumble through the door. Our strangely lonely Thanksgivings taught us to understand our home as a place in which sadness may be admitted, but also transformed. In the fallow soil of a lonely moment, we planted the seed of fellowship, and ah, how it has grown over the years into a harvest of friendship, of honesty in struggle, and of a gratitude that could only grow out of sorrow transformed.

A Great Thanksgiving

In the earliest days of the Christian church, the sacrament of communion had a special word associated with it, a word that has survived the long ages of church history and is still used regularly in many traditional churches today: *Eucharist*. This term for the body and blood of Christ as given in communion during a church service comes from the Greek word *eucharisteo*, which is approximately translated as "thanksgiving." In fact, the opening of the service of Eucharist is traditionally called the Great Thanksgiving.

It's easy to think of that word in terms merely of praise, the thanks we give for the gift of Christ. But the Eucharist, whether you see it as sacrament or symbol, is also a celebration of the Incarnation. Taking bread and (depending on the tradition) wine or juice reminds us in a very visceral way that what we celebrate in the Christian faith isn't just about our someday happiness in heaven. God's Incarnation in the world through Christ, His presence in His body and blood, tells us that He is profoundly with us now, healing life even here in the broken world.

The Eucharist reminds us that every aspect of our lives—physical and spiritual, joyous and grieved, present and future—is caught up in the story of God's ongoing redemption. It began long ago and continues now in love that transforms sorrow, in life that springs up in our loneliness, in grace that redeems our moments of despair.

The feast signaling this reality is called "thanksgiving" because through it we do more than just receive Christ; we also begin to live out the reality of His presence in us. Our lives become a reflection of His love, our generous actions a refrain of our gratitude for His life in us. Our lives themselves become a great thanksgiving.

That was the reality that entered our home on our first hodgepodge Thanksgiving. For many of us, that day, more than even the cozy family feasts of other more usual Thanksgivings, thrummed with the life of the Incarnation. We saw God at work so clearly that day, saw Him transforming loneliness into laughter, solitude and fear into fellowship and life. And the ground of that transformation, the table set for that feast—in its own way eucharistic—was our home.

In our exploration of what it means to create a lifegiving home, let us remember that home isn't a place where loneliness never happens, but a place where loneliness is transformed. Home is the place where the incarnational presence of Christ takes the dull stuff of our imperfect lives and turns it— remember?—into love. When we come to see our homes as the places in which God's gift of Himself, our daily bread, meets our brokenness and transforms it, the thanks and praise in us begin to make our very lives a prayer, a great Thanksgiving. In the words of a prayer that often follows the Eucharist in traditional Anglican churches,

> We offer you ourselves, our souls and bodies, to be a living sacrifice through Jesus Christ our Lord. Send us out into the world in the power of your Spirit, to live and work to your praise and glory. Amen.[2]

Home Is for Giving

One of my family's favorite movies is *Babette's Feast* (1987), a Danish film of sweeping beauty that chronicles the life of a small, strict religious community living on the windswept coast of the Jutland peninsula. Austere and pious in outlook, they eat only boiled fish and simple bread, live in austerity, and have little to do with art, beauty, or music. When a French woman lands on their shores as a penniless refugee, they take her in, and the capable Babette becomes servant and cook for the severe little community. Her only request comes after years of service. In thanks for the shelter she has received (and because of a sudden windfall of cash), she wants to throw a real French feast for the people who took her in. And what a feast it is, a feast whose lavish beauty communicates grace in a way the villagers, in all their moral rectitude, have almost never tasted.

I love Babette's gift because in her gratitude was a living, dynamic force. Babette's thanks became tangible in a feast that drew everyone around her into her joy. A deeply thankful heart creates an energy of its own, a forward motion of opening, creating, inviting.

Gratitude, in its very essence, yearns to give.

Even so, as we watch God transform and remake our loneliness within the refuge of home, our thanks will inevitably spill over into other people's lives. Gratitude isn't a gutting out of thanks, nor is generosity a painful sacrifice. Rather, both come from an overflow of joy. And neither is formed in a vacuum; both must come from recognizing that God's goodness to us is so extravagant that it must be passed on.

The essence of true thanksgiving is that we, having received the life of God into ourselves, then take His life into the world, drawing others into the feast of His grace. And that is the point at which generosity begins. That is the moment when we are compelled to open the doors of our homes, to open our hearts to the hungering people around us. Our thanks becomes incarnate in the grace we extend, the hospitality we offer, the love we speak—each of these things one more aspect of the lives we live as a great and constant giving of thanks.

One of the things I am most thankful for in the lifestyle passed on to me by my parents is a sense of stewardship of home. I was never taught to see our home just as something good for me. Yes, it was a gift and delight, a shelter, a place where I richly belonged. But that goodness was meant to create both joy and generosity in me. Through open houses and coffee dates, through Bible studies and Christmas parties, and through our ever-changing Thanksgiving guest list, I grew to realize that home was a gift I must learn how to give again.

In the rest of this chapter, then, we will look at some ways we can offer the gifts of our homes and selves to others, continuing the life we have found, the fellowship we've made, the grace we've known through a chosen practice of gratitude and generosity that opens heart, home, and time to those in need around us.

— In Our Home —

As with so many of home's best rhythms, gratitude and generosity are habits that must be practiced day by day and year by year in the cadence of home life. We had the larger occasions of open-house hospitality in which we shared the whole of home and table, the holidays in which the giving of thanks was the central theme. But we also had the workaday habits of kindness and the little mental disciplines of thanks: notes, meals, the small acts of service that speak of love. In each instance, there was a conscious choice to make both gratitude and giving an integral part of our home life. Following are some of the special days and regular ways in which we chose a home life shaped by generosity.

The Feast of Thanks

No matter who is coming or what else is happening, Thanksgiving at the Clarksons these days begins with a big breakfast (never mind the big dinner to come—that's hours away). The morning hours are packed with preparation, and we also try to catch a bit of the Macy's Thanksgiving Day Parade. But we try to take time before the guests arrive to read aloud one of David's jubilant psalms (like Psalm 100 or 103) and list out, either together or in a moment of private silence, the reasons for thanks that have marked our past year. If we have time, each prays his or her list out loud. If not, one of us says a prayer for the whole family. But by the time the doorbell rings, the turkey is nearly roasted, the table is set, and the rhythm of praise has already been established.

The Thanksgiving feast, as it ought and must be, is the centerpiece of our celebration. Considering the many guests we usually have, combined with whichever siblings are home, we always have quite a few places to set, but we believe a well-set table sets the scene for a happy feast. Our faithful oak table groans a bit as the extra leaves are laden with plates, the "special occasion" crystal, countless arrangements of candles, and place cards for everyone.

When we were very young and rubber stamps were all the rage, we made a set of place cards with a cornucopia stamp. Somehow the originals have survived with the family names intact, so we simply stamp a few more for new guests who come.

As the first guests arrive, we light the candles, put on some lilting Celtic music, and take off our aprons. Then we are ready for the feast.

And the food itself? It's always fascinating to see what friends will bring, which family recipe will make its time-honored way to our kitchen. But we always, no matter the amount of cooking required, include our own favorite dishes—lots and lots of turkey, two kinds of dressing or stuffing, Le Sueur brand peas (no substitutes allowed!), and usually an English trifle—guaranteeing leftovers for days.

During our feast, after all have eaten their fill, we pour another glass of something sparkly or brew a bit of coffee for those whom the after-dinner nap is calling. Before we leave the table, we pass a basket with dried corn kernels—one of the few traditions that has survived intact from my childhood days. Everyone takes five kernels and, for each one, shares something that fills his or her heart with thanks. The corn goes into a glass bowl as each one finishes, and before we know it, the bowl is filled with a beautiful golden pile, a visible reminder of God's goodness.

Prayer is the finale of this special time. All are invited to speak their thanks to God aloud as we bow our heads for a time of contemplation, with one person designated to close. When the amen is spoken, we linger as long as we please, "filling up the corners" as hobbits do at the end of an excellent feast.

For those made restless by the big meal and those needing to burn off a bit of dinner before dessert, we always have a walk. We wrap up in scarves and jackets and march out into the usually gray-day cold, often following a favorite trail that curves down around a huge old rock with a pond at its base. Then comes pie, coffee or tea, and maybe an old-fashioned hymn sing—or perhaps just having fun and relaxing with friends. (We are not spiritually focused all the time.)

Finally, when not another bite can be eaten or note sung, we pack everyone up with leftovers and hugs. Daylight is usually waning when we stand at the front door to wave them off, thankful beyond measure for one more feast of grace.

Remembering the Heroes of Faith

In many church traditions, November 1 is All Saints' Day, a feast day to remember and give thanks for men and women throughout Christian history who have left us examples of how to lead meaningful, godly lives. Those of a more evangelical persuasion might have a similar celebration on Reformation Day. Regardless, the day is an opportunity to showcase noble figures in history who have done great things. For many, it is also a day to celebrate that we are *all* saints, redeemed in the Lord and called to live our lives for Him.

To celebrate All Saints' Day, our family often hosted an evening party and asked the children in the group to dress up as someone they saw as a hero. (We love dress-up parties.) One year I dressed up as Florence Nightingale; another year Nathan performed a speech as William Wilberforce, followed by Joel as C. S. Lewis. This provided a way for us to associate with our heroes in a deeply experiential way, taking on the character and story of each. We read spiritual hero stories aloud, recited speeches, and memorized poems so that our hero day was a jubilant event celebrating brave deeds and gracious lives. It was a day in which we were made aware of the host of faithful people who have gone before us, the "great cloud of witnesses" (Hebrews 12:1) who modeled what it means to cultivate a life of heroic virtue for the Kingdom of Heaven. We especially loved it when parents joined in.

Harvest Festival

Throughout our years as a family, we have enjoyed creating our own seasonal celebrations in the midst of each season. As you might have gathered, our family always loved autumn, when we were most keenly aware of the comforts and grace of home. As the season progressed, we would gather in food, pile up wood for the fireplace, and bring out our cozy coats, sweaters, and scarves. We also typically planned some kind of a harvest festival. It was our way of keeping rhythm with older cultures, in which the gathering in of crops and drawing in for winter was a time for great thanksgiving. It was also great fun, something we all looked forward to.

A harvest festival can mean many things, but for us it meant a last gala of outdoor fun with a bit of good-natured competition and—of course—a lot of feasting. We usually tried to hold the festivals early enough in autumn that the weather was still warm. Living in Texas made this simpler; Colorado is always iffy with the chance of an early snow. But a bit of cold never hurt anyone, we found, and hot chocolate or cider was an easy cure.

The outdoor festivities included pumpkin carving, potato-sack races, foot races, egg tosses, and (if the weather was warm enough) water-balloon fights. When we lived with my grandmother on two hundred acres in rural Texas, we'd hitch two horses to a buggy and take people on hayrides. One event in particular that the boys always enjoyed was the hay-bale pillow fight. Each contestant stood on a small bale of hay, and the first one to knock the other off his bale won the round.

The races and competitions ended with a round of prizes—food, candy, gift cards, a small something for everyone. And of course, per Clarkson tradition, we served all sorts of treats—warm apple cake with caramel sauce, candy corn, caramel apples, roasted and salted pecans or almonds, and cinnamon apple cider.

Some years we held a Yankee swap as part of the event. Everyone would be asked to bring a small gift within a certain (very low) price range. The gifts would be shuffled and handed around, then each person got the chance to trade his or her gift with someone else. The mystery gifts were endlessly amusing, always the reflection of their giver's mischievous, generous, or straight-shooting personality.

The end of the night always came with a bonfire, kindled just as the sun sank down. As the stars came out, we would harmonize to all sorts of hymns, folk songs, and the old harvest melodies: "We gather together to ask the Lord's blessing . . ." As summer drew to its close and we felt the first chill, we knew ourselves wrapped warm in the friendship of those near us and the bonfire joy of the celebration. Winter could come, then, whenever it liked.

Habits of Gratitude and Generosity

Apart from more formal events that we take part in as a family in our home, we try to practice certain habits of generosity that bless others in different ways. Below are listed a few of our day-to-day practices:

Meals for Friends

A regular practice in our home was to make and bring meals for friends and families in times of stress, sickness, or discouragement. Something I watched my mom do over and over was make a huge pot of some deeply comforting soup (potato cheese or homemade chicken and noodle), bake a big batch of fresh bread and some cookies (or brownies or a pie), and pile it all into a box with a bunch of fresh flowers. She always put a handwritten note in, too, so that whoever was at the receiving end of that meal would know they were truly valued, deeply loved.

Handwritten (and Other) Expressions

The art of the handwritten note has grown out of favor with the age of e-mails and text messages, but there is still tremendous power in personal, handcrafted missives. Taking the trouble to write out thoughts by hand rather than typing them into a computer not only enhances the sentiment but also often makes the experience of expressing that sentiment more rewarding for the sender.

As opposed to the technical pragmatism of typing words onto a white background with a generic font used by millions around the world, a handwritten letter allows us to express our own personalities. In the lilt of each loop, the way we dot our *i*'s and cross our *t*'s, we infuse ourselves into our words. Being able to choose beautiful cards or stationery helps us personalize the notes even more. The very act of writing tends to bring out a greater depth of emotion in us, and it communicates to the receiving individual that we are invested personally in this gesture.

Handwriting is as particular to a person as a speaking voice—some voices are deep, some are light and expressive. And hearing the familiar voice of someone cherished brings a sense of warmth and happiness. The same can be true of a note written in a familiar hand. Seeing it immediately brings to mind a beloved face.

Handwritten thank-you notes were always a big deal in our house. From the time we were little, Mom insisted that we learn to write prompt, articulate thank-you notes after birthdays, Christmas, dinner at someone's house—whenever someone showed us a kindness. While we were first learning to write, she would dictate and spell the words; as we grew older, she would just make sure we had finished—and mailed—our notes.

She bought us each a set of good stationery, but we also stamped, stenciled, or otherwise crafted our share of handmade messages. And though we did our share of grumbling, Mom's training paid off in more ways than one. Our thank-you notes not only impressed the recipients but also helped us be more aware of kindnesses shown to us and thus become even more grateful. Today, the habit of writing thank-you notes is one we all use to great advantage in our adult and professional lives.

We also make it a habit in our family to write notes of encouragement to one another throughout the year. Typically these are tied to birthdays and holidays, but it isn't unusual for family members to receive handwritten notes on personalized stationery in their backpacks as they head out of town or to find one in their rooms when they are feeling down. Writing notes is a perfect way to cement encouragement that might have already been given in casual conversation.

Letters, too, are effective for creating a lasting record of a relationship. Though letter writing is admittedly a dying art, the beauty of a long-term correspondence conducted through handwritten letters is one that almost cannot be caught in words. When I was eleven and my best friend, Katrina, was nine, my family moved out of state, and we began to write each other letters. Twenty years later, we each have more than five hundred of these missives, evidence of the friendship that has followed us both through life changes, international moves, children, and more. Those letters are a narrative of friendship that cannot be replaced.

One last note in this regard. I am a firm believer in the power of handwritten correspondence. I revel in the act of writing by hand and enjoy developing the distinctive elements of my own handwriting. But that doesn't mean I don't communicate love and gratitude in other ways as well. Encouragement and gratitude can also be conveyed face-to-face in conversation and through e-mails and text as well, and in some circumstances, a quick word, a phone call, or a prompt e-mail or text can be more effective than a delayed handwritten letter. (But why not do all three?) What matters most is developing the habit of noticing and appreciating the gifts we are given and learning to express our gratitude, love, encouragement, and support in the most gracious and effective ways possible—in the words we speak, type, or write by hand.

Giving Out of Gratitude

Because of our belief in God's blessing upon our home and our understanding that He provides for us generously in our need, we always practiced tithing in our home. The word *tithe* comes from an old English word meaning "tenth" and is probably based on the Old Testament practice of giving a tenth of all produce and livestock to support the Levites (assistants to the priests) in their work.

Many people in the church today follow suit and tithe a set percentage of their income to the work of the church. Our family also tried to follow that principle. But to us the heart of tithing isn't in making sure to pay an exact amount, but rather in being prepared to give freely and generously of our money, our time, and our talents to support God's work in the world.

When we kids were young, we were each given a cash box with three envelopes—one for spending, one for giving, and one for saving. When we received our allowances, we tucked a bit of money in each. That practice of setting aside money right when we received it helped shape our giving habits to this day. As adults, we still follow this pattern—more or less haphazardly, according to personality.

From time to time we would eat cereal or oatmeal for dinner once a week instead of a more typical (and expensive) meal with meat, then fill a jar with the money we had saved. When our jar was full, we added up the money and sent a check to a ministry to the hungry and then included that ministry in our prayers. This practice helped inspire compassion in us and a sense of stewardship that we carry with us to this day.

As far as figuring out how and where to tithe as a family, we always started with our local church body. My parents often allowed us to help decide where we would send special gifts—sponsoring a child, supporting a missionary friend, contributing to a disaster relief fund, or something else. After that, we tried to keep eyes and ears open to the needs around us, whether through the church or official channels or on the more personal level—a friend without a job, perhaps, or a family we knew who was running a little short on cash.

There are endless ways to give. The key to choosing wisely is to pray for guidance and listen carefully, consider the passion you have for particular issues or topics, and invest in these with an open heart. Some of our chosen giving areas include the following:

- *Friends in missions.* Throughout our lives we have supported friends who are working independently in the mission field, both families and individuals. Most missions organizations require that their workers raise some or all of their own funds independently, so many missionaries rely on help from family and friends. We prayerfully give as much as we can to help make their work possible.

- *Child sponsorship programs.* These programs are built on missions in undeveloped countries and focus on the educational and spiritual growth of at-risk children. We have been longtime supporters of Compassion International, an evangelical sponsorship program with outreach in many countries all over the world, but there are other strong, ethically run organizations, such as World Vision and Children International, that do similar work.

- *Student ministries.* Some of the most vital evangelism work in the church today is done by organizations like InterVarsity Christian Fellowship, Campus Crusade for Christ (now called Cru), and The Navigators. Students all over the world are having their lives changed as they encounter Christ for the first time through student outreaches, and many form their values for Christian life through the student-focused ministry communities. Supporting these is a wonderful way to make an impact.

- *Independent artists.* As a family made up of writers, musicians, speakers, and filmmakers, we believe strongly in the power of artistic expression to shape culture. The books, movies, and music of our contemporary culture are having a profound effect on how people view their own lives and the lives of those around them, and we want to support those with a God-honoring voice. We have often tried to help independent artists keep their footing as they pursue projects. This might include helping to crowdsource a film, giving a love offering at a concert, or commissioning an artist or musician to create or write an original work.

- *Halfway houses.* For many people who struggle with homelessness or with poverty, these homes provide places to encounter true Christlike grace, start to learn to care for themselves, and find a way forward in the world. There are many different kinds of homes, from houses that remove children from the foster care system and put them in sponsor situations with church families to homes for single mothers needing a place to figure life out. Many of these homes are extensions of church ministries.

- *Shoeboxes for the homeless.* This is a great way to get kids involved in generosity, especially during the holidays. It involves taking shoeboxes (something we all have extras of lurking somewhere in our homes) and filling them with toys, treats, school supplies, and most important, hygienic items for kids in homeless shelters. This project provides a direct opportunity for children to have a hands-on experience of giving.

- *Rescue ministries for young women.* Organizations such as The Exodus Road are doing vital work helping women escape from prostitution or sex trafficking both in our country and abroad.

A Life of Prayer

A simple but effective way to develop grateful and generous hearts is prayer. Gathering regularly to pray for one another and for other people creates a habit of thinking compassionately and affirms God's hand at work in the world. When we children were young, my parents made sure to include us in their prayer times, even if they lasted a while, affirming our role in the prayers we offered as a family. Praying for the missionaries we supported, the children we sponsored through Compassion International, and those we knew who were going through difficulty helped us learn to see the needs of others in the world. And praying our thanks for God's good gifts helped us remember His graciousness toward us.

Interestingly enough, we found, the habit of regularly expressing our gratitude and our concerns to God actually made us *more* grateful and *more* determined to act generously on behalf of others. I think that's because regular prayer helps cultivate awareness, and awareness is key to both gratitude and generosity. We must learn how to nourish a heart that is keenly aware both of God's abundance as it comes to us and the needs of the world around us.

The grace of home is that it is a place where we are deeply nourished and given the capacity to be givers in our turn. That double rhythm of receiving, then giving—the drawn breath of praise and its release in generosity—creates the heartbeat by which we live lives rich in God's goodness—not just for ourselves, but for the world.

December
THE RHYTHM OF CELEBRATION
Seasons of Rejoicing in Family Life
(SARAH)

May you treasure wisely this jeweled, gilded time
And cherish each day as an extra grace.
ANDREW GREELEY

CHRISTMAS EVE HAD COME, and I stood in our woefully small kitchen, up to my elbows in salad dressing and green peas. Seven-layer salad with brown sugar ham had somehow become a family tradition after all the time we had spent in the South. That year, the careful layering had fallen to teenage me. I dotted the green peas with bits of red pepper for Christmas color and smothered it all in cheese. I was careful to cover each speck of green lest any one bite be bereft of its proper taste.

Absolute equality, in cooking and relationships, is something I learned from my mother.

I remember clearly that I sang as I worked that day, for the old favorite Christmas albums were trilling away, and however trivial the saying may be, work does go faster with song.

Joy sang along on the breakfast-nook couch, her swift, small hands in industrious flight through steel-blue yarn as she frantically knit a last-minute gift for Matthew, one of the teenage "adopted boys" of our home. She was determined to finish his gift before Christmas morning, but I could see that her fingers ached as she stood to measure the length of her work around her own neck.

"Do you think this is almost long enough?" she asked with a slight dramatization of stooped shoulders. "It almost comes to my waist, and you know Matthew's a bit short. How much taller could he really be than me?"

She stretched her legs to their full eight-year-old-girl height. Mom merely raised an eyebrow, and Joy sank back in resignation to keep on with her Christmas mission. I watched her and worked away myself, wondering abruptly what the world would do without the many Christmas-hearted souls who make last-minute surprises and knit not just physical but also spiritual gifts of well-kept traditions and fully realized celebrations.

How easy it is to miss the beauty woven into this work. We three there in the kitchen were the makers of all that our family most loved at Christmas—the good food, the gifts, the well-set table, the camaraderie.

My moment of insight began then, the realization that in the work I joined with my mother and sister I was a keeper of life's riches. That my oh-so-ordinary work helped weave the extraordinary celebration of Christmas.

I glanced at my mother behind me, her hands coated with flour and the dark specks of garlic and herbs she was working into the soft dough of our Christmas Eve bread. My eyes fixed on her hands with sudden reverence. Ah, how gentle those hands. They were deft and sure, taut with a wordless capability that brought order and life to all they touched. That day it was the bread; the night before it had been my heart as she soothed my fear and helped untangle my teenage emotions.

She gave the loaf its final twist and plopped it onto the baking stone. She sighed in relief, and I smiled. That was the last of the batch; already a toppling pile of plump rolls and intricate knots of cinnamon bread sat on the stove for the morrow. Potato soup simmered in a pot, and the ham was basting in the oven.

My mother, I realized, was a marvel.

The goodwill of mothers is like the goodwill of God. In that moment, I was keenly aware of its lack in myself and could only conclude that it was a gift that would come with time and generosity. My mother's will toward us, her children, was so persistently, so relentlessly good—a will to bless, to delight, whether or not we deserved it.

There was no pressing reason why she should so expend herself that day in fancy cooking and the wrapping of delightful presents in colored paper. But for some reason, and by a special grace, she did. If she didn't, I thought, the world might suddenly cease in kindness and lose its warmth.

The heartbeat of beauty that makes of our feasts something more than mere food, the rhythm of feasting by which families are knit together and knit also to a larger life—this is the daily, eternal work of countless generous hearts. The laughter by which homes are made not just functional but joyous is the chosen gift of every person whose work and words form the small worlds of home. There are myriad benevolent souls behind the smiles and sanity of humankind.

I too had finished my work. The phone rang upstairs, and my mother ran to answer it. I leaned against the counter and rested my stiff knees. My stomach was groaning with hunger at the wondrous smells nearby, but I had promised myself not a bite until the evening. I closed my eyes. I breathed. The scent of freshly cooked garlic and onion was heady stuff, and I felt a little woozy in my rare, sweet quiet.

Or maybe I was dizzy with the life of it all.

There, in that brief, still moment when my hands and head had ceased their spinning, I suddenly saw the rest of the world in its joyous dance. I perceived the music in our work, the haunting reverberation of eternal energy echoing in our actions, in the making of our feast and the decking of tables and trees and persons. There was, I realized, a rhythm in the click of Joy's needles and the clack of our tongues, in our constant turning from job to job, that reflected and enfleshed the ongoing life of God, the Incarnation invading the world to order, to enliven.

To love.

Why We Need to Celebrate

Children always seem to recognize the reality at the heart of celebration. Consider Christmas.

Since little girlhood, Christmas has been for me—and for most children, I think—a time rich in mystery. The day the Christmas tree went up in our home, the whole world seemed to shift. Even an ordinary day was extraordinary because the Christmas tree was alight, the Christmas carols playing on the stereo in their once-a-year lineup. It was as if the lights from the tree were scattered, star-like, throughout our existence, infusing the familiar with a sense of mystery. Everything seemed to wink and sparkle, speaking of some joy beyond the touch of my childlike words.

The joy of it was more than the sum of its parts. The wonder was certainly kindled by the fir scent and carols and jewel-toned colors of the wrapped gifts that began to appear beneath the tree. But even when I was tiny, I knew that all of that was somehow given, growing from the larger reality of what C. S. Lewis called "joy"—in the splendor of Christmas, the hint of the eternal delight for which my little heart already longed.

Because we live in a casual culture, in an age that tends to discount rather than treasure traditional rites of celebration and worship, it is easy for us to forget to mark what is deeply important. We don't want to be pretentious. We don't want too much fuss. We don't want to be materialistic. There is also the reality of exhaustion in our age, from the relentless forward motion of modern life that fights against any attempt to slow, to breathe, to notice with wondering eyes.

But in our lack of formal celebration, it is easy to lose the sense that there are immense things to celebrate in the first place. That some realities—like weddings and baptisms and Easter and the Christmas feast—require something of us, demand a response of heart, soul, and even appearance if we are to give them the kind of honor they deserve. We need to celebrate those things to the full so that we feel—in heart, touch, and memory—the full weight of their importance.

We need celebration because we need to remember the eternal. Adults as well as children need an occasional space in which to vividly picture and embody as much delight and laughter and song as they can because those lived realities allow them hope in what they cannot yet imagine, in the new heavens and new earth. We need high and holy days in which to remember the ultimate facts of our faith and history, to in some way enflesh the glorious reality of our hope.

Rediscovering Christmas

I encountered a renewed conviction of this as an adult during my first Christmas at Oxford. Christmas in a new country is always an experience to startle the soul and senses awake, but this time, in the traditional celebration of Advent expectation, I found a taut sense of the mystery and delight I knew so well as a child.

During my first weeks in Oxford, I stumbled into an old "high" church whose services were rich in the liturgy and language of the centuries. I was fascinated by the liturgical drama, with the sense of narrative that came to me each Sunday as the gospel story was lived anew in the forms, words, and actions of the Eucharist. There were actually feast days with prayers that changed to emphasize a new aspect of the gospel story as the whole of it was told in the liturgy of the church year.

But Christmas was, to me, the best, partly because of the expectation kindled in me by the weeks of Advent, the time before Christmas often called "Little Lent" because it is a solemn season, a period of reflection leading up to the Christmas feast. Advent made a space of contemplative time in which I focused on making room in heart and thought for the Christ child in all His joy. I learned that, except for the beautiful college carol services (held before Christmas since everyone would still be in town), Christmas carols would not be sung until the feast day itself. Instead we sang haunting Advent songs that spoke out the longing, the hope, the yearning of the human heart for a joy to sate all desire. I felt like a child all over again, my whole heart tingling with expectation and mystery.

The joy of Christmas itself came with a crashing beauty. When Christmas Day finally arrived, the altars were bedecked in gem-like tones of emerald and ruby, with evergreen draped round the church and Christmas carols being bellowed at the top of the choir's lungs. Joy had come blazing into the world in the coming of Christ. We tasted and touched and sang it in every aspect of worship and celebration. We dressed to the nines and feasted by candlelight and gave our best to the celebration of Jesus' arrival. In the magnificence of that ceremony, I had a small taste of what it must have been like to hear angels singing as they announced the coming of Christ to bring peace and joy to the whole world. And that was only the beginning, because in the traditional church year, I learned, there are *twelve* full days to celebrate Christmas.

In many of the theological books I encountered in my studies at Oxford, I was fascinated to note the ideas underlying sacramental and liturgical philosophy. Within those traditions is a profound understanding that our use of time and space, our physical experience, shapes our beliefs. The words we speak, the actions we perform, the days we set aside as holy enter into the rhythm of our experiences, shaping the way we taste and touch our faith.

Some philosophers, like Charles Taylor, argue that our increasingly secular culture is reflected in a total absence of sacred space or time.[1]

As I have contemplated this experience and many others, I have increasingly asked myself what we can do to bring an awareness of God back into our experiences of time and space. How can we "taste and see" His goodness, embody His life in our own lives? One of the ways, I think, is in the cultivation of celebration, a practice of fully honoring that which is holy or beloved.

Christmas is often seen as a season of excess. What it ought to be is a poignant season of *remembrance.* The point of all the food and song and gifts is not some hedonistic, once-a-year immersion in material overindulgence. The point is to put flesh and expression to joy. If we lose sight of the Christ child's coming, if we forget the heavenly joy we are trying to embody, then Christmas can easily become a season of mere excess. But when the Incarnation is at its heart, then every song, every special meal, every planned event becomes a pageant in which the drama of the heavenly story is lived out. The Christmas festival becomes a tiny taste of eternity, rising up in time.

I have been profoundly shaped as a person by growing up in a home where celebration was richly present. My heart and soul have been deeply conditioned by the spiritual formation attending occasions of fellowship and joy. My heart is rooted in a sense of goodness by my vivid memories of the traditions and celebrations of my home, a place deeply marked by the cadence of meaningful tradition.

From early in their marriage, my parents considered what traditions, parties, ceremonies, and practices they wanted to inaugurate in our family in order to communicate to us, their children, what was most valued in their lives. One of the things they came up with was our yearly shepherds' meal on Christmas Eve, a feast that has become a Clarkson touchstone of memory, meaning, and devotion (more about this follows). They also planned a series of events for the weeks before Christmas in which beloved friends were celebrated, new friends were woven into community, and family was honored.

Mom and Dad shaped our experience of Christmas to be one in which we encountered not only the fun of gifts but also the wonder of God come into the world as a human child. The point of the celebration (I can see now) was to hallow time, to create amidst the busyness of Christmas real spaces of experience in which we could taste and see the reality of God's love, the united love of family, and the beauty of old friendship.

My parents understood that what they taught us to celebrate was what we would learn to value most. (This book is, in many ways, a collection of those celebratory events: Family Day, birthdays, graduations, seasonal festivals.) They knew that the memories we formed together surrounding the key events of life and faith would be the ones that would shape our sense of the sacred, our value for human relationship, our recognition of God reaching out to us in every aspect of physical creation and personal relationship.

So Christmas, for us, was not simply a season of material experience. It was a season of renewal—because ultimately, the point of the Christian faith is that God has come to renew and redeem. The ending of the biblical story is a wedding feast, a Kingdom, a mysterious city with streets of gold and gates of pearl and jeweled foundation stones. This is the reality at which our Christmas celebrations hint. This is the real future we glimpse in the color and beauty, the feasting, laughter, and music of our most marvelous celebrations. Our remembrance is a kind of promise, our spoken hope in all the beauty that is to come. So let the feasting begin!

— *In Our Home* —

Seasons of Celebration

For many people, the church year is a foreign concept. Raised either outside of church or in churches with little to no liturgical practice, the idea of a whole church year with all sorts of designated dates and seasonal observances can sound, depending on your personality, either intriguing or overwhelming. The reality is simply that for hundreds of years, traditional liturgical churches around the world (Roman Catholic, Anglican, Orthodox, Lutheran) have formed the themes and structures of their worship around the narrative of the gospel story as embedded within the seasons and feasts of the church year.

The narrative cycle allows the life, birth, and death of Christ to be deeply remembered. It allows the church, in its worship, to form its use of time and space to memorialize and live the gospel narrative again and again, so that it becomes part of the collective psyche of God's people.

The church year begins on or about the first of December and usually, depending on what specific tradition you are following, includes the following seasons:

- Advent—four weeks of quiet reflection and preparation for Christ's coming
- Christmas—all twelve days of it, beginning on Christmas Day (that's where the song comes from!)
- Epiphany—the season commemorating Jesus' infancy, childhood, and ministry
- Lent—forty days of fasting and repentance prior to Holy Week and Easter
- Easter—the season to celebrate the Resurrection and events following
- Ordinary Time or Pentecost—the longest season, lasting from the feast of Pentecost until Advent

Within each of these seasons are special services, holy days, and memorial feasts commemorating different points within the life of Christ and the birth of the church.

The gift of the church year is that it gives believers the chance to live out the story of the gospel within their regular worship each year. With feast days surrounding events such as the angel's announcement to Mary (Annunciation), the coming of the Holy Spirit to the newborn church (Pentecost), or the presentation of Jesus in the Temple, believers are invited to contemplate the ways in which God has worked within the world to bring about redemption. They are able to remember and celebrate the people, events, and acts by which the story of salvation was accomplished.

The church year also, importantly, makes room for seasons of penitence as well as joy. It reflects and affirms both the sorrow (in Lent, a sharing of Christ's passion) and the celebration (in the twelve full days of Christmas glory) that mark the life of the Christian within the world. There is quiet reflection and waiting (Advent) and rejoicing at what has come (Pentecost), as well as the acknowledgment, in those "Ordinary" seasons, that God's work continues in our seemingly unremarkable, uneventful days.

While your own church may not embrace the church calendar, it is worth some study and consideration, even if only for your private devotion as a family or individual. Marking out a rhythm of celebration within space and time is one way of immersing ourselves in the ongoing narrative of Christ's real, advancing story. There is great beauty in the celebration of the church year, a sense of joining something much bigger than yourself.

If you are curious to find out more, Kimberlee Conway Ireton's *The Circle of Seasons* (2008) is an excellent place to begin. Her beautiful prose both evokes and explains the riches and spiritual resources to be found in a celebration of the church year, but she writes to those who may never have experienced that kind of liturgy before. Though currently out of print—not for long, I hope—it is not hard to find online.

Observing Advent

As mentioned above, the season of Advent is that of the approximately four weeks (four Sundays) leading up to December 25. The word *adventus* in Latin means "coming." In deeply traditional churches, Christmas hymns will not be sung and decorations will not be set up until Christmas Eve because Advent is seen as a time of waiting and preparation. Many churches (and homes) set up an Advent wreath with four candles, one for each of the four weeks of Advent. One candle is lit each Sunday, with particular Scriptures about the coming of Christ read aloud. The central candle, the Christmas candle, is lit on Christmas Eve as the nativity story is read and the feast of Christmas begins.

Though our family was not involved in a liturgical tradition when I was growing up, we did observe Advent through the simple practices of having an Advent wreath in our home and using a family devotional focusing on the Old Testament prophecies fulfilled in the coming of Christ. The wreath was the centerpiece of either the dining room table or the coffee table in the living room. We children helped decorate it, some years with bright baubles and some years with pinecones, nuts, and berries. On each Sunday of Advent, usually with the Christmas tree sparkling in the corner (we didn't really go for holding off on Christmas decorations until the actual day), we would gather to light the candles, read Scripture, contemplate the coming of Jesus, and pray together as a family.

In the midst of a busy and commercial modern season, the ancient rhythms of Advent rooted us in the divine story that is the cause of all the Christmas bustle and splendor. If you are interested in exploring this tradition and need a few ideas for devotionals to use, you'll find a list on www.lifegivinghome.com.

Christmas Tea

For as long as the Clarkson girls can remember, we've been hosting an annual Christmas tea. It began as a simple mother-daughter event, but over the years it expanded into a way to honor the women who have been special to us each year.

We set the table with the best china; ours comes from one of the grandmothers, an interwoven pattern of roses and butterflies. We light tall candles, brew big pots of black and herbal tea, and gather our friends round the table. We try to keep the numbers down, but we usually wind up with all the chairs full and three of us crammed on the rickety old piano bench.

Who could we leave out, after all? There are dear old friends, the ones whose faces link the present tea to past ones with a history of friendship and celebration. And then there are the new—one of my student friends, a new protégé of Mom's, a debate pal of Joy's. We gather in those we love and prize and those who might need to be woven into a circle of celebration at Christmas. And if that means crowding the table, so be it.

However the list of attendees may change, the menu, purpose, and party favors remain unchanged. We begin with a chilled raspberry soup steeped with cloves and cinnamon and served with a dollop of crème fraîche. Next comes a plated luncheon of thinly sliced quiche Lorraine; curried chicken salad; fresh greens with feta, roasted pecans, and dried cranberries; and a fresh-baked scone served with cream and jam. If anyone can stand it, the third course is a sliver of chocolate ganache cake, the specialty of a local bakery and our one store-bought item.

Halfway through the meal, Mom will ask a single question of each woman—something like one of the following examples:

- What has been the best gift of the past year?
- What are you most looking forward to this Christmas?
- What do you hope the next year holds?
- What is hard in your life right now?
- How have you seen God's kindness?
- How do you want us to pray for you this Christmas?

The question is different every year, and each guest takes a turn to give her answer. The answers that come always surprise us in their honesty and also in the gentle friendships they nourish.

Every year, as a favor, we send a tiny ornament home with our friends. Mom selects these, and she also keeps an eye out all year for the Christmas tea gift. She's brought back carved angels from Poland, tiny teacups from a conference, even crystal drops from Cracker Barrel. And she always ends the tea with an explanation of why she chose them and what she hopes will follow her guests into the next year.

The one everyone remembers best? The tiny teacup. "Drink the cup God has given you," said Mom, "and accept it as grace."

The purpose of the party, the ornament, and those questions is to clear out time for meaningful, connected friendship amidst the rush of Christmas. The Christmas tea is our celebration of the friendships that nourish and enrich our lives. The china and the food are simply the embodied half of the nourishment we want to give as Christmas gifts to the hearts of our friends in a meal that communicates how glad we are to have them in our lives.

Phyllis Stanley, a dear mentor and friend to all of the Clarkson girls, says that hospitality communicates value to the one being served. The Christmas tea is simply our festive way of telling our friends they are deeply valued and generously loved.

Christmas Books and Films—the Perennials

There's special delight in having a box of books and films that you only enjoy once a year.

Our Christmas books—picture books, art tomes, and yuletide novels—bring an aura of celebration when they are opened once again at the start of

December. The piling of Christmas books on hearth and table signals the beginning of read-aloud evenings by Christmas tree and firelight. Over the years a list of favorites has emerged, the books we always read one more time, the ones that each of us grown children has made sure to collect for our own home libraries. They range from classics like Charles Dickens's *A Christmas Carol* (1843) and O'Henry's *The Gift of the Magi* (1905) to more recent offerings like Lori Walburg's *The Legend of the Candy Cane* (1997).

As for films—our movie-loving family has gotten to the point where we rarely add a new film to the Christmas lineup; we want to watch the old ones whose familiar faces, lines, and scenes have enlivened our Christmas evenings for years. We wait until all the siblings are home to watch favorites like *It's a Wonderful Life* (1946) and *The Muppet Christmas Carol* (1992)—yes, our favorite rendition of Dickens's story features Kermit the Frog as Bob Cratchit.

For a list of our family's most beloved Christmas books and movies, visit our resource list at www.lifegivinghome.com.

Holiday Gatherings

Open House and Caroling

For us, the Christmas season would not be complete without a Christmas open house, to which we invite everyone we can think of. We usually set aside a Sunday afternoon to pile the dining room table with cookies, Christmas cake, and snacks galore and spend an afternoon in informal catch-up, feasting, and Christmas fun. We always wrap up the day with a good, long carol sing, with Clay on the guitar, Joel on the piano, and any number of others lending harmonies to the lead. It's simpler than it sounds to host—we just serve finger foods and the cookies we'd be making anyway—and the informal fellowship it creates has become one of our favorite parts of the Christmas season.

Progressive Dinner

Amidst the marking of high and holy things, one of the dearest things to mark in a season celebrating the great love of God is the fellowship of friends. Our first year in Colorado, we began a tradition with two other families of a holiday practice my mom had experienced in girlhood: a progressive dinner.

The idea is for each family to host a different course of the dinner in their home—appetizers at the first home, entrée at the second, dessert at the third. If you have more families, you add an extra course.

Over the years, the three families involved in the original dinner continued the tradition and developed all sorts of extra customs and fun. Some years we had all Asian appetizers. Another year we had a huge roast. One year we tried exotic cakes. The possibilities are endless, and the fun is that each family is only responsible for one course (and one set of dishes to wash).

We also formed our own traditions. One family was known for providing Christmas crackers (those little English favors you pop open to find trinkets and a paper crown). The Clarkson house was always the one for guitars and carol sing-alongs and another house became the traditional place where presents were given and received. Over the years, children grew, students graduated, marriages began. Each year we celebrated the progression of our collective stories with dinners that had become ever more creative with each passing year.

Our Shepherds' Meal

Our family likes to think we have an entirely unique Christmas Eve dinner tradition. For as the daylight dims and the restless expectation of the next day's glory sets in, we set to work to re-create, quite loosely and with great artistic license, the meal the shepherds ate in Bethlehem on the night that Jesus was born.

Our menu: fragrant potato soup; a round loaf of fresh-baked herb bread slathered in butter; cheeses of various sorts and sizes, all in a pile; a bowl of fruit; and some toasted nuts on the side (or our favorite, Worcestershire pecans). We figure that even if these foods aren't authentic, the shepherds would have liked them too. It takes every hand on deck to assemble and slice and ladle the meal into readiness, especially when we get home late from a candlelight service. But when all is ready, we set a grand table with the once-a-year Christmas dishes (more artistic license), pour the sparkling grape juice (or red wine for the more sophisticated among us), light as many candles as we can find, make sure the Christmas tree is sparkling like a starry night, and then turn off every light in the house. We want to be shepherds out in the darkness, you see, with warm soup and bread our comfort against the darkness.

Of course, our meal is almost always punctuated by laughter—that itself a feast when it comes down to it. But the feel of the house changes in the darkness, and we watch one another's faces in the shadow dance of the candle flames. The moment is rich in scent, in shadow and flame, in the music of the voices we love, and we draw very close round that table as we fill our bellies with what is, for most of us, one of our favorite meals of the year.

When the plates are empty and the talk dies down (though it never fully disappears in our opinionated household), Dad takes up his glasses, calls for a bit more light, and proceeds to read the story of the shepherds who were "keeping watch over their flock by night" when "the glory of the Lord shone around them" to announce the coming of a very special Child.

This tradition, with its unique blend of our own special meal, Scripture, and family ritual, has become the point for us at which Christmas really begins. We launched this tradition as a way of opening Christmas with a focus on Christ and family rather than just on the spectacle of gifts and food that would begin the next morning. There is a place for high and glorious celebration, but first we want to spend time contemplating the Baby whose coming was a gift beyond anything we can grasp, whose love is what binds us in faithfulness round that table, whose grace is the life in which we all stand. His is the light in the darkness, and with the shepherds, we begin our holiday in celebration of His brightness.

Saint Lucia

The Swedish celebration of Saint Lucia first came to our home when I was twelve years old. Having just finished the Kirsten books in the American Girl series, in which the Saint Lucia tradition was described, I was bright eyed with the idea of the eldest girl weaving a holly wreath, donning a white gown and red sash, baking saffron-infused Lucia buns, and waking her family with candlelight on Christmas morning.

While I may have gotten the dates mixed up—Lucia Day is actually December 13 in Sweden—and substituted Christmas cookies for Lucia buns, I did manage to make my debut a grand surprise. I borrowed an old white dress of Mom's, found Christmas ribbon for a sash, and wove a crown of cedar branches all by myself. Though the custom is to have candles in the crown, I chose to put them on a tray (much to my parents' relief). On Christmas morning, I carried the tray with lit candles, singing a carol, and woke each family member with a cup of hot chocolate or tea.

Joy watched the whole thing with glowing eyes, and the next year she, too, joined the Saint Lucia tradition. (The bit about Lucia being the eldest daughter bothered her not at all!) I'm afraid we never changed the date from Christmas.

Several years later, at the home of a dear Swedish friend, we ate actual Lucia buns and heard the more complete story surrounding the Lucia Day legends. The tales are various, but the one we heard has Lucia as a young Christian convert who sold her dowry to buy food for persecuted Christians. Unable to find her way through the dark catacombs where they were hiding, she wove a crown of evergreen branches, to which she fixed candles to light her way as she walked, carrying her gifts on a tray. She set out into the darkness, a figure of light and comfort, tray laden with food to sustain the suffering. When her betrothed discovered Lucia's conversion and the loss of her dowry, he handed her over to the Roman government, and she was martyred for her faith.

The legend came to Sweden with Christianity but was continued with the addition of another legend that had its beginnings in a time of famine. In a year when the Swedish people were starving, a ship sailed up the coast, and at its helm was a woman in white who emerged from the ship with great trays of food that saved the people from starvation. The people believed her to be Saint Lucia, come to deliver them as she had delivered others before, and began honoring her on December 13 with a special carol and saffron buns.

If the girls in your life want to try their hand at the tradition of Saint Lucia, it's simple to find a white nightgown or dress, cut a length of wide red ribbon for a sash, and weave a few branches of fir into a crown. If you're brave, you can affix a few candles to the crown—electric or LED ones are probably best. Or you can add that element to the Lucia tray as I did, along with Lucia buns (recipes are available on the Internet), Christmas cookies, or hot drinks of your choice. You can find all sorts of Lucia accoutrements in Swedish catalogs like *Hemslöjd*,[2] including some lovely crowns that can be used year after year.

A Seasonal Benediction

Dusk comes early on Christmas Day, the inexorable winter darkness spilling over the windowsills despite the lit candles, the small, starry lights on the Christmas tree, and the afterglow of a day of celebration. Shadows lengthen over the opened gifts and the festive table with its leftover feast; they gather under the tree and dance with whatever light remains after a day of hearty celebration. The coming of Christmas dusk usually finds each member of my family curled in some corner of couch or chair, at ease, exhausted, body and mind in that still place of satisfaction that comes with gifts successfully given, food happily devoured, traditions kept.

Every year I survey the jumble and joyous mess of Christmas strewn about the house. The love, both given and received, makes a hum of peace in my heart, while the happy weariness of the day stills my body and settles in my bones. I am happy. But I find that I often grow thoughtful in the dusk, and as the shadows deepen, a faint, wistful note of sadness or regret or even desire—for what I cannot say—sounds deep within my heart.

Christmas passes so quickly. The glory of it all is so long in coming, and the effort to make it all happen is immense. The beautiful work of the season, the feasting and gifts, the crafting of traditions—it all requires so much work. For a brief, marvelous day it blooms, everything at its zenith and fulfillment. But by evening it fades, and the long days of an ordinary winter stretch ahead.

And yes, we have eleven more days of Christmas to come, but for us those are typically quiet days, a kind of winding down. In the days to come I will often find my thoughts turning to January, to the work that must be done, the decorations to be stored, the pale gray light of quiet, ordinary evenings. So soon we must return to the work of the mundane, to the quiet days where all the beauty must be chosen and crafted all over again. The celebration never lasts as long as I desire, and something in me yearns to keep the joy of the day just gone. I hunger to grasp the Christmas splendor that so briefly embodied something my heart seems made to desire.

The truth is that yearning will always be present in our lives, a note of tangled hope and sorrow sounding right in the midst of even the best day, the happiest moment, the loveliest home. It, too, is part of the rhythms of the season. As it should be.

In a book that celebrates the marvelous gift of home, it is easy to present the life we make there as the end of life's journey, the place and fulfillment of all our hearts' needs and hopes. But the truth is that the homes we make, in all their refuge and comfort, are simply stand-ins for the true home we were made to desire. Our homemaking is but a way of walking well toward the place our Lord promised to prepare for us (see John 14:3). But ah, this is a rich and many-splendored way of walking by hope, of walking by faith in the goodness of the God who promises us the home of His own eternal presence.

The fact that there is yearning even in the heart of home's best celebration just points to the fact that we were made to desire an even greater beauty than it offers. And that is what my mom and I would have you remember as we close. Home is the place in which we picture, day after ordinary day, the fact that love will endure, that grief will be healed, that joy, one day, will last forever and the celebration will never end.

I have glimpsed that on hushed Christmas evenings. Amidst my yearning, I remember that Christmas exists to mark the coming of hope in Christ, a movement of redemption that we are invited to enter. The making of home, the keeping of love and faith is always a continuation of that coming, a forward motion, the incarnational movement that draws eternal goodness into time, helping us to touch, taste, and see the true home toward which we journey. Here on earth there is always an evening at the end of the day, a drawing in of the night after every day of celebration. But one day there will be no more darkness, and the feasting and music and togetherness will endure forever.

Night falls fully on Christmas as I sit and think. It always does. But so, too, does a touch on my shoulder or a hand in mine as someone sits close. Suppertime arrives (leftovers!) and the dancing fire invites conversation. Starlight shines in through the windows, mingling with the candlelight and the faint strains of whatever music we have chosen for the evening as we chat about what the coming year will bring. We rest in the shelter of one another and the space carved by years of tradition, hard work, and love. For a moment time falls away, and in the love we share, we taste the fullness of what it means to come home.

To be home.

To belong.

Notes

Part One: CHAPTER 2
1. Elizabeth Goudge, *Pilgrim's Inn*, Eliot Family Trilogy (New York: Coward-McCann, 1948), 48.

Part One: CHAPTER 4
1. Wendell Berry, *A Place on Earth* (Berkeley, CA: Counterpoint, 2001, first published 1967).
2. Nicholas Carr, "Author Nicholas Carr: The Web Shatters Focus, Rewires Brains," *Wired*, May 24, 2010, http:www.wired.com/2010/05/ff_nicholas_carr/2/.

FEBRUARY
1. Probably the best known of these is Gary D. Chapman, *The Five Love Languages: The Secret to Love That Lasts* (Chicago: Northfield Publishing, 2015, first published 1992).

MARCH
1. Owen Barfield, *Saving the Appearances: A Study in Idolatry*, 2nd edition (Hanover, NH: University Press of New England, 1988), 20.

APRIL
1. The original Middle English—which you may have had to memorize in school—was "Thanne longen folk to goon on pilgrimages." The very literal translation is my own.
2. As much as we enjoyed Kinder eggs, we have since learned that it is not legal to buy them or bring them into the United States. Apparently the FDA considers them a choking hazard, particularly to young children, because of the toy inside. I promise you—my parents had no idea at the time!
3. J. R. R. Tolkien, *The Lord of the Rings*, 50th anniversary one-volume edition (New York: Houghton Mifflin Harcourt/Mariner, 2004, first published 1954–1955), 35.
4. Ibid.

JUNE
1. Gerard Manley Hopkins, "As kingfishers catch fire, dragonflies draw flame," in *Poems and Prose* (New York: Penguin Classics, 1985, first published 1953), 51.

2. This extraordinary annual production began in 1989 and is still going strong! If you are interested in seeing a performance or becoming part of the cast or crew, visit http://thepromiseglenrose.com.

JULY

1. Wendell Berry, *Remembering* (Berkeley, CA: Counterpoint, 2008), 48.
2. William Shakespeare, "The Life of King Henry the Fifth," act 4, scene 3, *The Complete Works of William Shakespeare*, online edition, http://shakespeare.mit.edu/henryv/henryv.4.3.html.
3. This famous line comes from the opening stanza of Ralph Waldo Emerson's 1873 poem, "Concord Hymn."
4. *Goodbye, Miss 4th of July*, directed by George Miller (Walt Disney Television, 1988).
5. For tips on how to do this and other ideas on how to support our troops, visit http://www.operationwearehere.com/IdeasforSoldiersCardsLetters.html.
6. George Eliot (Mary Ann Evans), *Middlemarch* (New York: Bantam Classics, 1992, first published 1871–1872), 785.
7. J. R. R. Tolkien, *The Lord of the Rings*, 50th anniversary one-volume edition (New York: Houghton Mifflin Harcourt/Mariner, 2004, first published 1954–1955), 51.

AUGUST

1. J. R. R. Tolkien, *The Lord of the Rings*, 50th anniversary one-volume edition (New York: Houghton Mifflin Harcourt/Mariner, 2004, first published 1954–1955), 225.

SEPTEMBER

1. Bill Gallagher (writer), *Lark Rise to Candleford*, series 2, episode 2, dialogue transcribed from DVD (BBC Home Entertainment, 2010), episode first aired December 21, 2008.

NOVEMBER

1. George Herbert, "Prayer" (1633).
2. Colin Buchanan, ed., *Anglican Eucharistic Liturgies, 1985–2010: The Authorized Rites of the Anglican Communion* (Norwich, United Kingdom: Canterbury Press, 2011), 278.

DECEMBER

1. Charles Taylor's *A Secular Age* (Cambridge, MA: Harvard University Press/Belknap, 2007) is of great help here, as is James K. A. Smith's *Desiring the Kingdom: Worship, Worldview, and Cultural Formation*, vol. 1 of Cultural Liturgies series (Grand Rapids, MI: Baker Academic, 2009).
2. You can access this wonderful catalog at www.hemslojd.com.

About the Authors

SALLY CLARKSON is the beloved author of multiple bestselling books, including *Own Your Life* and *Desperate* (with Sarah Mae). As a mother of four, she has inspired thousands of mothers through Whole Heart Ministries (www.wholeheart.org), which she founded with her husband, Clay, in 1998. Since then, she has advocated relentlessly for the power of motherhood and the influence of home through her Mom Heart conferences (www.momheart.com), speaking to audiences on several continents. Sally encourages many through her blogs and websites—www.sallyclarkson.com and www.lifegivinghome.com (the companion site to this book)—as well as through her e-books and live webinars.

SARAH CLARKSON is a freelance writer and current student of theology at Wycliffe Hall, Oxford University. She is the author of three books: *Read for the Heart* (a guide to children's literature), *Caught Up in a Story* (on the formative power of story), and *Journeys of Faithfulness* (a creative, contemplative devotional for young women). She has worked extensively with family and student discipleship ministries, where she has gained a deep desire to help people discover the gift and importance of home. In blogs, books, and her current research, she explores the spiritual significance of story, the intersection of theology and imagination, and the formative power of beauty. She writes regularly about her adventures at www.thoroughlyalive.com and is at slow work on a novel. She can often be found with a cup of good coffee in one of the many quaint corners amidst Oxford's "dreaming spires."

DISCOVER THE SECRETS TO MAKING TREASURED MEMORIES FOR YOUR HOME—*all year long.*

THE Life GIVING HOME *experience*

A 12-Month Guided Journey

SALLY CLARKSON
with Joel Clarkson

978-1-4964-0539-5

Join Sally Clarkson on a journey to creating a space where your family longs to be. *The Lifegiving Home Experience*, a practical companion to *The Lifegiving Home,* will guide you through each month of the year, offering plans, ideas, and dreams for crafting a place of rest and sanctuary. Bring new life to your home and bless all those who enter it.

CP1048

Sally Clarkson
Books and Resources to
Help You Own Your Life

Sally has served Christ in ministry for four decades. She and Clay started Whole Heart Ministries in 1994 to serve Christian parents. Since then, Sally has spoken to thousands of women in her Mom Heart Conferences and written numerous inspirational books about motherhood, faith, and life. She is a regular mom blogger.

ONLINE

SallyClarkson.com – Personal blog for Christian women
MomHeart.com – Ministry blog for Christian mothers
WholeHeart.org – Ministry website, blog, and store
MomHeartConference.com – Ministry conference website

IN PRINT

Seasons of a Mother's Heart (Apologia Press)
The Mission of Motherhood (WaterBrook Press)
The Ministry of Motherhood (WaterBrook Press)
Dancing with My Father (WaterBrook Press)
The Mom Walk (Whole Heart Press)
Desperate (with Sarah Mae, Thomas Nelson)
10 Gifts of Wisdom (Home for Good Books)
You Are Loved (with Angela Perritt, Love God Greatly)

CONTACT INFORMATION

Whole Heart Ministries | Mom Heart Ministry
PO Box 3445 | Monument, CO 80132
719.488.4466 | 888.488.4466 | 888.FAX.2WHM